RADICAL DISCOURSES

ON

RELIGIOUS SUBJECTS.

DELIVERED IN MUSIC HALL, BOSTON, MASS.,

BY

WILLIAM DENTON.

BOSTON:
PUBLISHED BY WILLIAM DENTON.
FOR SALE BY WILLIAM WHITE AND COMPANY,
158 WASHINGTON STREET.
1872.

PREFACE.

THE following discourses, with the exception of the second, which was given before the Parker Society in 1864, were delivered in Boston Music Hall on Sunday afternoons, between the years 1868 and 1872, to the Spiritual Society meeting in that place. Several of them have been published in pamphlet form, and have met with a large sale. I send them out in a volume at the request of many who desire them in this more permanent form, and because it is thought that they may thus reach and benefit some who otherwise might not notice them.

WILLIAM DENTON.

WELLESLEY, MASS., Oct. 12, 1872.

CONTENTS.

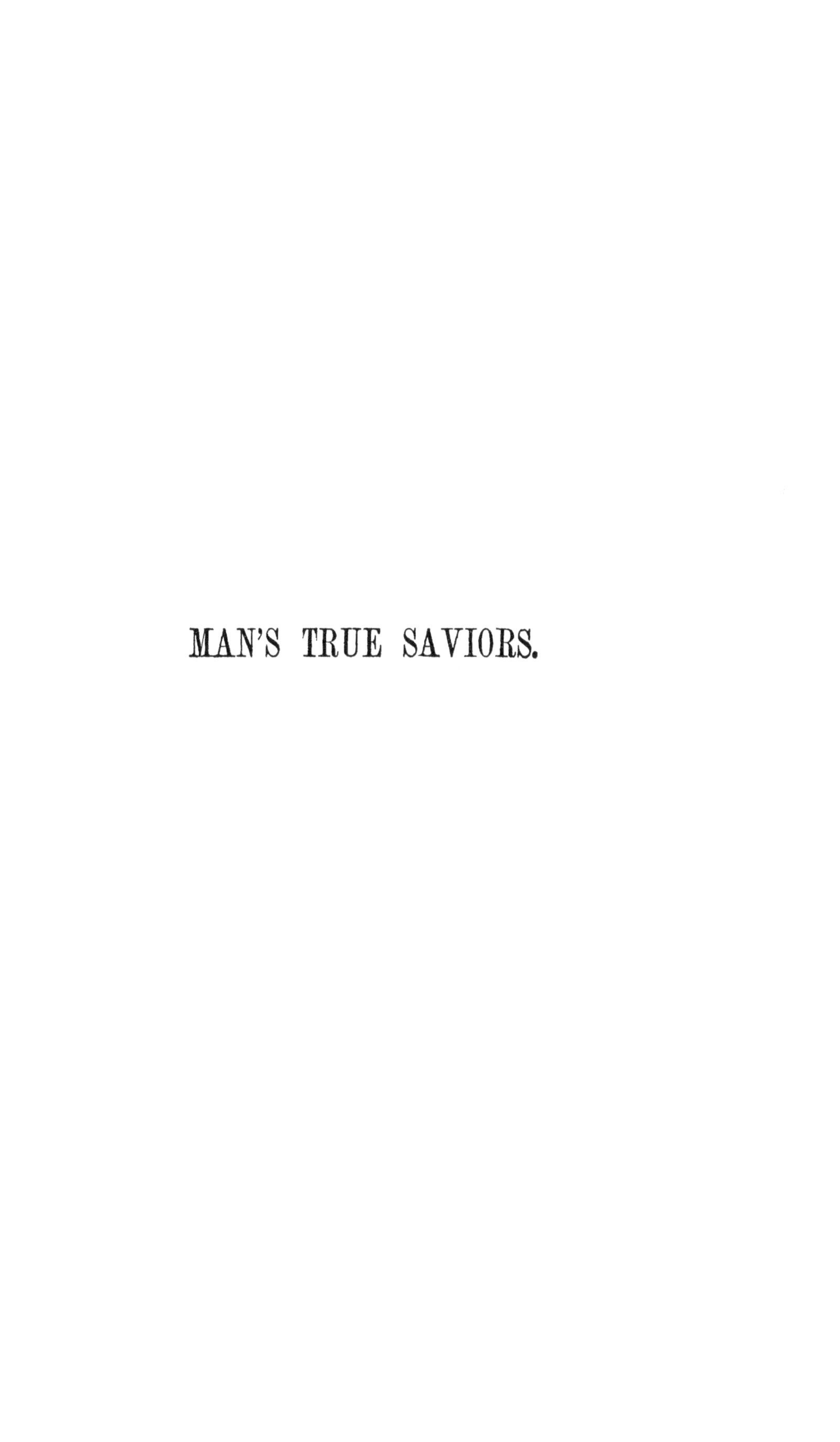

MAN'S TRUE SAVIORS.

MAN'S TRUE SAVIORS.

"WHAT must I do to be saved?" said a trembling jailer to his prisoners, eighteen hundred years ago. Since that time, millions, with tearful eyes, have asked the same question; and even to-day multitudes pause for the reply. The answer given to the jailer was, "Believe on the Lord Jesus Christ, and thou shalt be saved;" and the answer given by Paul and Silas then is the answer generally given by Christian clergymen to inquirers now.

Webster says, that "save" means "to preserve from injury, destruction, or evil of any kind." Does believing in Jesus save men in this sense? To believe is to take for true what is told us by another. Will believing that Jesus was born of a virgin; that he performed wonderful miracles; that he died on the cross, or rose again; that he was the son of God, or God himself, or any thing else respecting him, — will this preserve men from injury, destruction, or evil of any kind?

What are the evils that afflict mankind to-day, and from which we need to be saved? There is none greater than ignorance: it is the prolific parent of innumerable ills — of poverty, crime, and misery — that can never be told. The ignorant man walks through the world blindfolded, but with all the confidence of one who can see. He is always liable to fall down precipices and into pits, and is sure to choose a blind guide. Ignorant parents bring into the world children, that, by virtue of their generation, can never be healthy or wise, but must be a burden to themselves and their friends till death releases them. The ignorant farmer knows not how to treat his land, and his meagre crops only half satisfy the needs of his hungry family. The ignorant king makes the land mourn on account of his folly; and ignorant priests keep the multitudes who trust them constant slaves to grovelling superstitions. Ignorance fills our lunatic-asylums, almshouses, hospitals, and jails: it is, indeed, the fruitful soil in which vice of all kinds flourishes, and produces its baneful crops. Men drink intoxicating drinks, and boys learn to chew tobacco, because they are ignorant of the bad effects of these practices on the human system; and half the licentiousness of the world would be removed, were the perpetrators aware of the suffering that invariably follows.

Will believing in Jesus save us from ignorance? will it reveal to us a knowledge of our physical and mental systems, and their relation to the external world, so that we may reap the enjoyment that springs from a life ordered in harmony with natural law? Then, blessed faith! it shall be the first thing inculcated in the nursery; and a college professor destitute of this will lack the most essential qualification. Locomotives shall carry those who inculcate it on every train; balloons shall drop the saving creed, printed in all tongues, over all lands; and telegraphs flash the intelligence as wide as the race.

Alas! Jesus himself was ignorant, — so ignorant of the effect of the use of intoxicating drinks, that he not only drank them, but, if we are to believe one of his biographers, he even made them for other people to drink. He had such an incorrect idea of the size of our planet, that he supposed he had seen all the kingdoms of the earth from the top of a Syrian mountain; and was so ignorant of the inviolability of natural law, that he believed and taught that prayer could transport mountains from one locality to another. He never seems to have thought that the fabulous stories of the Old Testament were other than divine truths, and imposed them upon his unsuspecting believers. One of the greatest expounders of the Christian faith, that prince of believers, Paul, says that he counted all things loss for the excellency of the knowledge of this same Jesus. Writing to the Corinthians, among whom he had preached, he says he determined to know nothing among them, only Jesus and him crucified; and then declares that "the wisdom of this world is foolishness with God," and that "the Lord knoweth the thoughts of the wise, that they are vain." It is evident that Paul's belief in Jesus, instead of leading him to increase in knowledge, only led him to despise it. It is true that he recommends believers to grow in knowledge; but it is the knowledge of Jesus Christ: and how much ignorance will such knowledge dispel? He who grows only in the knowledge of Christ must be ignorant of what it is most important for him to know.

The Christian sentiment of more modern times is represented in one of Wesley's hymns: —

"Nothing is worth a thought beneath,
But how we may escape the death
That never, never dies."

That man's mind must be poorly stored with information, who is forever thinking about how he may escape an impossible death.

Take Christians as a body, and how ignorant of natural science they are! They seem to have been influenced by Paul's advice, "Beware, lest any man spoil you through philosophy;" and it is notorious, that generally, in the same proportion as a man becomes a philosopher does he become spoiled for a Christian. Christianity arose on the world like a baleful star; and the long night of the dark ages set in, that it took the invention of printing and the revival of philosophical literature to disperse. Christianity burned the books of the Greek and Roman philosophers, and would have burned the philosophers themselves, had they been living, and not recanted. When Christians are intelligent, it is where surrounding conditions have made them so, and in proportion to their outgrowth of the original spirit of Christianity. Belief in Jesus, then, does not save from ignorance.

Poverty is a great calamity. When it is so great as to produce hunger, it masters the man, possesses him, and sends him into society a human wolf. When it exists in less degree, it prevents a man from buying books, wearing good clothes, living in a comfortable house, and compels him frequently to dwell in an unhealthy neighborhood. It presses a man to the earth under its iron heel, and crushes, too often, the manliness out of him: it fetters the soul, stultifies the intellect, makes men mean, and keeps them so.

Will belief in Jesus cure men of poverty? Where could we find a poor believer if this was true? Jesus himself was poor, and very poor. He says, "The foxes have holes, the birds of the air have nests; but the Son of man hath not where to lay his head." He was dependent, indeed, during the latter part of his life, upon the charity of his friends. When a tax was demanded of him, a miracle was wrought, so the story goes, to obtain the paltry amount, which the scanty purses of Jesus and Peter were unable to furnish. Indeed, the early followers of Jesus were poor almost to a man, and consoled themselves by saying that God had chosen the poor of this world to be rich in faith, and heirs of the kingdom. If the present believers in Jesus were to believe in him implicitly, and obey him fully, they would be equally poor. If they were to cease to labor, lay up nothing, imitate the birds, and take no thought for to-morrow, how long would it be before poverty would have every one of them in its grip? Jesus exclaims, "Wo unto you that are rich!" and one of his poor followers, James, echoes his cry; while Paul says, "Having food and raiment, let us therewith be content." What a poverty-stricken people we should be if these statements were generally believed, and the commands of Jesus and his apostles obeyed! If we took no thought for food and raiment, we should soon be hungry and naked; if we did not lay up for ourselves when young and healthy, we should become paupers when old and infirm; and, if we were satisfied with food and raiment, where would be our railroads and locomotives, our steamships and telegraphs? Who would own a microscope or telescope? and in what condition would be the arts and sciences? It has only been by disbelieving Jesus, disobeying these commands of his, and practising the very opposite, that Christian nations have obtained the magnificent results of modern civilization. Believing in Jesus, then, does not save men from poverty.

Disease is a great and widespread evil. It shrouds man's life with gloom; it turns the blessings of nature into deadly curses; its venom rankles in the heart, dims the eye, palsies the hand, and binds the tongue. The diseased, it is said on good authority, actually outnumber the healthy; and, in consequence of this, misery, like a dark cloud, comes between millions and the sun of happiness that should shine upon all.

Will faith in Jesus bear away our infirmities, and make us whole, as the faith of the woman is said to have done, who but touched the hem of his garment? What a boon to the afflicted! We will indeed cast medicine to the dogs; and quacks, apothecaries, and doctors, who tinker the human system, may mourn for the days that are gone: Jesus shall be our great Physician, and a world of his healthy believers shall swell to the heavens their song of praise. But the flying pestilence heeds not even the blood of Jesus on the door-post: it enters and destroys the chosen people no less readily than it does the Egyptians. Sickness lays his hand on the Jesus-believing saint as heavily as on the Jesus-rejecting sinner; and, if there is any difference, the odds seem to be on the wrong side; for, as Solomon said of the conys, Christians are "feeble folk." They read in their oracles, "Bodily exercise profiteth little;" "Whom the Lord loveth he chasteneth, and scourgeth every son whom he receiveth;" and, if true to their faith, they bow, and kiss the rod that smites them, and neglect their bodies in this world that they may save their souls in the next. Christians are, no doubt, more healthy than special classes that might be mentioned, but nowhere near as healthy as those who, having outgrown Christianity, regard it as a duty they owe to themselves to learn the laws of health, and to live lives in obedience to them. Fevers burn Christians, and agues chill them; colds visit them, and consumption feeds upon them; and their salvation, instead of placing a barrier between them and the enemy, like a spy in the camp, invites his approach. The preachers of the Christian gospel are especially a weak, puny, sickly set of men: a robust man among them is an exception. After laboring "in their Master's service" for a few years, they are generally broken down, and require trips to Europe or the Holy Land to recruit their health. The more sickly of them rely upon doctors to heal their bodies, as their church-members rely upon Jesus for the cure of their souls, and generally with as little success.

Some of the ancient Christians, it is true, believed that Christianity included a remedy of disease: hence James says, "Is any sick among you? let him send for the elders of the church; and let them pray over him, anointing him with oil in the name of the Lord;

and the prayer of faith shall save the sick, and the Lord shall raise him up." What an easy, cheap, and expeditious way is this! But where is the Christian that believes in it, and practises accordingly? He sends for the elders only when they happen to be physicians, and then has more faith in their pills than their prayers, and in internal oleaginous applications rather than external; for the experience of long ago has demonstrated the uselessness of the practice that James recommends.

Death is spoken of by Christians as the "king of terrors," at whose approach the strongest fear and tremble. When men become subjects of King Jesus, does he deliver them from this potentate? Does he, at least, relieve them from all fear of what is inevitable? Then Christianity is still a boon, and its system of salvation worthy of acceptation; for life has little charm for that man who has continually before his eyes the fear of death. Jesus, the object of the Christian's faith, died young: he could neither deliver himself from death, nor from the terror that it inspired. Hear his prayer in prospect of approaching death: "If it be possible, let this cup pass from me." It was not possible; and in the anguish of his soul he exclaims, "My God, my God! why hast thou forsaken me?" Unable to deliver himself, how can he deliver his believers? So overcome by terror at the prospect of his own death as to "sweat, as it were, great drops of blood," it is not surprising that the believers in him tremble at the skeleton grim. Some Christians, it is true, die without fear, and some with courage, hope, and even joy; but we have no evidence that this is owing to their belief in Jesus, since it is true of believers in all religions, and in none. There is, indeed, good reason to think, even from the admissions of Christian ministers themselves, that unbelievers, as a rule, have much less fear of death than the majority of Christians. "In all my experiences," says the Rev. Theodore Clapp of New Orleans, "I never saw an unbeliever die in fear. I have seen them expire, of course, without any hopes or expectations, but never in agitation from dread or misgivings as to what might befall them hereafter. It is probable that I have seen a greater number of those called irreligious persons breathe their last than any other clergyman in the United States. . . . When I first entered the clerical profession, I was struck with the utter inefficiency of most forms of Christianity to afford consolation in a dying-hour." And this is what we might reasonably expect. Most Christians believe in a God who is angry with the wicked every day, — one who will damn a soul for one sin unrepented of: they believe in a devil of almost infinite power, and a hell of torment unutterable, to which the best of them are apt to feel that they are liable; while the worst that the unbeliever can fear is an eternal sleep, in which he will know no more than the violet which blooms on his grave. Your salvation, then, Christian, saves neither from death nor the fear of it.

Fire, when it obtains the mastery, is an evil to be dreaded, and any salvation from its ravages would be gladly received; but the Christian's belief does not save him from them. The fire licks up the very churches with its flaming tongue, and consumes alike the dwelling of Christian and infidel; and insurance societies are just as needful to the one class as to the other.

Is the believer in Jesus any safer in a thunder-storm for his belief? See that church-steeple shattered, and the minister in the pulpit struck dead upon his knees; while in awe his Christian brethren whisper, "Mysterious Providence!"

The floods are no respecters of persons. Christians drown as readily as their unbelieving neighbors, under like circumstances. Cast a Christian and an infidel into the sea: which will sink first? The one who knows not how to swim; and there is more salvation from drowning in a cork than in the faith of the one or the infidelity of the other.

In what respects, then, O Christian! does belief in Jesus, whom thou callest Christ and Saviour, save thee at all? "Our salvation," replies the Christian, "is from sin, from the wrath of God, and from eternal torments: it concerns not itself with sickness, poverty, floods, fires, and such trivialities, but with things of eternal moment." If the salvation by Jesus is indeed a salvation from sin, we will welcome it. From sin, — from lying, stealing, intemperance in all its forms; from anger, bitterness, and all uncharitableness; from jealousy, revenge, and all meanness; from war and all its horrors; from crime and all its results, — what a salvation that would be! I know that Jesus is said in Matthew to have received his name of Jesus, which means "saviour," because he should save his people from their sins; but where are the people that he has saved? Can those who call themselves Christians be in reality his people? Jesus himself acknowledged that he was not good. When one called him "good Master," he said, "Why callest thou me good? There is none good but one, that is God." John, the beloved disciple of Jesus, says, "If we say that we have no sin, we deceive ourselves, and the truth is not in us." It is evident, then, that he did not consider himself to be saved from all sin.

The Christians of to-day universally confess themselves to be sinners. In the Episcopalian church they repeat every Sunday morning, "Almighty and most merciful Father, we have erred and strayed from thy ways like lost sheep. We have followed too much the devices and desires of our own hearts. We have offended against thy holy laws. We have left undone those things which we ought to have done, and we have done those things which we ought not to have done; and there is no health in us. But thou, O Lord, have mercy upon us miserable offenders." Very similar are the confessions of Christian clergymen of all denominations, reiterated from the pulpit every seventh day; and the believing brethren, in whose name they pray, devoutly say, "Amen." And, in doing so, they acknowledge the statement to be correct. But what worse is an unbeliever than this? Some of them are not as bad. All Christians pray, "Forgive us our trespasses," as Jesus taught his disciples to pray; and it is evident, by his doing so, that he did not believe that their faith in him would save them from committing sin, as the confessions of modern Christians show its helplessness in their case. Where is the Christian that is saved from sin, or that even professes to be? Should any man claim to be, and he a married man, let his wife be questioned "separate and apart" from her husband; and, if she be truthful, her statement will prove the worthlessness of his claim. Indeed, Christians seem to take pride in confessing what great sinners they are, and unblushingly sing, what can only be true of one of them, —

> "I the chief of sinners am;
> But Jesus died for me."

The very reason why they should not be sinners at all, according to their theology. What merchant will credit another the sooner because he is a Christian, or place more confidence in him when making a bargain? Some have done so only to find themselves grievously disappointed. We are surrounded by believers in Jesus, — men and women who profess to have been born again, and passed from a state of nature into a state of grace; who profess to have been saved by this great salvation: but where are those that never lie, nor prevaricate; who never take advantage of another in a bargain; who are never angry, nor sulky, nor greedy, nor refuse to help the needy; who are temperate in all things, — never use tobacco or intoxicating drinks, nor injure their bodies by any indulgence? Where are those that are never bigoted, intolerant, or uncharitable, and whose consciences absolve them every evening, so that they have no need to pray, "Forgive us our trespasses," for they have no trespasses to be forgiven? The Christian Church, with all its pretensions, cannot furnish a single one. What, then, are we to think of the statement that Jesus saves men from sin?

Christianity did not save the South from slavery, where it was commenced and carried on by Christians and Christian ministers, whose hands were strengthened by their Christian brethren of the North: the one forged the fetters and applied them; the other riveted them, and cursed in the name of Jehovah all who attempted to break them; while most of those who wrote and lectured against slavery were men whom the Church branded as infidels.

Belief in Jesus does not save men from war and cruelty. Christian nations have been notoriously fighting nations; and Christian wars have been among the most cruel and bloody. "There are no wild beasts as ferocious as Christians who differ concerning their faith," said the heathen in the fourth century; and, if we are better now, it is due not to the superiority of our faith, but to the advance which the best types of our race present in accordance with the operation of natural law. "What a dreadful picture," says Dr. Dick, "would it present of the malignity of persons who have professed the religion of Christ, were we to collect into one point of view all the persecutions, tortures, burnings, massacres, and horrid cruelties, which in Europe and Asia, and even in the West Indies and America, have been inflicted on conscientious men for their firm adherence to what they considered as the truths of religion!"

It must be confessed, that, if some of the teachings of Jesus were obeyed, war would be impossible; but when he declares that the punishment of a false faith will be damnation, and that damnation everlasting fire, that man must be more than mortal who believes, and is not led in some degree to persecute those whose faith is, in his opinion, erroneous.

Christianity does not save from intemperance; for, while men almost universally believed in Jesus where the evil was, it grew till it overshadowed the land. It invaded the pulpit, and dragged to untimely graves hosts of the strongest Christian believers. The first temperance paper was published by Joseph Livesay of England, who was what is called an infidel; and it was not till outsiders had done the heavy work, and they saw a prospect of assistance from it, that Christians took much interest in the temperance movement. The Bible is the bulwark of moderate drinking, and the example of Jesus one of its principal supports.

Christianity does not save from bigotry and intolerance. No people in our country are as bigoted as Christian believers; and it is no wonder. Jesus looked forward to the time when he should sit on the throne of his glory, and say to those who had neglected the believers in him, "Depart from me, ye cursed, into everlasting fire." If he had possessed the power, he would evidently have given his enemies a taste of earthly fire, as so many of his followers subsequently did. Paul was charged with bigotry to the lips, and fulminates his anathemas like a pope's bull; and even the "loving John" would have turned Theodore Parker out of his house in the name of Jesus, as the Boston Christian bigots tried to pray him out of the world.

The religion of the despised Nazarene, peaceful

while an infant, became a fighting bully as soon as it could use its fists. It imprisoned, banished, and burnt; it inaugurated war for the religious opinion's sake, and deluged Europe and Asia with blood. When this was over, dungeons were filled, racks invented, and the fagot burned the refractory sceptic that milder means failed to convert. Do not suppose that this spirit is extinct. A revival of orthodox religion is a revival of uncharitableness and hate; then men think most of its damnatory creed; their hatred of infidelity and the infidel is proportioned to their love of souls. Here is a prayer that was offered in the Young Men's Christian Association of Boston only a few days ago, and reported in "The Boston Herald." "Lord, if that infidel that Brother C. told us about is at work this morning writing his tracts, Lord, paralyze his arm!" Who cannot see that this praying brother would have paralyzed the arm himself, if he had possessed the power?

Lying clings to Christian nations as creeds do to Christian churches. Leading Christians are notorious falsifiers for God: their religious tracts and books abound with calumnies against unbelievers, sophistry and special pleading that would have disgraced a Roman lawyer in the days of Cicero; and it is no wonder that they practise occasionally on their own account what they so frequently do for their religion and their God.

It may be said, that, although Christianity does not save men from all sinning, it still does much to restrain them from vice; and this cannot be denied. Mohammedanism does the same thing: it restrains its believers from the use of intoxicating drinks. Professors of the Christian religion are frequently restrained by it from the commission of such sins as the Church denounces; but, on the other hand, the Church upholds sins by virtue of its belief in Christianity. It was thus that it upheld slavery, and to-day upholds woman's degradation. It has two vices peculiarly its own: it robs man of one-seventh portion of his time, which it generally employs in idleness or superstition; it has invented a sin which it calls sabbath-breaking, and spends more time and effort to prevent men from committing this imaginary crime than it does to hinder them from doing what justice universally condemns. The bigotry and intolerance so generally manifested by it in proportion to its influence have made it the greatest engine ever invented to fetter the human mind; and it is only as its power decreases, and the soul is liberated from its influence, that the large-brained races of the world attain to those results of enlightenment in which now even Christianity makes its boast.

The salvation that is said to come from a belief in Jesus is not a salvation from sin, — nothing can be much more certain, — and we still ask, "What does Jesus save men from?" — "From the wrath of God?" Does your God, then, become angry? — he whom you believe made worlds more numerous than drops of water in the ocean by the word of his mouth; he who is perfect in love, a perfect father, and we his children. I know men who would be ashamed to be angry, men who would blush to have their wrath excited by a man — their equal: and yet you believe in a God who is angry, and angry with man. It cannot be so. But, if so, what makes God angry? You tell me it is sin; for your Scriptures say that God is angry with the wicked every day. But you confess every day that you are wicked: how, then, can you be saved from the wrath of God? If you are telling the truth morning and evening, you are a sinner; and the book in which as a Christian you believe declares that the soul that sinneth shall die: it also declares that "the wrath of God is revealed from heaven against all unrighteousness and ungodliness of men," and asks, — what should be to you a solemn question, — "If the righteous scarcely be saved, where shall the sinner and the ungodly appear?" Your God must hate you if you are a sinner: so that your salvation does not even save you from the wrath of God.

"But our faith enables us to appropriate the merits of Jesus, so that we receive the reward of his perfect obedience. Jesus is called the Lord our righteousness; for, though we can do nothing that is acceptable to God, we clothe ourselves by faith with his virtue, and he becomes all in all to us." Can it be that I understand you? You may injure both your body and your soul by licentious indulgence; but, by exercising faith in Jesus, God will reward you for his chastity. You may lie and steal, since these vices are human; but only believe, and you appropriate the divine honesty and veracity of your Saviour, and all is well. What a gospel of rascality is this! What a comfortable doctrine for the man who wishes to excuse his shortcomings, and escape the just penalty of his misdeeds! No wonder that immorality flourishes wherever it is preached! Under its influence men are content to confess themselves sinners every Sunday, and trust in Jesus to save them; while they are just as content to go on sinning during the week: for the Sunday confession must be made, and the Sunday trust exercised, at all events. But it is certain that nothing can be more false than this doctrine. Paul truly says, "Whatsoever a man soweth, that shall he also reap." Nothing more true, as our daily experince demonstrates. No man can break a physical law, and another bear the consequences; nor can any man sin, and Jesus suffer the penalty for him; nor did he suffer it eighteen hundred years ago in anticipation of the offences the Christian sinner would commit in coming time. Jesus had no merit to spare: fanatic as he was, he felt and acknowledged his own deficiency; and the structure of the universe forbids any appropriation of the merits of another.

But we are told that the salvation that comes by faith in Jesus saves us from eternal torments. But what evidence is there that any such torment exists? The very lightning that in its fury knows no respect of persons; the bounteous rain that distributes its blessings upon all; the smiling moon, peeping into the fevered face of the debauchee; the sunshine, looking through the gloomy bars of the prison, and whispering hope to the doomed criminal, that gilds alike the gallows and the church-vane with its glory; the calm evening, cooling the sultry air, lighting the lamps in the hall of night, and hushing the birds, that saint and sinner may sleep, — all teach the absurdity of this orthodox fable. Should there be any eternal torment, the Christian is as likely to suffer it as any, if his Bible in which he trusts is to be credited. It is only those who obey the commandments of Jesus that have a right to the tree of life, and may enter through the gates of pearl into the celestial city. But Christians do not obey them. They resist evil; they lend, hoping for something; they judge; they lay up treasures on earth; they take thought for to-morrow, and act in all respects as if Jesus had never said a word in reference to these subjects. Jesus teaches that they only are founded on the rock who obey his teachings: all others are to be swept into perdition when the tide of God's wrath shall flow over a ruined world. In no wise is there any hope for thee, Christian: thy salvation is a sham, thy great Physician a quack; the only diseases that he cures being imaginary ones that faith in him has produced.

The Christian doctrine of salvation is built on the Christian doctrine of damnation; and the doctrine of damnation rests upon the doctrine of original sin; and this upon the story of man's fall from a condition of original purity and goodness. But of this story science may be said to have proved the utter falsity. Geology has settled the question as far as our planet is concerned. It has not fallen from an originally perfect condition to one in which volcanoes belch, storms howl, earthquakes heave and ingulf, and ferocious beasts devour. Geology proves, that, in all these respects, the world has improved, and is to-day a better abode for human beings than at any past period in its history. Archæology, a younger sister of geology, has in like manner proved that man has not fallen from a state of sinless perfection to one in which lying, stealing, drunkenness, and licentiousness characterize him, but that, from the condition of a savage, he has climbed during ages to the civilization of the present. The opinion held by those who have made archæology a study is well represented in the address of Lord Dunraven to the Cambrian Archæological Association: "If we look back through the entire period of the past history of man, as exhibited in the result of archæological investigation, we can scarcely fail to perceive that the whole exhibits one grand scheme of progression, which, notwithstanding partial periods of decline, has for its end the ever-increasing civilization of man, and the gradual development of his higher faculties." And in the statement of Sir John Lubbock, in the closing chapter of "The Origin of Civilization," "Existing savages are not the descendants of civilized ancestors. The primitive condition of man was one of utter barbarism; and from this condition several races have independently raised themselves."

Archæology has demonstrated that chiliads of years before the world was made, according to biblical chronology, man in England, Scotland, France, Belgium, and Europe generally, was a savage. The remains of his cannibal feasts which have been found show the amazing distance that he has since travelled on the road to perfect manhood. What lifted him out of this pit, and gave to the world the architecture of Egypt, the art of Etruria, the poetry and philosophy of Greece, the morality of Gautama and Confucius, and the jurisprudence of Rome? All this long before Jesus was born, and probably before a chapter of the Bible was written. That advanced man which advanced the planet, his dwelling-place, for millions of years before his foot trod it. What pushes the tree on from the sapling, struggling for existence, to the towering pillar of living beauty? The spirit in the tree, pushing, urging day and night, and that never allows it to rest. What carried the earth upward from the monotonous wilderness of heated rock to the ocean-bearing, lake-gemmed, mountain-crowned planet of to-day? and life, from the polype of the sea-bottom to the croaking frog and the thinking man? The all-controlling Spirit, never resting, never far away, as inseparable from the universe as a man's soul is from himself; and this, in the first rude men, carried them on, awakened thought in their souls, lit a fire of love in their hearts, whispered of heaven in their ears, and to-day reveals to them a condition of perfection to which humanity must yet attain, and for which the best men are daily striving.

Man, then, has not fallen: the foundation of damnation and the necessity for orthodox salvation is gone. God did not make a pure fountain, allow the Devil to poison it, and then compel the whole human race to drink of it, and at the same time threaten them with eternal torment if they should manifest its evil effects.

But, if man did not fall from an originally pure condition, then he did not receive from that fall that never occurred a corruption of his nature, whereby he is "inclined to evil, and that continually." I never can remember the time when I was not inclined to good, when I did not love truth, honesty, temperance, purity, manliness; and I do not believe that I am an exception in this respect. I believe this to be the general feeling of all men. The protest which the soul makes against absurd forms, useless ceremonies, and false notions, is mistaken for opposition to virtue and goodness. I cannot say that I was naturally fond of Sunday ; it was the most melancholy day of the week : nor did I take much delight in sermons ; not because I disliked the goodness inculcated in them, but because there was so little in them attractive to my youthful mind. The goodness that supports asylums, that establishes schools, that founds temperance, peace, and antislavery societies, that calls for justice to woman and to the laborer, and that overthrows tyranny, is the goodness of human nature, that throbs with more or less intensity in every breast, and which Christianity ostentatiously claims for itself, while it conveniently passes over to the credit of what it calls " the world " the evils which are its own legitimate fruit.

Are Mohammedans less temperate than the Christians who tempt them with intoxicating drink ? Are Hindoos less honest than British Christians, who have stolen from them their country, and who enrich themselves by impoverishing the inhabitants ?

But we are told that all persons do wrong; that is, they knowingly violate natural law. I grant it; but, if that proves original sin, it will not be at all difficult to prove original virtue. All persons do right; and they do right ten times where they do wrong once. No man was ever known to tell more lies than truths, or to be for a longer time angry than good-natured. The fact is, that human beings are born neither in virtue nor sin, but capable of both : and, with each succeeding age, man's ability to master his animal propensities increases ; and he thus grows into virtue, as he does toward perfect manhood, for which he started at the beginning, but to which he cannot attain without the time essential for that growth.

If the doctrine of original sin is false, then the notion that God doomed the race to endless perdition on account of a condition resulting from it is false. Man was never lost, nor in danger of being lost: that in his history that looks most like it is his belief of such a fable. The damnation from which Jesus is supposed to save men only exists in the imagination of those who believe in this soul-enslaving superstition. When I ask for the evidence on which the faith in eternal damnation rests, I am pointed to the Bible, which I am told is God's word. Before believing such a doctrine on the statement of the Bible, you ought to be as certain that the Bible is true as that your head is on your shoulders. The very fact that the Bible teaches it is sufficient evidence that the Bible is untrue. Where, O Nature, my mother! dost thou teach such a horrible doctrine as these ignorant children of thine are blasting men's souls with? Not in the south wind, that sweeps over the land to-day with life and beauty following in its path. Out of the cold arms of winter springs the land; the loosened streams are leaping from the hills with musical cadence; the green grass is peeping; the buds are swelling; and the long-silent birds are pouring their melody into our souls. How these voices give the lie to this howling blasphemy! Thou sun, that turns the world over, and warms it into life; that kisses the cheek of the cottager's child, and smiles on the beggar as sweetly as on the pompous bishop; that lights up the malefactor's cell as gloriously as the cathedral, — thou preachest a gospel in which no such soul-harrowing dogma is found.

The headache of the drunkard is but the voice of Nature saying to him, "Do thyself no harm." The burn of the child is painful; but the pain teaches it a lesson that it needs to learn: and, if the burn is so severe that it must die, Nature wraps her arms about the little one, sends it into a precious sleep, and wakens it for a start in a higher life.

How could damnation be the penalty for man's doing what by virtue of his very constitution he must do? Man was as certain to sin as a green apple is to be sour; and time and favorable conditions are as necessary to cure him as to ripen and sweeten the apple.

But, if men were never liable to damnation, the necessity for evangelical salvation never existed. God never allowed the Devil to rend the world; and there never was any need for his Son to come from heaven to patch it. God never hurled the world into the pit of perdition with his right hand; and there was therefore no necessity for him to lower the rope of salvation down with his left for the lost wretches to seize by faith. Men never were far from God; and they consequently need no one to bring them nigh. They were never damned, nor in danger of it; and Orthodox salvation is as unnecessary as a lightning-conductor in a coal-mine.

The method by which God is supposed to save men through faith in Jesus shows monstrous absurdity and cruelty on the part of God who offers it, and great unmanliness on the part of those who accept it. Man, the finite, has sinned against an infinite God; he has broken his most holy law: and God justly consigns him to eternal torments; and it is only by an exercise of his infinite mercy that a way of escape has been provided. So much Orthodoxy assumes. It is evidently false; for nothing can be more unjust or unreasonable. All men sin everywhere, and have always done so: it is therefore evident that wrong-doing is inevitable. What God could punish men, and, above all, eternally punish them, for doing what, in the nature of things (and these he had himself made), all of them must do? Tie up your boy's legs, and flog him till his back is gory, because he does not run six miles an hour; keep him without food for three days, and then kill him because he steals a crust from your pantry, — and you are a kind, considerate parent, compared to a God who makes men with a strong disposition to do wrong, permits a Devil to tempt them, and then annexes the penalty of eternal damnation to the crime of wrong-doing.

God is angry with the sinner: the wrath of his indignation boils. With the sword of vengeance in his hand, he is ready to strike the fatal blow. Just as the glittering blade is about to descend, the innocent Jesus appears on the stage. "Spare, oh, spare the sinner!" says Jesus. "Only on one condition." — "Name it," says Jesus. "Thou must die in his stead, or my justice can never be satisfied." — "I will: let the blow descend." God plunges the sword of his justice into the heart of Jesus, and then receives the sinner to his bosom graciously; and he goes on his way, singing, —

"Jesus has paid the debt we owe,
And God is satisfied."

To save man by such a plan, supposing it to be possible, is to sink him in meanness and degradation. So instinctively do men scorn it, that mesmeric excitements, under the name of revivals of religion, are got up to overcome this natural repugnance. We have sinned, — such is the doctrine, — and are justly subject to punishment; but an innocent being offers to bear the penalty, if we will believe in him, accept him, and bow down to him. "No, thank you, Jesus, no! I much prefer to bear the consequences of my own transgressions, that I may learn the lesson from them that nature inculcates, and whose tendency is to make me wiser and better. There may be men who wish to dodge the consequences of their deeds: they may accept your offer; but I cannot, — still less if, in accepting it, I am at the same time to accept of you as my master." If to hell I must go, I will go a free man, and with that sense of manhood that must transform the pit of perdition into paradise.

I charge this doctrine with being not only false, but dreadfully pernicious. If Jesus bears away the consequences of our guilt, takes our place, washes us in his blood, so that, though black as ink, we can in an instant be made white as snow, why should we struggle for purity? why should we wrestle with temptations daily, and strive earnestly to live lives in harmony with our ideal of manhood? Faith in Jesus must be of infinitely more importance than faithfulness to principle: to obtain the cloak of his righteousness, and skulk under it, and be credited with the merit that belongs to another, becomes much more important than to live a righteous life; and thus the Church, by its acceptance of this doctrine, makes men satisfied with a tenth-rate morality, and puts off the day of the world's redemption.

What, then, shall we do to be saved? Evils are around us like mosquitoes in July: like bloodhounds, whose scent can never be baffled, they dog our footsteps. Not a soul but needs salvation from them: how shall it be obtained? Let us see what has saved us in times past.

Once, man trod the wild, a naked savage. The sun scorched him by day, and the cold wind chilled him as he lay on the branches of a tree at night. The sleet fell upon his bare breast, and, melting, ran in streams to his feet. He searched the woods for wild fruit, and dined on acorns, crab-apples, wild plums, and chestnuts, or roots that he scratched out of the ground. At times, he outran the wild rabbit, sucked its warm blood, and ate its quivering flesh, nor thought of better fare. What saved him from this pitiable condition? What taught him to build a house, clothe himself with befitting garments, and thus bid defiance to the elements? Nature, that brought man into existence, did not launch him on the ocean of life without a pilot or charts, merely promising to supply them at some future time. She did not send Jesus with a beacon-light four thousand years afterwards, and make the success of millions of vessels depend upon their ability to see what to most of them in the nature of things was invisible. The first man carried his savior in his soul, and no man since has ever been destitute; and just in proportion as men have attended to this savior have they been delivered from evil, saved from sin and suffering, and led into truth and right, and the heaven that invariably accompanies them. By using his mental powers, man learned to spin and weave, and make for himself garments for all seasons and all weather: it was thus he learned to fashion the wooden club, the hammer and axe of stone, then of bronze, and, lastly, of steel, to fell the trees, to dig the stone, to burn the lime, and rear his household home; and, in process of ages numerous, the naked, houseless savage was transformed into artistic man. And all this long before Adam rose or fell, before the snake was cursed, or the Bible Saviour promised.

In the times of old, man wearily wandered over the earth: if he wished to go a hundred miles, every step had to be taken by his own feet. He climbed the rugged mountain-steeps, waded or swam the streams, threaded his way through the wilderness, and with bleeding feet and exhausted body arrived at his destination. He saw the wild steed; and increasing intelligence taught him its use: with a stem of a vine for a bridle, he mounted, and with exultant spirit bounded the country over. As his intelligence further increased, he levelled the hills, filled the valleys, bridged the streams, united distant lands by highroads and railroads, over which flies the locomotive, outstripping the eagle in its flight.

Where we now assemble, and hundreds of thousands find ample subsistence, a hundred savages would have starved three hundred years ago. Take a glance backward, and view this region as it was. The beasts of the chase have fled; deep snow covers the ground, and hunger dwells in every miserable hut; hollow-eyed men and women look into the wan faces of their famishing children, who vainly cry for food; the last bone is picked, the last scrap of skin roasted and eaten: death calls them one by one, and with returning spring the prowling wolves pick their bones. What saves us from such a fate to-day? Our increased intelligence. This taught us to plough, to sow, to reap; and over our broad land waves bread for a world. The salvation of Orthodoxy never produced a blade of grass nor a grain of wheat: it is as powerless to stay the hunger of the savage as it is to quench the deep thirst of the enlightened soul.

Ignorance once covered the land like a pall, and Nature's preachers discoursed for ages to deaf souls. The thought, as it slowly rounded itself in man's brain, had no power of projection from the mind that gave it birth, but lay there shrouded, and died with its possessor. By the development of his inherent nature, man grew into speech, formed signs for sound, shaped the reed, and then the feather that dropped from a passing bird's wing; from the waving flag by the river-side first, and then from a nation's tatters, brought forth paper, and made the wisdom of one the property of the many. He ransacked the sunless caves, and brought to light the iron and the lead, and formed the printing-press,—the multiplier of thought, the long-wished-for lever that moves the world.

In his infancy man was terrified by eclipses that swallowed the day, and comets whose fiery hair streamed over the evening sky, and portended to him most fearful calamities. He saw in storms, tornadoes, volcanoes, and earthquakes the presence of angry gods or devils, whose wrath could only be turned away by bloody and cruel ceremonies. Science soothed and comforted him: she put into his hand the telescope, and brought these monsters of the sky into his home, tamed them, and they became agreeable visitants. She has not destroyed storms, volcanoes, and earthquakes; but she has taught us how to foretell storms, informed us where earthquakes are most likely to occur, and pointed out the natural causes that produce them.

There was a time when war was man's universal trade, and its curses came to every door; when whole regions were ravaged, and neither age nor sex was spared. Man's growth in intelligence and benevolence has assuaged its horrors; made distant nations acquainted, and united them by the bonds of commerce; has given them peaceful pursuits, and promises in time to destroy all war, and usher in the reign of universal peace.

Man's intelligence does not enable him to cure all sickness; but it does better. It teaches multitudes how to prevent sickness, and will ere long instruct all, as it has already by the discovery of anæsthetics robbed pain of its terrors.

What is it that saves us now? It is a summer's evening: a dark cloud rolls its sable folds over the sky. Who shall save us from the bolt launched apparently for our destruction? It strikes: we are stunned; but that slender rod saved us: along it the fiery flash descended harmless to the ground. Franklin is our savior, and science instructed him.

The rain descends in unremitting showers. The heavens seem dissolving, and threaten to wash the land into the sea. The river rises. Down go madly the rushing waters; away the piers of the bridge are swept; the bridge itself swings, sways for an instant, and is gone; its timbers are hurrying down the stream. The toll-house still remains, a frail island in the rushing river; but the waters are rising: they are washing away its foundations. See that boy on the housetop waving his handkerchief, a woman at the window, looking at the angry waters, and wringing her hands in despair! Hear the hoarse cries of the father as he calls for help! In vain is faith. Prayers, psalms, hymns, Bibles, can do nothing. Neither the virgin nor her Son can aid the perishing family, and we shudder as we see what must be their fate. But here comes a boat rowed by strong arms. They are saved! Children, mother, father, all are saved just as their home goes dashing down the boiling flood. What saved them? Science and benevolence,— science, that taught men to build the boat; and benevolence, or kindly feeling, which is the heritage of humanity, of which no church has a monopoly; which the people called wicked by the Orthodox often manifest more strongly than those they consider most pious: these were the saviors of this family, as they are the great saviors of mankind.

It is night: the last lamp has shut its eye, and calmly the stars look down on the sleeping city. Wrapped in soundest slumber we lie as the hours unconsciously fly. We are aroused by clanging bells: what a glare lights up the room! Hear the tramp of hurrying feet in the street below, and that most fearful cry of "Fire, fire!" We follow the rushing throng. There is the building: how the flames lick it with their fiery tongues, and then leap as if in ecstasy above their victims! How well it is, we think, that all have escaped! But they have not. Hear those screams, louder than the crackling fire. It is a mother's voice, "Save, oh, save my child!" The flames, like fiery serpents, are on every side, ready to devour her, and there is no prospect of escape. "O God," she cries in her anguish, "save my child!"

Hearts throb, and eyes are dim with tears. What is that rising through the smoke? A ladder! I hear the oath of the fireman, though I cannot see him, as he calls to his men. It is placed against the devoted building: the hose from a steam fire-engine play on each side of the window, and beat back the flames; and the arms of the kind-hearted, though rough-handed and rough-tongued fireman, bear mother and baby in safety to the ground amid the joyful shouts of the delighted spectators. They are safe! What saved them? Prayer, in her case, was powerless as the breath that utered it: the salvation of the Christian, if trusted in, could but have paralyzed the arm of endeavor. What church would open its doors to the fireman that saved her? What future awaits him if Orthodoxy is to decide? Yet he was a savior: science aided him, benevolence impelled him. Intelligence and love, man's great deliverers in every age, — they have cured a thousand ills under which we suffered in the past, and promise to cure or relieve all that remain.

Science has sunk wells in the desert, opened fountains by hundreds in the sandy waste, and made it blossom as the rose. It has dug mines innumerable, and brought up blessings from the flinty bosom of the earth. It has clothed us, heated our apartments, and shorn winter of its rigor. It has robbed the small-pox, that terrible scourge, of its horrors, cleansed our cities, and said to the dreaded cholera, "Touch not my children, and do those who obey me no harm." Aided by benevolence, it has reformed our prisons, and banished the tortures that were so prevalent when the Church ruled the land, and the Bible was regarded as the fountain of all law. They have entirely changed the character of our insane-asylums. Wretched creatures are no longer chained in bare rooms, and left in nakedness, filth, and cold, to howl and scowl their miserable lives away, as they were not a hundred years ago, but are treated with better sense and greater kindness, and generally restored to their friends in the possession of health of body and soundness of mind.

By railroads and steamships science is uniting us with all mankind in bonds so firm that war can never sever. Already we are shaking hands with China and Japan. The barriers are falling that our mutual ignorance erected; and in time we shall become so well acquainted with other nations, and our interests be so inseparably connected with theirs, that war will become impossible.

By physiology science is teaching us daily the laws of health, and supplying us with motives to obedience; and, wherever its instructions are heeded, the average duration of human life is increasing. By geology it has enabled us to discard the old biblical fables of the earth's and man's creation, and shown us the orderly development of organic beings during ages of which the Jewish cosmogonist never dreamed; and by phrenology it has revealed to us the cause of the strong propensities to wrong-doing which some persons possess; and thus, by placing a double guard where the danger was greatest, much evil has been nipped in the bud. In demonstrating to us that the basis of all intoxicating drinks is alcohol, and that this is an acrid poison, it has saved countless thousands from drunkenness and all its attendant evils, and it will in time banish it from the earth.

Science, or knowledge, does more: it robs death of its terrors. It has revealed to many of us a spirit in all organic existences, and its conscious, continued existence in man; and comforted millions by giving them the absolute assurance of life after death has destroyed the body. It says to the mourner, "Dry up your tears: they are not dead, but born anew into a higher life. The earth claims the body; but that which you loved, the spirit that animated it, is yet in existence, and you shall meet again." It reveals no hell, it tells of no Devil, and shows the impossibility of both. It preaches no forgiveness, it is true; but it shows the possibility of outgrowing the effects of wrong-doing and how to enjoy by right-doing the bliss that invariably flows therefrom.

What is it, my brother, that curses you, and from which you wish to be delivered? There are but few evils from which a man cannot be saved in this life; and all that this life fails to cure, the next will, in my opinion, accomplish. "*I am poor:* my poverty troubles me." Give me your hand, my brother: I have been just where you are, and I can sympathize with you. You can be saved. If there had been as much pains taken in Boston to save men's bodies as there has been to save their souls, you would not be poor. But you must never remain where you are. Cursed is the man who is poor; but doubly cursed is the man who is content to be poor. You must be economical; and I will not ask you to be more so than I have been. Stop tobacco chewing and smoking instantly. "My tobacco only costs me three cents a day." Yes; but three cents a day is nearly eleven dollars a year. Stop that glass of lager-bier: there is no value in it to you, and it costs money, which you cannot afford. Let rich men waste money on such folly if they choose: you must not do it if you would conquer poverty. Drink no longer tea and coffee. "Why, you would take away all my comforts," I hear you say. When you have ceased from the use of them, you will find that it was the use that made the appetite for them, and caused them to appear necessary. Hot water, and milk and sugar taken with it, as with tea and coffee, is more wholesome, cheaper, and in time you will like it just as well. Cease eating rich cakes and lard-crusted pies; live simply; buy nothing because it is fashionable. You may save, the poorest of you, by strict economy, fifty dollars a year. Buy with that a piece of land (if you had what is justly yours, you might get it without buying): build a house of your own on it as soon as possible, if there are no more than two rooms in it. I have lived in a house with one, and know the happiness of the man who has a foothold on this planet, and a home that does not belong to another.

You are sick, and that makes you unhappy. But

what a blessing it is that the best of medicines can be had for nothing! and, if you have vitality enough left, they can cure you. If not, you will be better without your body; and death will relieve you from its burden. Exercise in the open air, sunshine, pure water, plain food, — these are the medicines I recommend to you: the medicines you buy of the apothecary are generally as useless as they are dear.

You are a drunkard. I do not despise you. I do not tell you to wash in the blood of Jesus; for if you could you would be no cleaner, and the same quantity of whiskey would make you just as drunk. You must abandon all intoxicating drinks, from brandy to hard cider: that is the only way by which you can obtain salvation. In time, all taste for these drinks will die out, and you will be a free man. This remedy is infallible, and as good for prevention as it is for cure. It has saved every man that fairly tried it, and its benefit has been incalculable.

You have large amativeness, and at times this passion is your master. Do not suppose that you are the only man in the world in the same condition. This passion is the strongest; for only by its exercise can the race be perpetuated. But you must not allow it to master you. The man, the essential man, the reasonable man, the moral man, must be the master; and this can be done. You must be temperate in all things: abandon tea, coffee, tobacco in all its forms, and intoxicating drink in every shape. The use of these increases the power of the animal propensities, while at the same time it weakens the will, and obscures the judgment. Pepper, mustard, spices, and all condiments, if used at all, should be used very sparingly. Never read books that appeal to amativeness, and arouse it. Work hard, so that sleep will overtake you as soon as your head reaches the pillow. Do not loiter in bed after you are awake in the morning, — not even on Sunday. Have worthy objects of thought, and they will banish unworthy ones. If you are unmarried, and over twenty years of age, find a suitable companion, and marry: a good wife is worth more to most men than a thousand Christs.

"*I am ignorant*, and wish to be saved." The man who knows he is ignorant is on the highroad to knowledge. You feel what the wisest and best have felt, and you have no need to be discouraged. Resolve to learn a little daily, and your acquisitions in a few years will surprise you. Read, but be sure to write; think for yourself; make some branch of knowledge a specialty, and give a little time to it daily. One thing well learned will give you a taste for many others, and help you to learn all others; and you will not be ignorant in all respects, whatever you may still be in many.

"*But I fear to die.*" Cheer up: that is the last thing that should trouble you. Find a good medium for communication with the spirit-world, and you can receive evidence, as thousands have done, of the existence of your friends, with warm and loving hearts, enjoying existence more than they did while here. Death will lead you to them, and make you one of their number; and, when you are satisfied of this, your fear of death will be gone, and you will be saved.

"Is Jesus, then, a savior in no sense?" All good men, and in fact all men, are, to a certain extent, saviors. The man who gives a hungry man a dinner saves him in one sense: the woman who stands by her friend in sorrow, and comforts her in affliction, is also a savior. The wagoner who gave the young girl his great-coat on a wet night, — he too was a savior. Little is said about them; but there are thousands of women who are saving men, children, and other women, daily and hourly. To call this fanatic of Nazareth the Saviour of the world is to do injustice to the noblest of mankind. What a grand list is the list of saviors! — Moses, Jesus, Confucius, Gautama, Socrates, Plato, Watt, Joan of Arc, Fulton, Arkwright, Herschell, Thomas Paine, Theodore Parker, Fanny Wright, Humboldt, John Brown, Garrison, Phillips, and hosts of others. To many of them we owe vastly more than we do to Jesus; and justice has yet to be done them in the more intelligent future.

Science and benevolence, in all ages, have done the work of salvation, and Orthodox religion and superstition have as constantly claimed the credit. "We have done it!" exclaim these impudent charlatans. "See that dashing locomotive, with a thousand passengers at its heels! We fashioned him with our hands, breathed the air of life into his iron body, and started him on his world-wide mission. We gave wings to the telegraph, life to the printing-press; and by us the world has advanced to the noontide of glory." The fact being, that they lay dozing in the darkened church till the scream of the engine and the galvanic shock of the telegraph awakened them to a knowledge of their existence. Take from man all that science has done, and leave him all that orthodox Christianity can do apart from science, and what would he be ? No house to shelter him ; no garment to clothe him; no machinery to assist him ; the great universe a sealed book ; himself little more than a blank on one of its pages. In a cave he would sleep ; and, when the sunbeams shone therein, he would waken to recite his prayers to the Mumbo Jumbo of his creed, who grumbles in the thunder, and shows his anger in the oak-splitting lightning.

If science and benevolence are our great saviors, let us cultivate them.

> " Science is a child as yet ; but her scope and power shall grow,
> And her triumphs in the future shall diminish toil and woe."

Let halls of science be multiplied, and opened on Sunday, free for all. Let us have lecturers dealing in facts, rather than priests dealing in fables. Instead of Bible societies and tract societies, let us have societies for the distribution of knowledge on which the soul can feed, and by which man can make the most of his present position. Let people understand the glorious truths of astronomy ; and let telescopes be as plentiful as Bibles. Let the truths of geology, which are destined to supplant many of the fables of theology, be familiar to all. Let every child be taught a knowledge of its own body, and its relation to food, drink, air, light, &c. ; and thus will the ravages of disease be stayed, and a foundation for long life and happiness secured. Let the producers of the world's wealth be secured the product of their labor, and let all idlers be compelled to work or starve. Let Fashion die, and Use and Beauty take her place, and the true millennium will be here. The fever-breeding swamps will be drained, and fruitful gardens take their place: where the reed and the flag grow, the apple, the pear, and the peach shall flourish; the wild woods will fall, and stately palaces for humanity rise. The slave of capital shall stand erect, a man, and rejoice in the fruit of his labor; and the prison for the felon will be no longer needed. The pope and the priest, the king and the captain, will be loved and feared and hated no more. War will only be known in history, and Love shall be at home in every bosom.

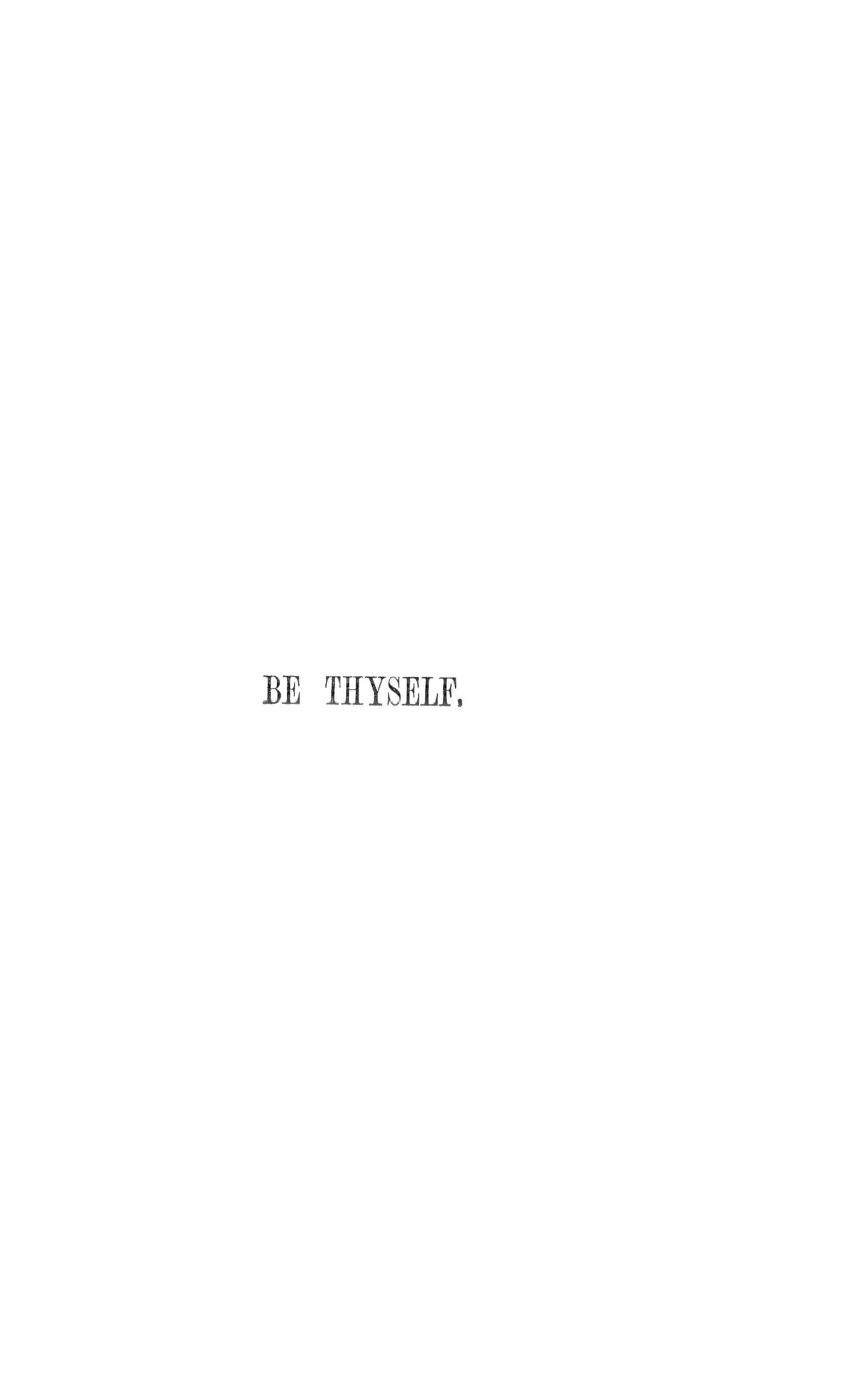

BE THYSELF,

BE THYSELF.

We live in a universe abounding with variety. The heavens present us with systems, suns, stars, planets, comets, meteors, and clouds. Systems differ from systems in shape, suns from suns in size. "One star differeth from another star in glory." One planet is belted, another girt with rings; comets and meteors are as varied as their numbers. Clouds are never twice alike: pile upon pile they lie, with rosy-topped mountain-peaks; skip like silvery sheep across the blue meadow of the sky, or lie like golden islands in a silver sea.

The earth is not less varied than the heavens. Here the mountains lift up their hoary heads in silent majesty, white with the snows of a thousand winters; and there lie the dusky valleys, ten thousand feet below them, where twilight holds continual holiday. The boundless plain stretches before us, a wide expanse without a hillock, an ocean of drifting sand unblessed by a green blade, or a grassy prairie in its virgin green, or clad in flowery beauty; the placid lake, the leaping rill, the dark cañon, the river, rolling forever on, and the ocean girt by low sand-banks or frowning precipices, calm as a frozen lake, or, waked to wrath by furious storms, howling to the moaning of the winds.

Nor are the organic productions of the earth less varied, — from the cedar that rears its symmetrical head three hundred feet above its roots, to the velvet moss that carpets the ground at its feet. The lichen clings to the boulder, the algæ to the wave-washed rock; the pine's leaves are spines, while a leaf of the talipot palm will cover a company of soldiers. The condor scales with unwearied wing the heights of the Andes; the katydid chirps in the meadow its evening hymn; the whale floats, an island in the ocean; the animalcule explores a drop.

What diversity! No two planets, no two animals, no two things, alike. Not only does the oak differ from the pine, and the pine from the cedar, but no man ever saw two oak-trees alike, nor any two leaves upon an oak. There are no two grains of sand alike: to microscopic eyes they would be as diverse as boulders. To a stranger the sheep in a flock seem all alike; to the shepherd they are as different as the individuals comprising it, and he can call them all by name. Nature never casts two articles out of the same mold: when one is cast, she cracks the mold, and makes a new one for the next, and thus secures endless variety.

Man is no exception to this rule. Look at the variety of races, — the blushing Caucasian, the oblique-eyed Mongolian, the dark-skinned African, the black-haired, beardless American, the dumpy Esquimaux, and the spindle-shanked Australian. Heads differ, eyes differ, fingers differ, all parts differ, in every man from every other man, the world over. That passing from us which is invisible to all differs from the invisible aura of others, or how could the dog track his master through the crowded street? There are said to be from three to four thousand languages on the globe, from the harsh and guttural Esquimaux to the smooth and liquid Italian. Every individual has, in fact, peculiarities of speech that distinguish him from all others. The voice reveals the person when we have no other clue; and we say that is John, Mary, or Thomas, when the persons speaking are unseen.

This variety that we thus notice in Nature is a continual blessing. Suppose it otherwise. Let all the heavenly bodies be alike in size and brightness, and placed at equal distances, and we should have a celestial checker-board, true to the line, and pretty for one look, but tame forever. Make all the flowers roses, and who would not miss the violet? The rose itself would lose half its beauty for want of contrast with its less fair floral sisters. If all leaves were alike, and all trees after the same pattern, how the dull landscape would fatigue the eye! Make all men like pins in a paper, mold candles in a box, or shot in a barrel, the fat thin, or the thin stout; elongate the short, or stunt the long; give all eyes the same expression; make all noses aquiline or Roman, — and what a desert of faces would surround us! Let it occur to-day, what terrible mistakes would take place before morning! There is not an ugly sinner but would pray for the return of his old face to rescue him from the dead level of humanity.

Minds differ more widely than faces. "Many men, many minds," is a proverb as true as it is old. More varied than flowers in the garden, leaves in the forest, or stars in the sky, are the minds of mankind. Look into our libraries and see the products of those minds,—books on every conceivable subject, and no two alike even on the same subject.

This difference is seen in boys as soon as the intellect is awake, and manifests itself continually. Here is a little mechanic saving his cents and buying a jack-knife, with which he whittles mimic water-wheels. See him in the brook, his little pants tucked up to his brown knees, while he rejoices, as his wheel spins round, like an angel over a new world. Give him a chance to develop in his own peculiar line, and, like a Watt or a Fulton, he will yoke new steeds to the car of progress, and drive on the world at a diviner speed.

Another little fellow is drawing horses on the barn-door with chalk, or making little dogs out of dough in the kitchen. An artist is he in the germ; full blossomed and fruited, the business of his thinking soul and obedient hand shall be to embody the creations of his genius, that shall bless the world for long centuries after he has gone to more than realize his most glorious conceptions in a higher school of art.

Here is a born orator; mounted on a stump, he harangues the village boys. Proud ships may sail, they attract him not; wheels may spin, what cares he? Could he enchain an audience by his eloquence, earth has no greater blessing, heaven itself could grant no more. To this he devotes himself; his soul leads, he obediently follows, till multitudes hang breathless upon his words, while he talks as a spring leaps from the mountain-side.

This farmer cares more for his cattle than a monarch for his crown. Spring has driven winter from the land, the birds are singing, and he rejoices as he drives his "jocund team a-field." Nothing could induce him to leave these incense-breathing fields for the din and dust of the city; but the merchant despises the dull round of the farmer, and is never happy but in the crowded mart,— a busy man among busy men.

It is well that it should be so. Were all to become merchants, the stock would soon be spent; the river of commerce would dry up, for the rills of production would cease to flow. Were all producers, goods would accumulate as water does in lakes, and there would be no rivers to distribute the surplus to the needy lands. If all were poets, painters, or orators, bread and butter would be sadly deficient; and if all were plain, prosy farmers, how much that makes life joyous we should lose!

As men's intellectual endowments differ, so do their moral faculties and religious sentiments. One is a born sceptic; he must see, hear, feel, and is hardly satisfied without tasting and smelling, what is marvellous, in order to give it credence. He may desire to believe; but the arms of his faith are so short that they can not reach the distant object. Another believes at once: it is only necessary to present the statement, and he swallows it in a moment, though "gross as a mountain." He reads that the whale swallowed Jonah, and he lived three days in his belly; if he had read that Jonah swallowed the whale, he would swallow both, and make no bones about either. He has no need to pray, —

> "Stretch our faith's capacity wider and yet wider still.'

The door of his soul is wide enough to take in all company; no more to be reasonably praised for the width of his spiritual gullet, than the sceptic blamed for the narrowness of his.

One is firm as a mountain: he feels like Fitz James when he exclaimed, —

> "Come one, come all! This rock shall fly
> From its firm base as soon as I."

Another is pliant as the wheat-stalk, that waves in the June breeze.

This man is spiritual; every breath that he draws is redolent of heaven; he mounts as naturally as the freed bird, and carols in the sky; that man gravitates to the earth like a thunder-cloud big with a shower.

The arms of the benevolent would all mankind embrace. If he were made of gold, his sympathy would lead him to give himself away for the benefit of man kind. Some such give away all that they have, and more than they have; while the economical man's purse-strings are twined around his heart, sometimes with a hard-to-be-loosed knot in them, and he thinks ten times before he gives once.

If all were credulous as some, the world would feed on lies, and dire would be the consequence. If all were sceptical as others, new truths and strange facts might stand knocking at the world's heart for centuries before they gained admission. If all were firm and unyielding, progress would either be impossible or very slow; and, if all were equally pliant, revolutions would be as plentiful as showers in spring, and peace and stability would be at an end. If all were spiritual as Swedenborg in his later days, corn and potatoes would be sadly deficient; and if all were "of the earth, earthy," we should be no better than the savage in the wild.

There may be too wide deviations from a normal standard morally, as there are intellectually; for some are born morally asquint, as others are physically,—deviations that require careful culture and training to overcome. But men as naturally differ in their moral natures as they do in their physical constitutions, and the difference thus existing is of the greatest value to the race. One's religion is like the sun, fervid and intense; another's like the moon, calm and beautiful; and another's like the stars, bright and saint-like; yet all lovely as the varied flowers of the meadow, or the tints of the evening sky.

Hence the importance of the exhortation of my text,—BE THYSELF. There is no originality, no complete manhood, without it. It is the highest prerogative of the animal kingdom, the crowning glory of humanity. Among the coral polyps, at the base of the animal kingdom, we have millions of animals united in one community; what is eaten by one is as if eaten by all; and the will of the individual is lost in that of the group, harmoniously forming their stony structures at the sea-bottom. Among the mollusks, countless multitudes lie in one oozy bed, with little scope, as there is little inclination, for individual action. Among the fishes there is more scope; but, living in shoals, the will of one is lost in that of the many. Among the birds a few leaders control the flock. Beasts possess more independence; but the strongest horse leads the band as it sweeps over the prairie, and the old male buffalo decides the course of the entire herd. Ascending to man, there is more individuality, and the most among the most highly developed.

Even the savage is an individual who comes into direct communication with Nature for himself. His parents say, "Shift for yourself," and Nature says the same. He learns where the fish hide, and he spears them; he watches the beaver, and traps it, that he may clothe himself with its skin. He knows the ridge on which the chestnut grows; and, when the leaves fall, he makes for the winter a secret hoard. He builds his own tent, supplies his fire, communes with Nature, and forms ideas of the world in which he finds himself. But he must be obedient to his chief, even to death; and his individuality is sacrificed continually. But here is the philosopher in whom humanity blossoms, and brings forth fruit. In him we see the highest exemplification of self-hood. In him Nature's great endeavor is fulfilled, her work of the ages is completed. Reason sits on the throne; and the lawless propensities are subject to her sway. He reads, hears, investigates; and what his judgment decides upon, that he does, and hears the continual plaudit of a good conscience, saying, "Well done!"

The benefits that flow from the exercise of this self-hood are inconceivable. Among men who practice it are Emerson, the most original mind on this continent, and whose private life is pure as his intellect is clear; Garrison, whose manliness no force could bend, and whose love for the bondman was only equaled by a fearless denunciation of his oppressors; in science, Lyell, Darwin, Huxley, Spencer, Draper, independent free-thinkers, who are delivering the world from ignorance, enlarging the domain of thought, and breaking the bonds of priestly bigotry and intolerance. On the other side are the tools of Popish superstition, who dare hardly call their souls their own; with whom the word of a priest is potent as a law of God; who kneel, and swallow the God baked but yesterday by the cook, and dare not open their shutters to let in one ray of heaven's pure light; the slaves of Episcopal domination, whose priests swear never to be wiser than the Thirty-nine Articles, and who must perjure themselves if they ever step beyond the narrow, creed-made pale that the first step of an infant mind would almost overstride; and, along with these, the millions of abject ecclesiastical subjects, whose spiritual bondage is their pride, and who tremble when they hear a free thought, lest the heavens fall, or the earth gape, and swallow both speaker and hearers.

The world's heroes in poetry, philosophy, mechanics, and reform, have been heroic by virtue of their self-hood. Leave this out of the composition of a man, and you have, in poetry, a verse-wright who never dared to write an original line; in philosophy, a peddler of defunct ideas; and in war, a poltroon. What made Homer the prince of song, and enabled the old "blind man of Chio" to chant a strain which the hills of Greece echoed for centuries, still heard across the wild ocean, and amid the din and roar of this nineteenth century? He wrote in his own inimitable style the beautiful thoughts that crowded into his brain: from the heaven of his own creation, he poured down those melodies which a busy world on tiptoe stands to hear.

Who was Shakspeare's model? Whence did he draw the supplies of which millions have drunk and been refreshed? With no broken pitcher did he go to another's well, but drew from the exhaustless fountain of his own soul. He stands to-day like a granite mountain, whose head is lost in the clouds, and whose culminating point no traveler has reached: as men ascend, untrodden hights lie still above them. Had he been a mere imitator, the molehill of his production would have been long since trodden to the dead level of the plain.

How did Bunyan write his "Pilgrim's Progress"? As the brook babbles, taking no counsel of other brooks, but telling its own story in its own way; and, in spite of its many absurdities, the tinker's book will live for centuries. Copernicus and Galileo, taking counsel of their own souls, heeding not the monkish fable-mongers who believed the world to be flat as a table, and the stars little shining points, boldly marched into the untrodden realm, explored its seas of worlds, and came back laden with glorious truths.

Columbus, advising with no Past, old and decrepit, who had bounded the world, and inscribed on its boundary, "No more beyond," launched his bark to cross the unknown ocean; and for weary weeks and months sailed steadily on, on, — the cloudy sky above, the inky sea around, — spite of the frowns, tears, and entreaties of the cowards who accompanied him, till a new world, like a radiant maiden, leaped into his arms, and blessed him for his manliness. We are here to-day because Columbus dared to be himself.

It was this self-hood that made Raphael the prince of painters, and Napoleon of warriors. "He does not fight according to the rule," said the European fogies. No; but he had a rule of his own to fight by, and thus he conquered. In Watts, it gave us the steam-engine, with its hundred hands and its restless soul; and in Fulton, the boat that heeds not wind or tide, whose steam-arm paddles day and night, and never tires. By it, Socrates climbed the hights of philosophy, from which it was but a step to the heaven into which he entered.

Mere imitators in art never scale the hights; but, placing their feet in the prints left by former travelers, they tire themselves out with a step that is unnatural to them, and faint and die by the way, leaving no sign behind that they have ever been. In life's battle, they never make heroes, but wearing another man's armor which never fits them, and wielding a weapon never made for them, they accomplish little, and fall an easy prey to the enemy.

Of the hundreds who have imitated Shakspeare, how many live in remembrance? They have gone like the smoke of the Indian wigwam from our land, while he shines on like a star. Books written by these imitators are mere repositories of twaddle, mountains of chaff, great in bulk, but small in nutriment for the hungry soul. A bonfire of them would give more light to the world than they can give in any other way. Most of our theological works are of this class, — embalmed hosts of dead men's foolish thoughts: a library of them is a catacomb or a mummy pit; how useless to look for light or life in them! Men throw overboard their own thoughts, richer than pearls, and load their barks with cast-off, water-worn shells of conservatism.

Books written by thinkers—men who thought and dared to express their thoughts — are always worth reading. I care not whether their authors were Atheists or Methodists, Heathen or Mohammedan; the life's blood of the author circulates through them, and in reading you feel its pulsations. But books written by men who never saw through their own eyes, who never put out their hands, and felt the world for themselves, nor took one manly step, are the faintest echoes from the distant hills, compared with the heaven-shaking thunder that produced them.

Self-hood is as necessary in religion as in art, science, and literature. The world has been cursed for centuries by men who have sought to shape the religious element in all after the same model. Placing the soul of man in the crucible of sect, it has been melted down, and poured into some creed-made mould: its beauty marred, its original proportions destroyed, it stands a monument of man's folly, a warning to all, and speaks in loudest tones the language of my text, Brother, sister, BE THYSELF!

All great religious reformers have acted more or less on this principle. The more fully they have carried it out, all other things being equal, the wider has been their sphere of influence, and the more good they have accomplished. What enabled Moses to rise above the multitude, like a mountain in the midst of a vast plain, so high, that, at the distance of thirty-five hundred years, he stands out still in bold relief against the horizon? What magic was there in his name, that Oblivion swallowed it not with the millions that have disappeared in his never-to-be-satisfied maw? Snapping the fetters with which the priests of Egypt sought to bind his soul, he listened to the promptings of his heart as it taught him a better religion than he had ever before heard; and he hesitated not to obey its requirements. Leaving behind him the enchantments of Egypt, and the pleasure of Pharaoh's court, he became a wanderer in the desert,— an excellent place for a man to commune with himself. Thence he came, and stamped his soul upon the Jewish nation.

He dared to think for himself on religious matters, to face the great universe and question it; and with a rare originality he taught his countrymen a religion — the answer, as he believed, to his questions — far in advance of its predecessors. But every Jew had just as much right to question for himself and cherish the answer as he; but this Moses would by no means allow: the answer to him must be the answer for all. Hear him! "If thou wilt obey the statutes and commandments that I command thee this day, then blessed shalt thou be in the city and in the field; blessed in thy going-out, and blessed in thy coming-in; blessed in thy basket and in thy store. But, if thou wilt not obey them, cursed shalt thou be in the city and in the field; cursed in thy going-out and coming-in, in thy basket and in thy store." Liberty, spontaneity, selfhood, all must be sacrificed to rigid conformity. The

Jew must be a Mosean, or destruction awaited him. Moses regards the seventh day as holier than all others, and consecrates it to rest for all generations; and the independent Israelite, who gathered sticks upon that day, is stoned to death. Moses thought an angry God could be appeased by burning sheep, oxen, and doves; and the man who has advanced beyond this, who does not believe that God can be pleased with the smell of roasting beasts, must kill and roast his cattle notwithstanding; for Moses speaks, and will be obeyed.

You tell me that Moses received his commandments from God; yes, from the God that is in you and me, and in the same way that we receive ours. He talked with him as we talk with him when we converse with our brother; and he saw him as we see him in the starry sky, or the grassy spear at our feet pointing heavenward. Man three thousand years ago was no nearer to God than we are to day; and the New-England thinker can see God on Mount Katahdin as well as Moses did on Sinai.

Moses thus became the model man for the whole Jewish nation. Every child was taught, that just in proportion as he became like Moses, was he a true man, and sure of God's blessing; as far as he fell short of this, so far had he departed from the right, and was subject to a curse.

After the death of Moses, he was elevated by priest and Levite, sabbath after sabbath, and feast after feast; his holy law unrolled, and weekly read to the assembled multitude. Moses was king, the children of Israel his subjects. Moses was the die, and the Jews the coin, stamped by the repeated blows of their priests with his image and superscription. To be like Moses was the highest ambition of the noblest and best; greater than he could no man be; to be wiser was impossible, and to dream of being better was blasphemous.

Thus crept the nation snail-like through the dull centuries; an oppressive ritual upon their backs like a mountain of lead, and Moses before them, a dark cloud shutting out the blue sky from their wistful gaze.

But Nazareth produced a man who refused to bow any longer to the God, Moses, that had been set up. "One man dared to be true to what is in you and me." In an age of slaves he was free; in an age of cowards he was a hero. While the whole nation was crawling in the dust, Jesus stood upon his feet, and allowed his manhood to speak. "Ye have heard that it hath been said by them of old time (that is, by Moses and the Moseans), An eye for an eye, and a tooth for a tooth: but I say unto you, Resist not evil; but whosoever shall smite thee on the right cheek, turn to him the other also." "Again: ye have heard it hath been said by them of old time, Thou shalt not forswear thyself, but shalt perform unto the Lord thine oaths; but I say unto you, Swear not at all. Let your communication be, Yea, yea; Nay, nay: for whatsoever is more than these cometh of evil." We find him saying, in opposition to old Jewdom, "Why judge ye not of yourselves what is right?" He proclaimed himself Lord of the sabbath, as every sensible man is, and boldly set at defiance all who attempted to fetter his soul. What a consternation was there among the scribes and Pharisees, the soul-mongers of Judæa! "Have you heard that mechanic of Galilee, who is traveling about the country preaching heresy? He addressed a rabble the other day, when he made himself superior to Moses, and set at naught the law given by God himself on Mount Sinai. I understand that he has been saying, Why judge ye not what is right your selves? thus making men their own lawgivers, and taking away the necessity for our services. He is a bold blasphemer, whose mouth must be stopped; away with him, away with him, crucify him, crucify him, he is not fit to live!" The multitude echo the cry, "Away with him, crucify him!" and so they did; and doubtless thought there was an end of his doctrine, and their craft was forever safe. Never did men make a greater mistake. Bury a truth and it is a seed; it springs up, grows, and bears fruit a thousand-fold. Kill a reformer, and his ghost does a hundred times more than the man could ever have done if alive. The doctrine of Jesus could not be killed, and his death seemed to give it life; it spread far and wide; mounted the hills, crossed the valleys, was wafted over the seas; it mounted the throne of the Cæsars, and conquered the conquerors of the world. Now the despised Nazarene, the young reformer of Galilee, has become the esteemed Saviour. While he lived, he was no better than the publicans and sinners with whom he associated; he had a devil, and was mad; he was a pestilent fellow, whom no Jewish aristocrat would be seen in company with for the world. But now he is a good man, a great man, a prophet; nay, a greater prophet than Elias himself, then the greatest and best man that ever lived; the Son of God, yea, the only-begotten Son of God; and lastly, God Almighty from heaven! Men were not satisfied until they had unseated the Omnipotent, and set the man Jesus upon his throne. This is the way the world serves reformers; there is nothing too vile to say about them while they are alive, and nothing too good when they are dead, and the world has accepted their doctrine.

Moses was now dethroned, and Jesus made king; henceforth all must be his obedient subjects. Moses was knocked unceremoniously off the pedestal, Jesus placed thereon, and made the model for the whole human race. "Looking unto Jesus" now becomes the duty of all. The path of life bears the impressions of his feet, and it is our duty, not to make our own impressions, but walk implicitly in his; for "he has left us an example, that we should tread in his steps."

Thus have men destroyed one idol and set up another; and the business of our modern scribes and pharisees is to induce people to worship it. In the name of Jesus the freeman, souls are robbed of their birthright, and the most terrible threatenings denounced against those who, like him, dare to be themselves. In the name of humanity, I protest against this. Jesus our helper, our friend, our teacher, but never our master or tyrant, who holds the lash of future torment over the trembling captive.

Supposing the Jesus of the New Testament to be the veritable God-man, who lived and died that we might live, his example is not such as it would be well for mankind generally to follow. Could each man be a Jesus, it would still be infinitely better to be himself. Looking at his character, as drawn by his four biographers, let us see what would be the consequence of a universal attempt to imitate the example of Jesus.

He lived to be above thirty years of age, yet never was married, never had a wife to call him husband, nor a child, father. On one occasion he said, "There are some eunuchs which were so born from their mother's womb; and there are some eunuchs which were made eunuchs of men, and there be eunuchs which have made themselves eunuchs for the kingdom of heaven's sake. He that is able to receive it, let him receive it." Paul, who seems to have regarded Jesus as a perfect example, never was married, and he advised others to imitate him, as he did his master. Suppose men universally were to shape themselves thus after this model, would not the consequence be most disastrous? The whole world a Shaker community, and in less than a hundred and fifty years a wilderness of wild beasts without a human inhabitant.

According to Mark, Jesus worked at the trade of a carpenter. At the age of thirty he abandoned his business and went out to preach the Gospel. Walking by the sea of Galilee he found Simon and Andrew, James and John, fishing; he called them, saying, "I will make you fishers of men;" they left their fishes and nets, and followed him. Matthew sat at the receipt of custom; Jesus passed by, and said, "Follow me;" and, strange to say, although a Jew, he left his money-gathering business, and followed Jesus. When he had in this way taken twelve men from their avocations, and they and a multitude were assembled together, he preached to them thus: "Take no thought for your life, what ye shall eat or what ye shall drink; nor yet for your body, what ye shall put on. Is not the life more than meat and the body than raiment? Behold the fowls of the air; for they sow not, neither do they reap, nor gather into barns; yet your heavenly Father feedeth them. Are ye not much better than they? Why take ye thought for raiment? Consider the lilies of the field, how they grow: they toil not, neither do they spin. Therefore take no thought saying, What shall we eat, or what shall we drink, or wherewithal shall we be clothed? For after all these things do the Gentiles seek; for your heavenly father knoweth that ye have need of all these things. Seek first the kingdom of God, and his righteousness, and all these things shall be added unto you. Take, therefore, no thought for the morrow, for the morrow shall take thought for the things of itself." Again he says, "Sell that ye have, and give alms." Suppose that men were to commence imitating Jesus in this respect. The tailor leaves the shopboard and cloth, the blacksmith the hammer and anvil, the farmer the plow, and the weaver the loom; millers cease to grind, and bakers to bake, and each commences to preach; and as they preach, they say, "God has given you life, will he not, also, give you food to sustain that life? Cease working, then, and trust in him. He has given you bodies without any effort of your own; will he not much more clothe those bodies without any labor on your part? Look at the sparrows and the pigeons; they neither sow nor reap, and yet God feeds them. Consider the wild roses; see how beautiful they are, and how well clothed; the purple robe of a king is not equal to theirs, and yet they neither spin nor weave. Therefore take no thought about what you shall eat or wear, but trust in God, who feeds the sparrows and clothes the grass, and it will all be well."

The consequences of generally practicing such unphilosophical doctrine would be starvation and ruin. It might answer well for Jesus and his disciples to do thus, for others were sowing, reaping, baking, and fishing for them, and supplying their necessities. If it had not been so, their preaching and practice would have by no means corresponded; for they would have discovered that loaves do not grow on bushes, nor clothes on trees, and that though birds may be fed without sowing and reaping, it is otherwise with human beings.

On one occasion, Jesus went into the temple, and found there money changers, and the sellers of oxen, sheep, and doves; and after he had made a scourge of cords he drove them out, poured out the changers' money and overthrew the tables; this, too, after preaching non-resistance to its utmost extent. An imitation of such conduct would hardly be tolerated, nor would its influence be beneficial. His denunciation of the Scribes and Pharisees is terrible; they were surely not all bad, all "serpents" and of the "generation of vipers," all "fools and blind;" yet he makes no exceptions, but fulminates his woes against them in the most offensive manner. If they were thus bad, how much would his denunciations do toward reforming them? And among a large class like this, there must have been some noble characters.

He told his disciples in the beginning of his ministry not to preach his doctrines to the Gentiles, and states himself that he preached in parables that others "seeing might not see, and hearing, they might not understand." When the people ask him very reasonably for a sign of his Messiahship, he calls them an "evil and adulterous generation." He makes himself the head, and teaches that all are to be subordinate to him. "One is your master, even Christ;" "I your lord and master." If a city would not receive his disciples, nor hear their words, as they wandered round rehearsing the gospel of the Nazarene, when they departed from it they were to shake off the dust of their feet as a testimony against it, and he informs them that it would be more tolerable for Sodom and Gomorrah in the Day of Judgment than for that city. He seems to have had some of the feeling that exists in the little souls of our sectarian bigots. Their sect is comprised of the chosen few, to whom it is the Father's good pleasure to give the kingdom. They are not of the world, and they will have the pleasure of seeing the destruction of their enemies, those who would not believe, bow down to, and support their church. The notions of Jesus with regard to property, prayer, and non-resistance, are very far from reasonable; and though he said and did many excellent things, taking the narratives concerning him to be true, still it is evident that he is no model for the race.

And of this the church generally seems to be aware, though professing continually to practice his precepts and live his life. Jesus says, "Lend, hoping for nothing again;" but where are the Christians that do it? Do outsiders demand six per cent, ten per cent, or two per cent a month, if they find any one whose necessities compel him to pay such usurious interest, then Christians do the same; and no difference, in this respect, is observable between them. Jesus said, "Resist not evil, and if any man smite thee on the one cheek, turn the other also;" "Love your enemies." Christians generally pay no more attention to these commands than if they had never been uttered; in fact, every sect has made an artificial Jesus of its own, generally less fanatical and extravagant, and more fashionable and better suited to the times. We have a Quaker Jesus, who wears a broad-brim, and says "thee," who never enters a "steeple house," and looks upon music and dancing with horror. The Methodist Jesus believes in class-meetings where every one tells his experience; in prayer-meetings where men and women shout and scream as if God was afar off or asleep, and has great faith in John Wesley's sermons and the Methodist discipline. The Episcopal Jesus, unlike the real one, thinks much of forms and ceremonies, loves the tones of a solemn organ, and the dim, religious light that streams through a stained glass window; believes in the thirty-nine articles, and thinks the creed of Athanasius, "which in damning souls is very spacious," one of the best compositions outside of the Bible. The Shaker Jesus believes in "Mother Ann," regards marriage as a mortal sin, thinks all the world Sodom, and Shaker communities so many Zoars to which the righteous Lots have fled from the impending destruction.

This conduct is probably better than it would be to follow literally the example of Jesus, for this, we have seen, would be most disastrous. The obligation of my text is strengthened, then, by our review of the life of Jesus and the conduct of his so-called Church. Man, woman, be thyself, and thou shalt be as great as Jesus, too, or greater than he.

In obedience to this principle, Luther, singlehanded, coped with the banded hosts of Popery, shook the triple-crowned Pope himself, though sitting on the throne of ages, made the Roman hierarchy tremble at the sound of his name, and delivered from priestly tyranny a host of noble souls. Had he been content to shroud his manhood in the monk's cowl, and keep down the rising aspirations of his soul, we might still have been moping about in the dark night of priest-craft, by the pale light of the stars, nor dreaming of a dawning day, and he, a poor Popish slave, had crept long since to the silent grave.

Had he been more faithful to his soul, walked according to its dictates without looking to the right or the left, we might have been much farther advanced to-day. What a multitude of Lutherans are wearing his cast-off clothes, ragged and thread-bare, fitting no one, in place of their own natural and beautiful apparel!

George Fox was a poor shoemaker in Drayton, Lincolnshire. Feeling the fire of truth burning in his bosom, he went out to warm the cold, dead world with its divine influence; casting down his boots and lasts, he went forth to preach the Gospel. What Gospel? The Gospel of George Fox, and no other. And this poor shoemaker, with no more than an ordinary amount of brain and intelligence, shook every steeple in the land. Bold, fearing nothing when his soul led the way, pre-eminently self-reliant, and ever turning to "the light within," we find him entering the old vaults of gloomy superstition, club in hand, breaking the sectarian images, opening the prison doors, flashing light into the dark corners, and enforcing by precept and example the sentiment of my text. When the priests heard that the "man with the leather breeches" was coming, they left their pulpits and fled; and George mounted the deserted pulpits and distributed to the famished multitude the bread of life. At one time we find him wading through the bogs of Ireland, at another roaming in the wilds of America. The phlegmatic Hollander is stirred by the indefatigable Drayton shoemaker, nor could the cold prisons of England quench the fire of his zeal. Had all the Quakers been as much themselves as George, the promised millennium had dawned long ere this. This, alas! they never dreamed of being. George was good, great, and useful; and they, to be so, must be like him; the nearer the resemblance the better. He wore a broad-brim, had no collar on his coat, said "thou" and "thee;" and every genuine Quaker does the same to this day; and should he depart from the faith, he is soon told "Thee is not following Friends' rule." When George went into a church, he kept on his hat, to show that he had no faith in "holy houses;" the Quakers, imitating their model man, wear hats in their own meeting-houses, which no one regards as holy, and that to the detriment of their health. Unfortunately George could not sing, and had a small organ of ideality, so that he had no taste for pictures, and little or none for the fine arts generally. Henceforth, every Quaker must be dumb; music is a sin, and paintings and sculpture awful waste of time and labor. Friends' meeting-houses are built like barns, and their worship is so dead and monotonous that the young gladly escape from it to something more attractive. The spirit may move one Friend to sing as much as it does another to preach; but all singing spirits are "demons," and must be exorcised. In short, every Quaker must be a Fox, whereas to be a man, he must needs be himself.

John Wesley was somewhat manly; and his obedience to himself, despite of ecclesiastical laws, made him a reformer; but when he said to the members of his church, "It is your business to obey our rules, and not to mend them," he evidently did not intend others to be as noble as he had been.

If thou wouldst be a man, bend at the shrine of no mortal; walk in no pathway because others tread it; be thy cwn leader, thy own sect; when all are so, then will come the true church. Who was Wesley, that thou shouldst be a Wesleyan? or Luther, that thou shouldst be a Lutheran? or Christ that thou shouldst be a Christian? all men; art thou not equally so? When the priest threatens thee with damnation, and would load thee with his gyves to secure thy soul's salvation, say, "Hands off, sir! I am, also, a man! Rather let me be lost, being a free man, than be saved to be an eternal slave!"

Sects are engines that crush the soul; priests direct them! Keep out of their power. They are sand-pits where ignorant or interested men pretend to dig treasures; keep from their brink; once enter, thou mayest lose the light of day. They are man-traps set on "holy ground;" beware of them; let not thy feet wander on their domain.

But, says an objector, some men's sense of right is very defective, and when they think they are doing right they are really doing wrong. I most willingly grant it; but what then? Shall we tell the man that he must do what he thinks is wrong? or shall we tell him that we are right and he must bow to our authority? This would make the man a slave, and that could never be right. If a man should be so blinded as to conscientiously believe right to be wrong and wrong to be right, I should still say to him, "Do what you believe to be right, but the consequence of your ignorance will fall upon your head." Whether men sin ignorantly or willfully, they suffer, and this suffering tends to make them wiser continually,—tends to bring their sense of right side by side with Nature's actual right.

But, says another, must man discard all models, cast aside all examples, refuse all guides? Destruction would assuredly be his fate. There is no necessity for this; all models, all examples, all guides are useful to enable us to form our own. A man's model must be in his own soul, all others with which he is conversant assisting in forming it.

Ever there floats before the real
The bright, the beautiful ideal.
And as, to guide the sculptor's hand,
The living forms of beauty stand,
Till from the rough-hewn marble starts
A thing of grace in all its parts,
So ever stand before the soul
A model, beautiful and whole:
The perfect man that we should be,
Erect in stern integrity.
Keep this, oh soul, before thy sight,
And form the inward man aright.

Be true to this model to-day, and to-morrow it is fairer and more beautiful and perfect, always advancing as we advance, and ever before and above us beckoning us on. All we read, hear, and learn helps us in the formation of this true self that must be our model; hence we must disdain no advice, even from a child. We all have much to learn. Moses, Jesus, and Joseph Smith may teach us something; let us thankfully receive all they can give. But let no man take us off our feet; let the officious help of none prevent us from exercising our faculties and unfolding ourselves in accordance with our own law.

Religious imitators, like all others, fall short of their original, and copy its defects, rather than its excellences. The Pharisees imitated the sectarian pride, the narrow-souled bigotry of Moses, who could see no virtue outside of the tents of Israel, rather than the wisdom that dictated sound laws, and the meekness that is said to have characterized their model man. Of the million imitators of Jesus, we have many that can denounce with his vehemence, proclaim damnation to all unbelievers, and speak of outsiders as "dogs;" but how few imitate his manliness, his contempt of riches, his active benevolence and unswerving adherence to right? Of the thousands of Quakers who imitate the little, and in some cases ridiculous, peculiarities of George Fox, where will you find the man as bold and self-reliant as he, daring to utter his thoughts though they differ from those of every living mortal?

Absurd imitation of the past has characterized the masses in all ages. The worship of the Greek and Roman deities continued after all faith in them was gone. Altars smoked and priests officiated in the temples long after the gods had departed; for the dead absurdities of the Past ruled the living Present; and even the philosophers did not possess sufficient self-hood to throw off their allegiance to the defunct tyrants. In our own time, the foolish dictates of fashion are scrupulously obeyed by millions who know no higher law; and multitudes of intelligent men and women become the mere playthings with which she sports at her pleasure.

Instead of one fashion-monger dictating to the world, how much better would it be if all developed their natural taste and love of the beautiful, and dressed accordingly. How much we lose from the stupid folly of those who allow the taste of one, or it may be the lack of taste in one, to govern and mold the whole.

All who take the privilege of being themselves should be equally willing to give the same privilege, and not seek to impose their conditions upon others. The water is very well for a fish to live in, but a poor place for a bird; and though grass makes a good dinner for a horse, a lion would soon starve on it. The road I travel may suit me, but what right have I, when others are unwilling to go the same way, to knock them down and drag them into it? Every planet may revolve on his own orbit, so it comes into collision with no other; and there is room in the wide universe even for the eccentric comet.

Many reformers decry and despise those who are operating in other fields. Their pet reform is the one upon which the world hangs, or the central sun around which the universe revolves. All others are fragmentary, theirs integral. Men advocate one reform, read about it, hear every one talk about it where they lecture, until it assumes a mountain magnitude and shuts out all else from their gaze. The Temperance Reformer says nothing can be done to elevate and bless the masses till they are made sober, for drunkenness is the parent of crime and misery. Let all become temperate and the day of the Lord is at hand; and he is astonished that all reformers do not lend their aid to the great work until it is accomplished. The Antislavery Reformer assures us that slavery is the curse of curses; the canker-worm that is eating out the nation's heart; the sum of all villanies; a fire burning to the lowest hell. Hence the Antislavery Reform is the most important; all others are comprehended in it, and he who does not advocate it is recreant to truth and duty.

The Land Reformer is certain that his reform underlies all others, — the soil must be the foundation. Let the land be equally divided, or every man have possession of what he can cultivate, and poverty, and the vice and misery consequent upon it, will flee, and the golden age return. Slavery could not exist, intemperance would be no more, and the voice of rejoicing would be heard through all the land.

"This reform all should labor for," says he. "Hold!" says the advocate of Woman's Rights. "Men are what their mothers make them, and they make bad laws because women who mold them are robbed of their rights, and hold a degrading position in the world. Give woman her true position, educate her for her high destiny, and every reform will follow, as spring the flowers when summer warms the soil."

All these are useful, all necessary; but no one or two reforms include the whole. Make the world sober to-morrow, licentiousness, tyranny, war, and ignorance would still abound; destroy slavery, and an army of evils would still remain for the reformer to combat.

"Find thy work and do it," my brother, my sister.

The business of one is to enter the untrodden wild, axe in hand, and with sturdy strokes bring to the ground the giant trees; of another, to grub up the bushes and pile the brush for burning; the work of a third, to turn up the virgin soil to the sun's bright eye, while others follow to scatter broadcast the good seed, attend the growing crops, and gather in the glorious harvest. All are necessary; none can say, "I have no need of thee;" for the final result can only be obtained by the diversified labor of all.

Heed not the teachers who tell thee to deny and crucify thyself. Thou art thy own law, thy own Bible, thy own model. There are no Scriptures so sacred as those written in thy soul; read them carefully, and obey them faithfully, ever seeking for new light to scan aright their pages, from the world around thee, transcribed in books, or engraven upon the ever-living page of Nature herself. So shalt thou develop into a noble, sound, whole-souled being, happy in thyself, and diffusing happiness, as the rose its fragrance, to all around.

Be thyself; a nobler gospel
  Never preached the Nazarene;
Be thyself; 'tis holy Scripture,
  Though no Bible lids between.

Dare to shape the thought in language
  That is lying in thy brain;
Dare to launch it, banners flying,
  On the bosom of the main.

What though pirate knaves surround thee;
  Nail thy colors to the mast;
Flinch not, flee not; boldly sailing,
  Thou shalt gain the port at last.

Be no parrot, idly prating
  Thoughts the spirit never knew;
Be a prophet of the God-sent,
  Telling all thy message true.

True, the coward world will scorn thee,
  Friends may fail, and fiends will frown;
Heaven itself grow dark above thee,
  Gods in anger thence look down.

Heed not; there's a world more potent
  Carried in thy manly heart;
Be thyself, and do thy duty;
  It will always take thy part.

If the God within say, "Well done!"
  What are other gods to thee?
Hell's his frown; but where his smile is,
  There is heaven for the free.

THE DELUGE.

THE DELUGE IN THE LIGHT OF MODERN SCIENCE.

If the Bible is God's book, we ought to know it. If the Creator of the universe has spoken to man, how important that we should listen to his voice and obey his instructions! On the other hand, if the Bible is not God's book, we ought to know it. Why should we go through the world with a lie in our right hand, dupes of the ignorant men who preceded us? It can never be for our soul's benefit to cherish a falsehood.

Science is, perhaps, the best test that we can apply to decide the question. Science is really a knowledge of what Nature has done and is doing; and since the upholders of the divinity of the Bible believe that it proceeded from the Author of nature, if their faith is true, it cannot possibly disagree with what science teaches.

Science is a fiery furnace, that has consumed a thousand delusions, and must consume all that remain. We cast into it astrology and alchemy, and their ashes barely remain to tell of their existence. Old notions of the earth and heavens went in, and vanished as their dupes gazed upon them. Old religions, old gods, have become as the incense that was burned before their altars.

I purpose to try the Bible in its searching fire. Fear not, my brother: it can but burn the straw and stubble; if gold, it will shine as bright after the fiery ordeal as before, and reflect as perfectly the image of truth.

The Bible abounds with marvellous stories, — stories that we should at once reject from their intrinsic improbability, not to say impossibility, if we should find them in any other book. But, among all the stories, there is none that equals the account of the deluge, as given in the sixth, seventh, and eighth chapters of Genesis. It towers above the rest as Mount Washington does above the New-England hills; and, as travellers delight to climb the loftiest peaks, I suppose that many would be pleased to examine this lofty story, and see how the world of truth and actuality looks from its summit.

According to the account, in less than two thousand years after God had created all things, and pronounced them very good, he became thoroughly dissatisfied with every living thing, and determined to destroy them with the earth. He thus expresses himself: "I will destroy man, whom I have created, from the face of the earth, — both man and beast, and the creeping thing, and the fowls of the air; for it repenteth me that I have made them." Again he says to Noah, "The end of all flesh is come before me; for the earth is filled with violence through them, and behold I will destroy them with the earth."

Why should the beasts, birds, and creeping things be destroyed? What had the larks, the doves, and the bob-o-links done? What had the squirrels and the tortoises been guilty of, that they should be destroyed?

He proceeds to inform Noah how he will do this: "And behold I, even I, do bring a flood of waters upon the earth, to destroy all flesh, wherein is the breath of life, from under heaven; and every thing that is in the earth shall die." And we are subsequently informed that "every thing that was in the dry land died." But why not every thing in the sea? Were the dogs sinners, and the dog-fish saints? Had the sheep been more guilty than the sharks? had the pigeons become utterly corrupt, and the pikes remained perfectly innocent? It may be, that the apparent impossibility of drowning them by a flood suggested to the writer of the story the necessity of saving them alive.

But Noah was righteous; and God determined to save him and his family, eight persons, and by their instrumentality to save alive animals sufficient to stock the world again after its destruction.

To do this, Noah was commanded to build an ark, three hundred cubits long, fifty broad, and thirty high. It was to be made with three stories, and furnished with one door, and one window a cubit wide. Into this ark were to be taken two of every sort of living thing, and of clean beasts and of birds seven of every sort, male and female, and food sufficient for them all.

There are differences of opinion about the length of the cubit: most probably it was about eighteen inches; but taking it at twenty-two inches, the largest estimate that I believe theologians have made, the ark was then five hundred and fifty feet long, ninety-one feet eight inches broad, and fifty-five feet high. Leaving space for the floors, which would need to be very strong, each story was about seventeen feet high; and the total cubical contents of the ark were about one hundred and two thousand cubic yards. Scott, in his commentary, makes it as small as sixty-nine thousand one hundred and twenty yards; but the necessity for room was not as well understood in his day. Each floor of the ark contained five thousand six hundred and one square yards, and the three floors sixteen thousand eight hundred and three square yards, the total standing-room of the ark.

Into this were to be taken fourteen of each kind of fowl of the air or bird. How many kinds or species of birds are there? When Adam Clarke wrote his commentary, two thousand three hundred and seventy-two species had been recognized. Ornithology was then but in its infancy, and man's knowledge of living forms was very limited. Lesson, according to Hugh Miller, enumerates the birds at six thousand two hundred and sixty-six species; Gray, in his "Genera of Birds," estimates the number on the globe at eight thousand. Let us not crowd Noah, but take the six thousand two hundred and sixty-six species of Lesson. Fourteen of each of these would give us eighty-seven thousand seven hundred and twenty-four birds, — from the humming-bird, the little flying jewel, to the ostrich that fans the heated air of the desert, — or over five for every yard of standing-room in the ark. If spaces were left for the attendants to pass among them, to attend to the supply of their daily wants, the birds alone would crowd the ark.

But, beside the birds, there were to be taken into the ark two of every sort of unclean beast and fourteen of every sort of clean beast. The most recent zoölogical authorities enumerate two thousand and sixty-seven species of mammals, or, as they are commonly called, beasts. Of cetacea, or whale-like mammals, sixty-five; ruminatia, or cud-chewers, one hundred and seventy-seven; pachydermata, or thick-skinned mammals, such as the horse, hog, and elephant, forty-one; edentata, like the sloth and ant-eater, thirty-five; rodentia, or gnawers, such as the rat, squirrel, and beaver, six hundred and seventeen; carnivora, or flesh-eaters, four hundred and forty-six; cheiroptera, or bats, three hundred and twenty-eight; quadrumana, or monkeys, two hundred and twenty-one; and marsupialia, or pouched mammals, like the opossum and kangaroo, one hundred and thirty-seven. If we leave out the cetacea, that live in the water, and the cud-chewers, which are the clean beasts, we have one thousand eight hundred and twenty-five species; and male and female of these, a total of three thousand six hundred and fifty.

But, besides these, there were to be taken into the ark fourteen of every kind of clean beast. And what are clean beasts? The scriptural answer is, animals that divide the hoof and chew the cud; and of these at least one hundred and seventy-seven species are known. Fourteen of each of these added, make a total of six thousand one hundred and twenty-eight mammals, from the mouse to the elephant. These beasts could not be piled one upon another like cord-wood; they could not be promiscuously crowded together. The sheep would need careful protection from the lions, tigers, and wolves; the elephant and other ponderous beasts would require stalls of great thickness; much room would be required to enable them to obtain needful exercise, and for the attendants to supply them with food and water; and a vessel of the size of the ark would be taxed to provide for these beasts alone; and to crowd in, and preserve alive, beasts and birds, was an absolute impossibility.

But there are of reptiles six hundred and fifty-seven species; and Noah was to take into the ark two of every sort of creeping thing. Two hundred of these reptiles are, however, aquatic: hence water would not seriously affect them; but crocodiles, lizards, iguanas, tree-frogs, horned frogs, thunder-snakes, chicken-snakes, brittlesnakes, rattlesnakes, copperheads, asps, cobra de capellos, whose bite is certain death, and a host of others, must be provided for. It would not do to allow these disagreeable individuals to crawl about the ark; and nine hundred and fourteen of them would require considerable space, whether they could obtain it or not.

By this time, the ark is doubly crowded; but its living cargo is not yet completed. A dense cloud of insects, and a vast army destitute of wings, make their appearance, and clamor for admission. The number of articulates that must have been provided for is estimated at seven hundred and fifty thousand species, — from the butterflies of Brazil, fourteen inches from the tip of one wing to the tip of the other, to the almost invisible gnat, that dances in the summer's beam. Ants, beetles, flies, bugs, fleas, mosquitoes, wasps, bees, moths, butterflies, spiders, scorpions, grasshoppers, locusts, myriapods, canker-worms, wriggling, crawling, creeping, flying, male and female, here they come, and all must be provided for.

Nor are these the last. The air-breathing land-snails, of which we know four thousand six hundred species, could never have survived a twelve months' soaking; and they must therefore be cared for. The nine thousand two hundred of these add no little to the discomfort of the trebly-crowded ark.

Now let the flood come: all are lodged in the ark of safety, and are ready for a year's voyage. But we forget: the ark has not yet received one-half of its cargo. The command given unto Noah was, "Take thou unto thee of all food that is eaten, and thou shalt gather it to thee; and it shall be for food for thee and for them;" and we are expressly told that "according to all that God commanded Noah, so did he."

Food for how long? The flood began in the "sixth hundreth year of Noah's life, in the second month, the seventeenth day of the month." Noah, his family, and the animals, went in seven days before this time, and left the ark the six hundred and first year of Noah's life, the second month, and the twenty-seventh day of the month. They were therefore in the ark for one year and seventeen days.

What a quantity of hay would be required, the material most easily obtained! An elephant eats four hundred pounds of hay in twenty-four hours. Since there are two species of elephants, the African and the Indian, there must have been four elephants in the ark; and, supposing them to live upon hay, they would require three hundred tons. There are at least seven species of the rhinoceros; and fourteen of these, at seventy-five tons each, would consume no less than one thousand and fifty tons. The two thousand four hundred and seventy-eight clean beasts, — oxen, elk, giraffes, camels, deer, antelope, sheep, goats, with the horses, zebras, asses, hippopotami, rodents, and marsupials — could not have required less than four thousand five hundred tons; making a total of five thousand eight hundred and fifty tons. A ton of hay occupies about eighteen cubic yards; and the quantity of hay required would fill a hundred and five thousand three hundred cubic yards of space, or more than the entire capacity of the ark.

If these animals were fed on other substances than hay, the extra difficulty of obtaining and preserving those substances would counterbalance any advantage that might be gained by the economy of space.

A vast quantity of grain would be necessary for thousands of birds, rodents, marsupials, and other animals; and large granaries would be required for its storage.

What flesh would be needed for the lions, tigers, leopards, ounces, wild-cats, wolves, bears, hyenas, jackalls, dogs, and foxes, martens, weasels, eagles, condors, vultures, buzzards, falcons, hawks, kites, owls, as well as crocodiles and serpents! Not one but would eat its weight in a month, and some much more. A full-grown lion eats fifteen pounds of flesh in a day: there are two species of lions; and the four would eat twenty-two thousand pounds in a year. There would be, at least, three thousand animals feeding upon flesh; and, if we calculate that they averaged two pounds of flesh a day, this would give a total of more than two million and a quarter pounds of flesh to be stored up and distributed. And since dried, salted, or smoked meat would not answer, this flesh must have been taken into the ark alive. It would be equal to more than thirty thousand sheep at seventy-five pounds each; a great addition to the original cargo, and necessitating an extra quantity of hay for their food, till their turn came to be eaten.

Fish would be required for the otters, minks, pelicans, of which there are eight species, and must therefore have been fifty-six individuals in the ark; one hundred and five gulls, for there are fifteen species; one hundred and twelve cormorants, forty-nine gannets, one hundred and forty terns, two hundred and eighty-seven kingfishers, beside storks, herons, spoonbills, penguins, albatrosses, and a host of others; mollusks for the oyster-catcher, turnstone, and other birds.

The fish could not be preserved after death in any way to answer for food, and must therefore have been alive: large tanks for the purpose of keeping them would take up considerable of the ark's space. The water in such tanks would soon become unfitted for the respiration of the fish, and there must have been some provision, by air-pumps or otherwise, for charging the water with the air essential to their existence.

Many animals live upon insects; and this must have been the most difficult part of the provision to procure. There are nineteen species of goatsuckers;

and there must have been in the ark two hundred and sixty-six individuals. These birds feed upon flies, moths, beetles, and other insects. What an innumerable multitude must have been provided for the goatsuckers alone! But there are a hundred and thirty-seven species of fly-catchers; and Noah must have had a fly-catcher family of nineteen hundred and eighteen individuals to supply with appropriate food. There are thirty-seven species of bee-eaters; and there must have been five hundred and eighteen of these birds to supply with bees. A very large apiary would be required to supply their needs. But, beside these, insects for swallows, swifts, martins, shrikes, thrushes, orioles, sparrows, the beautiful trogans and jacamars, moles, shrews, hedgehogs, and a multitude of others, too numerous to mention, but not too numerous to eat. Ants, also, for the ant-eaters of America, the aard-vark of Africa, and the pangolin of Asia. The great ant-eater of South America is an animal sometimes measuring eight feet in length. It lives exclusively on ants, which it procures by tearing open their hills with its hooked claws, and then drawing its long tongue, which is covered with glutinous saliva, over the swarms which rush out to defend their dwelling. Many bushels of ants would be needed for the pair of ant-eaters before the ark landed on Ararat. How were all the insects caught, and kept for the use of all these animals for more than a year? A hundred men could not catch a sufficient number in six months. And, if caught, how could they be preserved, together with the original stock of insects necessary to supply the world after the deluge? Some insects eat only bark;

others, resinous secretions, the pith, solid wood, leaves, sap in the veins, as the aphide, flowers, pollen, and honey. Wood, bark, resin, and honey might have been supplied; but how could green leaves, sap, flowers and pollen, be furnished to those insects absolutely requiring them for existence? Thirty species of insects feed on the nettle, but not one of them could live on dried nettles. Rösel calculates that two hundred species subsist on the oak; but the oak must be in a growing condition to supply them with food. In no other way, then, could the insects have been preserved alive than by large green-houses, the heat so applied as to suit the plants of both temperate and tropical climates, and the insects so distributed among them, that each could obtain its appropriate nourishment.

Fruit would be necessary for the four hundred and forty-two monkeys, for the plantain-eaters, the fruit-pigeons of the Spice Islands that feed on nutmegs, for the toucans and the flocks of parrots, parroquets, cockatoos, and other fruit-eating birds. As they did not know how to can fruit in those days, and dried fruit would be altogether unsuitable, there must have been a large green-house for raising all manner of fruit necessary for the frugivorous multitude.

How were the various animals obtained? The command given to Noah was, "Two of every sort shalt thou *bring* into the ark."

Animals, as is now well known, belong to limited centres, outside of which they are never found in a natural state; and naturalists know that these centres were established ages before the time when the deluge is supposed to have occurred.

Thus, Hugh Miller, in his "Testimony of the Rocks," says, "We now know that every great continent has its own peculiar fauna; that the original centres of distribution must have been, not one, but many; further, that the areas or circles around these centres must have been occupied by their pristine animals in ages long anterior to that of the Noachian Deluge; nay, that in even the latter geologic ages they were preceded in them by animals of the same general type. There are fourteen such areas, or provinces, enumerated by the later naturalists;" and Cuvier, quoted by Miller, says, "The great continents contain species peculiar to each; insomuch, that whenever large countries, of this description, have been discovered, which their situation had kept isolated from the rest of the world, the class of quadrupeds which they contained has been found extremely different from any that had existed elsewhere. Thus, when the Spaniards first penetrated into South America, they did not find a single species of quadruped the same as any of Europe, Asia, or Africa."

The white bear is never found except in the arctic regions; the great grizzly bear is only found in the neighborhood of the Rocky Mountains. Nearly all the species of mammals found in Australia are confined to that country, as the wingless birds of New Zealand are confined to that, and the sloth, armadillo, and other animals, to South America.

A journey to the polar regions would be necessary to obtain the white bear, the musk-ox, of which seven would be required, since it is a clean beast; seven reindeer, likewise; the white fox, the polar hare, the lemming, and seven of each species of cormorant, gannet, penguin, petrel, and gull, some of which are as large as eagles, as well as mergansers, geese, and ducks, certain species of which are only found in the frigid zone. Noah or his agents must have discovered Greenland and North America thousands of years before Columbus was born: they must have preceded Behring, Parry, Ross, Kane, and Hayes in exploring the Arctic regions. They searched the ice-floes and numerous islands of the Arctic seas, snow-shoed, over the frozen *tundras* of Siberia, to be certain that no living thing escaped them; then, after catching and caging all the animals, conveyed them, with all manner of food necessary for their sustenance, together with ice to temper the heat of the climate to which they were for more than a year to be exposed, returned to the nearest port, and, after a toilsome journey from the sea-coast to Armenia, arrived at their destination. How many of these animals would survive the journey? and, of those that did, how many would survive the change of climate and habits?

Another party must have visited temperate America; traversed New England in its length and breadth, forded wide streams, made their way through unbroken wildernesses, traversed the Great Lakes, roamed over the Rocky Mountains, and secured the black bear, cinnamon bear, wapiti or Canadian stag, the moose, American deer, antelope, mountain sheep, buffalo, opossum, rattlesnake, copperhead, and an innumerable multitude of other animals — insects birds, reptiles, and mammals, that are only to be found in the temperate regions of America.

A voyage to South America must have been made

to obtain tapirs, pumas, peccaries, sloths, ant-eaters, armadilloes, fourteen each of the llama, alpaca, and vicuna, beside monkeys, birds, and insects innumerable. A vessel nearly as large as "The Great Eastern" must have been employed, or a number of smaller ones, to accommodate the collectors, the animals, and food for a voyage across the Atlantic. There must have been, at least, a thousand men, wandering through the woods of Brazil, along the valley of the Amazon, the Orinoco, and the La Plata; paddling up the streams, scaling the mountains, roaming over the pampas, climbing the tall trees, turning over every stone and log, and exploring every nook, to discover the snails, bugs, insects, worms, reptiles, and other animals indigenous to South America, from the Isthmus to Terra-del-fuego.

There must have been obtained four elephants, for there are two species, the Asiatic and the Indian; fourteen rhinoceroses, one of which is found only in South Africa, another in the island of Java, and a third in Sumatra; two hippopotami, and possibly four, for some authorities say there are two species. Fourteen giraffes, since they are clean beasts, must have been caught and driven from Central Africa (many more, indeed, must have been caught, that the required number might reach the ark and be preserved); twenty-eight camels, two hundred and eighty oxen (for there are twenty species, and they are clean); and no less than thirteen hundred and eighty-six deer and antelope, of which there are ninety-nine species recognized: these to be collected in various parts of Europe, Asia, Northern and Southern Africa, and America.

New Zealand must have been visited to obtain its

wingless birds; Mauritius for its dodo, then living; Australia for its marsupials and other peculiar animals; and every large island, and most of the small ones, to obtain those forms of life that are only to be found in each. From the island of Celebes, they must have taken the eighty species of birds that are confined to it, which would require them to catch, cage, feed, and convey eleven hundred and twenty specimens: a no small job of itself. Ten men that could accomplish that, and carry them safe to Armenia, would do all that men could do in ten years. From the Philippine Islands, the seventy-three species of hawks, parrots, and pigeons, peculiar to them; which would require, since fourteen of every kind of bird were to be taken into the ark, no less than one thousand and twenty-two specimens. From New Guinea, and the neighboring islands, two hundred and fifty-two of the magnificent birds of paradise, since there are eighteen species.

A faint idea of the difficulties encountered and overcome by Noah's agents may be gathered from what Wallace, in his recent work on the Malay Archipelago, informs us respecting these birds of paradise. "Five voyages to different parts of the district they inhabit, each occupying in its preparation and execution the larger part of a year, produced me only five species out of the fourteen known to exist in the New-Guinea district." If it took Wallace, with all the assistance that he had from various officials, five years to obtain five species, represented by dead birds, how long did it take Noah's agents to obtain eighteen species represented by two hundred and fifty-two live birds? Wallace could only obtain two alive, and for these he had to pay five hundred dollars.

If the antediluvian sinners were any thing like the modern ones, Noah must have been richer than the Rothschilds, or he never could have obtained their services; which he must have done, or it could never be truthfully said, "according to all that God commanded him, so did he."

The collection of the land-snails alone would be no small tax. Seventy-four are peculiar to Great Britain: hence there must have been a hundred and forty-eight snails collected from that island. Six hundred species are found in Southern Europe alone, and twelve hundred must have been collected from there; eighty in Sicily, ten in Corsica, two hundred and sixty-four in the Madeira Islands, a hundred and twenty in the Canary Islands, twenty-six in St. Helena, sixty-three in Southern Africa, eighty-eight in Madagascar, a hundred and twelve in Ceylon, a hundred in New Zealand, and others on every large and some of the small islands of the globe. The world must have been circumnavigated many times before the vessel of Magellan was built, and every island visited and ransacked ages before the time of Captain Cook. But it seems surprising, since these voyages must have been performed by the sinful antediluvians, that they did not save themselves in their ships when the flood came; for vessels that could perform such voyages would certainly have survived the flood more readily than the clumsy ark.

But was it really done? A thousand men in ten years, with all the appliances of modern art, — steamboats, railroads, canals, coaches, and express companies, — could not accomplish it in ten years; nor ten times the number of men keep all the animals alive in one spot for one year, if they were collected together.

"But," says the Christian, "Noah never did collect them: no intelligent person in this day ever supposes that he did." What then? "The Bible expressly declares that 'they went in unto Noah into the ark.' By instinct, such as leads the swallow to take its distant flight at the approach of winter, they came from all parts of the globe to the ark of safety."

It is true that one account does say that they came in unto Noah, for there are two very different stories of the deluge mixed up in those chapters of Genesis; but, although flying birds might perform such a feat as going twelve thousand miles to the ark, which would be necessary for some, how could other animals get there? It would be impossible even for some birds. How could the ostriches of Africa, the emus of Australia, and the rheas of South America, get there, — birds that never fly? There are three species of the rhea, or South-American ostrich; and forty-two of these would have a journey of eight thousand miles before them, by the shortest route: but how could they cross the Atlantic? If they went by land, they must have traversed the length of the American continent, from Patagonia to Alaska, crossed at Behring's Strait when it was frozen, and then travelled diagonally across nearly the whole continent of Asia to Armenia, after a journey that must have required many months for its completion. The sloths, that have been confined to South America ever since the pliocene period at least, must have taken the same route. How they crossed the mountain streams, and lived when passing over broad prairies, it would be difficult to say. A mile a day would be a rapid rate for these slow travellers, and it would therefore require about forty years for them to arrive at their destination. But, since the life of a sloth is not as long as this, they must have bequeathed their journey to their posterity, and they to their descendants, born on the way, who must have reached the ark before the door was closed. The land-snails must have met with still greater difficulties. Impelled by most wonderful instinct, they commenced their journey full a thousand years before the time; and their posterity of the five hundredth generation must have made their appearance, and been provided with a passage by the venerable Noah.

Scott, who wrote a commentary on the Bible seventy or eighty years ago, must have seen some of these difficulties, though with nothing like the clearness with which science enables us to see them now. He says, "There must have been a very extraordinary miracle wrought, perhaps by the ministration of angels, in bringing two of every species to Noah, and rendering them submissive to him and peaceable with each other; yet it seems not to have made any impression on the hardened spectators."

Think of a troop of angels fly-catching, snail-seeking, and bug-hunting through all lands, lugging through the air, horses, giraffes, elephants, and rhinoceroses, and dropping them at the door of the ark. One has crossed the Atlantic with rattlesnakes, copperheads, and boas twined around him, almost crippling his wings with their snaky folds; and another with a brace of skunks, one under each wing, that the renewed world may not lack the fragrance of the old. What a subject for the pencil of a Raphael or Doré! Had the "hardened spectators" beheld such a scene as this, Noah and his cargo would have been cast out of the ark, and the sinners themselves, converted by this stupendous miracle, would have taken passage therein.

Not only must there have been a succession of most stupendous miracles to get the animals to the ark, but also to return them to their proper places of abode. But few of them could have lived in the neighborhood of Ararat, had they been left there. How could the polar bear return to his home among the icebergs, the sloths to the congenial forests of the New World, and all the mammals, reptiles, insects, and snails to their respective habitats, the homes of their ancestors for ages innumerable? To return them was just as necessary as to obtain them, and, though less difficult, was equally impossible.

How could eight persons, all that were saved in the ark, attend to all these animals! Nearly all would require food and water once a day, and many twice. In a menagerie, one man takes care of four cages, — feeds, cleans, and waters the animals. In the ark, each person, women included, must have attended each day to ten thousand nine hundred and sixty-four birds, seven hundred and sixty-six beasts, one hundred and fourteen reptiles, one thousand one hundred and fifty land-snails, and one hundred and eighty-seven thousand five hundred insects.

Few persons have an idea of the difficulty of keeping even the common birds of a temperate climate alive in confinement for any length of time. Food that is quite suitable in a wild state may be fatal to them when they are kept in the house. Linnets feed on winter rape-seed in the wild state, but soon die if fed upon it in-doors. "They are to be fed," says Bechstein, "on summer rape-seed, moistened in water; and their food must be varied by the addition of millet, radish, cabbage, lettuce and plantain-seeds, and sometimes a few bruised melon-seeds or barberries." Nightingales, he says, should be fed on meal, worms, and fresh ants' eggs: but, if it is not possible to get these, a mixture of hard egg, ox-heart minced, and white bread may be given; but this often kills the birds. No such food would do for Noah's nightingales, then, or where would have been the nightingale's song? They must have been fed on meal, worms, and *fresh* ant's eggs. How they were obtained, we have, of course, no knowledge. Bechstein says that larks may be fed with "a paste made of grated carrot, white bread soaked in water, and barley or wheat meal, all worked together in a mortar. In addition to this paste, larks should be supplied with poppy-seed, bruised hemp, crumb of bread, and plenty of greens, such as lettuce, endive, cabbage, with a little lean meat or ant-eggs occasionally." He says the cage should be furnished with a piece of fresh turf, often renewed, and great attention should be paid to cleanliness. The care of the birds in the ark probably fell to the women. As they had not read Bechstein, or any other author on bird-keeping, — and thousands of the birds must have been total strangers to them, — how did they know what diet to supply them with, and where could they get it, supposing they had time to supply them at all?

If the difficulty was great to keep the birds of a temperate climate, how much greater must it have been to keep tropical birds in a climate altogether unsuited to them? The two birds of paradise bought by Wallace were fed, he says, on rice, bananas, and cockroaches: of the last, he obtained several cans from a bake-house at Malta, and thus got his paradise birds, by good fortune, to England. But how many cans of cockroaches would be necessary for two hundred and fifty-two of such birds, — the number in the ark? and where were the bake-houses from which the supply might be obtained?

To keep this vast menagerie clean would have required a large corps of efficient workers, especially when we remember that there was but one door in each story, as some suppose; or one door to the whole ark, as the story seems to teach, and this door was closed; and but one window, and that apparently in the roof. The Augean stable, the cleansing of which was one of the labors of Hercules, can but faintly indicate what must have been the condition of the ark in less than a month, supposing the animals to subsist as long.

Whence came the water that covered the earth to the tops of the highest mountains? "All the high hills that were under the whole heaven were covered. Fifteen cubits upward did the waters prevail; and the mountains were covered," says the record. And to do this, it rained for forty days and forty nights. A fall of an inch of water in a day is considered a very heavy rain in Great Britain. The heaviest single rain recorded fell on the Khasia Hills in India, and amounted to thirty inches in twenty-four hours.

If this deluging rain could have continued for forty days and nights, and had it fallen over the entire surface of the globe; the amount would only have been one hundred feet; which, instead of covering the mountains, would not have covered the hills. But, of course, such a rain is only possible for a very limited time, and on a small portion of the earth's surface.

Sir John Leslie, in "The Encyclopedia Britannica," says, "Supposing the vast canopy of air, by some sudden change of internal constitution, at once to discharge its whole watery store, this precipitate would form a sheet of scarcely five inches thick over the surface of the globe." But if the water that covered the earth above the tops of the highest mountains came by rain, it must have rained seven hundred feet a day for forty days! or there must have fallen each day, according to Sir John Leslie's estimate, more than fourteen hundred times as much water on the earth as the atmosphere contained!

But the writer says, "The fountains of the great deep were broken up." To the Jews, who supposed, with David, that God had founded the earth upon the seas, and established it upon the floods, this meant something; but, in the light of geology, we see that it only demonstrates the ignorance of the man who wrote and the people that believed the story.

Adam Clarke, commenting on this passage, says, "It appears that an immense quantity of water occupied the centre of the antediluvian earth; and, as this burst forth by the order of God, the circumambient strata must sink in order to fill up the vacuum occasioned by the elevated waters." If true, it would not have assisted in drowning the world one spoonful. For if the strata sank anywhere to fill the hollow previously occupied by the water, it would only make the mountains so much higher in comparison: hence it would require just that much extra water to cover them. In the light of geology, however, the notion is sufficiently absurd. A mile and a half deep, the earth's interior is hot enough to convert water into steam; there is, therefore, no chance for water to exist in its centre, or anywhere near it.

It is as great a difficulty to discover where the water went when the flood was over. We are told that the fountains of the deep and the windows of heaven were stopped, and the rain was restrained. But this could do nothing towards diminishing the water. All that it could possibly accomplish would be to prevent the rise of the water. But we are also told that "God made a wind to pass over the earth." All that the wind could do, however, would be to convey to the atmosphere the moisture it took up in vapor; and this could not have lowered the water a yard. The highest mountain, Kunchinginga, is more than twenty-eight thousand feet high; the flood prevailed one hundred and fifty days, and abated two hundred and twenty-five; and if this abatement was done by the wind, it must have blown an ocean of water from the entire surface of the earth, one hundred and twenty-five deep, every day for eight months! All the hurricanes that ever blew, blowing at once, would be the gentlest zephyr of a summer's eve, compared with such a wind as that; and by what possibility could such a craft as the ark survive the storm?

A question, proper to be asked is, *How were the*

animals supplied with light? and how did the attendants see to wait upon them in the first and second stories of the ark? There was but one window, and that only twenty-two inches in size, and it appears to have been in the third story. It was a day when kerosene was unknown, and tallow dips were uninvented. How did these animals live in the darkness? and, above all, how did Noah and his family supply their wants? It could have been no easy or pleasant thing to wait upon hungry lions, tigers, crocodiles, and rattlesnakes in the dark, to say nothing of the danger.

How did they breathe? There was but one twenty-two inch window; the ark was "pitched within and without with pitch;" "The Lord shut him in." Talk of the Black Hole of Calcutta: it must have been pure as the breath of morning compared with the condition of the ark in one day.

Where did they obtain water for drink? Supposing all the additional water needed to drown the world was fresh, when mingled with the water of the sea, as much as one-tenth of it would be salt water, and this would render it utterly unfit for drink. Provision must therefore have been made for water; and a space certainly half as large as the ark must have been taken up for the water necessary for this immense multitude.

The fish, mollusks, crustaceans (such as our crabs and lobsters), and all corals, must have died if such a flood had taken place, — the fresh-water fish from the salt water at once added to their proper element, and the salt-water fish and other marine forms from so large an addition of fresh water. For months, there could have been no shore: what is now the margin of the sea was buried miles deep; and all the fucoidal vegetation, upon which myriads of animals subsist, must have perished, and the animals with it, if the change in the constitution of the water had not killed them. Every time a man swallows an oyster, he has evidence that the Noachian deluge did not take place.

The plants must have perished also. How many of our trees, to say nothing of the grasses and feeble plants, could endure a soaking of nearly twelve months' duration? Some of the very hardiest seeds might survive, but the number could not be large. The present condition of vegetation upon the globe is another evidence, then, that this deluge did not take place.

When the ark landed on Mount Ararat, and the animals went forth, how did they subsist? As they went down the mountains, the carnivorous animals would have devoured a large portion of the herbivorous animals saved in the ark. Beside the lions, tigers, leopards, ounces, and other carnivorous mammals, amounting to eight hundred and ninety-two, there were in the ark six hundred and sixty-six eagles, for there are forty-eight species; one hundred and forty-four buzzards, fourteen hundred and forty-two falcons, one hundred and forty hawks, two hundred and thirty-eight vultures, and eight hundred and ninety six owls. What chance would a few sheep, rabbits and squirrels, rats and mice, doves and chickens, have, among this ravenous multitude? How could the ants escape, with ant-eaters, aard-varks and pangolins on the watch for them as soon as they made their appearance? There were as many dogs as hares, as many cats as mice. How long a lease of life could the sheep, hares, and mice, calculate upon? Before the herbivorous animals had multiplied, so as to furnish the carnivorous animals with food, they must all have been destroyed, after all the pains taken for their preservation. Noah should have given the herbivora, at least a year's start, especially since the vegetation of the globe was so deficient.

But we are told that the species of animals may have been much fewer in the days of Noah; and, therefore, much less room would be necessary. A single pair of cats, say some, may have produced all the animals of the cat kind; a pair of dogs, all the animals that belong to the dog family. Such an explanation might have been given when zoölogy was little known, and geology had no existence; but there is no place for it now. Animals change, it is true, and all species have probably been produced from a few originals; but the process by which this is accomplished is so slow in its operation, that we have no knowledge of the formation of a new species. We know that lions, tigers, and cats of various species, existed long before the time of the deluge, and dogs, wolves and foxes; and we find mummied cats, dogs, and other animals in Egypt, as old or older than the deluge, so little changed from those of the present time in the same locality, that we cannot recognize any difference between them.

"*You seem to forget that all things are possible with God: he could have packed these animals into an ark of one-half the size, brought them altogether in the twinkling of an eye, and returned them as rapidly.*"

And you seem to forget that the account in Genesis gives us no hint of any such miracle. Noah was to take the animals to him, and to take unto him of all food that is eaten; and, as Hugh Miller remarks, "the expedient of having recourse to supposititious miracle in order to get over a difficulty insurmountable on every natural principle, is not of the nature of an argument, but simply an evidence of the want of it. Argument is at an end when supposititious miracle is introduced." But, if a miracle was worked, it was not one, but ten thousand of the most stupendous miracles, and entirely unnecessary ones. This, the Rev. Dr. Pye Smith saw, when he said, "We cannot represent to ourselves the idea of all land animals being brought into one small spot, from the polar regions, the torrid zone, and all the other climates of Asia, Africa, Europe, and America, Australia, and the thousands of islands, — their preservation and provision, and the final disposal of them, — without bringing up the idea of miracles more stupendous than any that are recorded in Scripture. The great decisive miracle of Christianity, — the resurrection of the Lord Jesus, — sinks down before it."

It is a favorite method with the advocates of special revelations to show their agreement with the operations of natural law, till a difficulty is met with that cannot be answered, when they flee at once to miracle to save them. But, in this case, miracle itself cannot save them.

Geology furnishes us with evidence that no such deluge has taken place. According to Hugh Miller, "In various parts of the world, such as Auvergne in Central France, and along the flanks of Etna, there are cones of long-extinct or long-slumbering volcanoes, which, though of at least triple the antiquity of the Noachian deluge, and though composed of the ordinary incoherent materials, exhibit no marks of denudation. According to the calculations of Sir Charles Lyell, no devastating flood could have passed over the forest-zone of Etna during the last twelve thousand years."

Archæology enters her protest equally against it. We have abundance of Egyptian mummies, statues, inscriptions, paintings, and other representations of Egyptian life belonging to a much earlier period than the deluge. With only such modifications as time slowly introduced, we find the people, their language, and their habits, continuing after that time, as they had done for centuries before. Lepsius, writing from the pyramids of Memphis, in 1843, says, "We are still busy with structures, sculptures, and inscriptions, which are to be classed, by means of the now more accurately determined groups of kings, in an epoch of highly flourishing civilization, as far back as the fourth millennium before Christ." That is one thousand six hundred and fifty-six years before the time of the flood. Lyell says that "Chevalier Bunsen, in his elaborate and philosophical work on ancient Egypt, has satisfied not a few of the learned, by an appeal to monumental inscriptions still extant, that the successive dynasties of kings may be traced back without a break, to Menes, and that the date of his reign would correspond with the year 3,640 B. C.;" that is nearly thirteen hundred years before the time of the deluge. Strange that the whole world should have been drowned and the Egyptians never knew it!

From the "Types of Mankind," we learn that the fact

is "asserted by Lepsius, and familiar to all Egyptologists, that negro and other races already existed in Northern Africa, on the Upper Nile, 2,300 years B.C."

But this is only forty-eight years after the deluge. What kind of a family had Noah? Was amalgamation practised by any of Noah's sons? If all the human occupants of the ark were Caucasians, how did they produce negro races in forty-eight years? The facts again compel us to announce the fabulous character of this Genesical story of the deluge.

"No intelligent person now believes that it was a total deluge: Buckland, Pye Smith, Miller, Hitchcock, and all Christian geologists, agree that it was a partial deluge, and the account can be so explained."

How strange that God should dictate an account of the deluge that led everybody to a false conclusion with regard to it, till science taught them a better. But let us read what the account says, and see whether it can be explained to signify a partial deluge. To save the Bible from its inevitable fate, such men as Buckland, Smith, Miller, Hitchcock, and other Bible apologists, it is evident from their writings, were ready to resort to any scheme, however wild.

I read (Gen. vi. 7), "I will destroy both man and beast, and the creeping thing." How could a partial deluge accomplish this? (v. 13); "The end of all flesh is come before me. I will destroy them with the earth." How could all flesh be destroyed with the earth by any other than a total deluge? (v. 17); "I do bring a flood of waters upon the earth, to destroy all flesh wherein is the breath of life, from under heaven; and every thing that is in the earth shall die." Not only is man to be destroyed, but all flesh wherein is the breath of life, from under heaven, and every thing in the earth is to die. Can this be tortured to mean a partial deluge? (vii. 19); "And the waters prevailed exceedingly upon the earth; and all the high hills that were under the whole heaven were covered; and all flesh died that moved upon the earth, both of fowl, and of cattle, and of beast, and of creeping thing that creepeth upon the earth, and every man. All in whose nostrils was the breath of life, of all that was in the dry land, died. And every living substance was destroyed which was upon the face of the ground, both man and cattle, and the creeping things, and the fowl of the heaven; and they were destroyed from the earth, and Noah only remained alive, and they that were with him in the ark." Had the man who wrote this story been a lawyer, and had he known how these would-be-Bible-believers, and at the same time geologists, would seek to pervert his meaning, he could not have more carefully worded his account. It is not possible for any man to express the idea of a total flood more definitely than this man has done. He does not merely say the hills were covered, but "*all*" the hills were covered; and lest you should think that he certainly did not mean the most elevated, he is careful to say "all the *high*" hills were covered; and lest some one should say he only meant the hills in that part of the country, he says expressly "all the high hills that were *under the whole heaven were covered*." He is even so cautious as to introduce the phrase "*whole* heaven," lest some one in its absence might still think that the deluge was a partial one. To make its universality still more evident, he says, "All flesh died that moved upon the earth." This would have been sufficiently definite for most persons, but not so for him; he particularizes so that none may escape, — "both of fowl, and of cattle, and of beast, and of creeping thing that creepeth upon the earth, and every man." To leave no possibility of mistake, he adds, "all in whose nostrils was the breath of life, of all that was in the dry land, died." Can any thing more be needed? The writer seems to see that some theological professor may even yet try to make this mean a partial deluge; and he therefore says, "Every living substance was destroyed which was upon the face of the ground, both man, and cattle, and the creeping things, and the fowl of the heaven; they were destroyed from the earth." Is it possible to add to the strength of this? He thinks it is; and he therefore says, "Noah only remained alive, and they that were with him in the ark." Could any truthful man write this and then mean that less than a hundredth part of the earth's surface was covered. If not a total flood, why save the animals, above all the birds? All that Noah and his family need to have done would have been to move out of the region till the storm was over. If a partial flood, how could the ark have rested on the mountains of Ararat? Ararat itself is seventeen thousand feet high, and it rises from a plateau that is seven thousand feet above the sea-level. A flood that enabled the ark to float on to that mountain could not have been far from universal; and, when such a flood is accounted for on scientific principles, it will be just as easy to account for a total flood.

"*The flood was only intended to destroy man, and therefore only covered those parts of the earth that were occupied by him.*" The Bible states, however, that it was intended to destroy every thing wherein was the breath of life; and your account and the Bible account do not at all agree. But, if man was intended to be destroyed, the flood must have been wide-spread. We know that Africa was occupied before that time, and had been for thousands of years, by various races. We learn, from the recent discoveries in the Swiss Lakes, that man was in Switzerland before that time; in France, as Boucher's and Rigollet's discoveries prove; in Great Britain, as the caves in Devonshire show; in North America, as the fossil human skull beneath Table Mountain demonstrates. Hence, for the flood to destroy man alone at so recent a period, it must have been as wide spread as the earth.

Even according to the Bible account, the garden of Eden, where man was first placed, was somewhere near the Euphrates; and in sixteen hundred years the race must have rambled over a large part of the earth's surface. The highest mountains in the world, the Himalayas, are within two thousand miles of the Euphrates. That splendid country, India, would have been occupied long before the time of the deluge; and, on the flanks of the Himalayas, man could have laughed at any flood that natural causes could possibly produce.

"How do you account, then, for these traditions of a deluge that we find all over the globe?"

Nothing more easy. In all times floods have occurred; some by heavy and long-continued rains, others by the bursting of lake-barriers or the irruption of the sea; and wherever traditions of these have been met with, men with the Bible story in their minds have at once attributed their origin to the Noachian deluge.

"But Jesus and the apostles indorse the account of the deluge."

Granted; but does that transform a fable into a fact? They believed the story just as our modern theologians believe it; because they were taught it when they were children, and had not learned better. Jesus says (Matt. xxv. 37–39), " But as the days of Noe were, so shall also the coming of the Son of man be. For, as in the days that were before the flood they were eating and drinking, marrying and giving in marriage, until the day that Noe entered into the ark, and knew not until the flood came and took them all away; so shall also the coming of the Son of man be." If the man had regarded the story as false, he never would have referred to it in such a manner. And, in this manifestation of credulity on the part of Jesus, we can see the very false estimate placed upon him by so large a portion of the people of this country. Let the truth be spoken, though Jesus and all other idols be overthrown. So he would say, if alive, or he was not as good and intelligent a man as I think he was.

By this story the Bible stands or falls as a divine

book. It falls, as we see, and takes its place with all other human fallible productions. For knowledge, we go to Nature, our universal mother, who gives her Bible to every soul, and preaches her everlasting gospel to all people.

IS SPIRITUALISM TRUE?

IS SPIRITUALISM TRUE?

It is useless to tell us that a doctrine is popular. Paganism was once more popular than Presbyterianism; the world to-day would have been flat as a table, if the belief of a majority could have made it so. "But our doctrines are old: they have stood for eighteen hundred years." If such an argument is good for any thing, it overturns all Protestantism, and establishes Catholicism in its place; for Protestantism is only a protest against Catholicism, which must, therefore, be the older. But Buddhism, which was established twenty-five hundred years ago, says to Catholicism, "Out, you baby of yesterday!" but, scarcely seats itself in the temple, before it is unceremoniously ejected by hoary Paganism, the son of the ages.

For a doctrine to commend itself to the thinkers of the nineteenth century it must be true. It matters not whether one or one million believe it; whether it is declared by the beggar, whose shivering body the rags but miserably protect, or comes from heaven with a voice of thunder and the answering response of archangels. The only significant question that we can ask is, Is it true? If not, God himself cannot save it from the perdition that awaits it.

Is Spiritualism true? What is Spiritualism? It is not a belief in the writings of Andrew Jackson Davis. It is not an indorsement of the manifestations that are said to occur through the Davenports, or Eddys, Miss Ellis, or Mrs. Blair; nor is it to believe all that is published in "The Banner of Light," or declared by the thousands of mediums who speak in the name of the departed throughout the land. Whatever truth there may be in them, I object to making Spiritualism responsible for all these things, many of which can only be known to be true by examinations that one may have neither time nor ability to make, and that the parties concerned are sometimes unable, and sometimes unwilling, to permit.

What is Spiritualism, then? Webster gives the following definition of it: "Spiritualism is a belief in the frequent communication of intelligence from the world of spirits, by means of physical phenomena commonly manifested through a person of susceptibility, called a 'medium.'" A better, because a more accurate definition is, "Spiritualism is a belief in the communication of intelligence from the spirits of the departed, commonly obtained through a person of susceptibility, called a 'medium.'"

The spirit is something that exists when the body dies; but, since we see nothing depart, it is invisible; it communicates, according to our definition, with the living; it has, then, organs by which its communications are made: hence Spiritualism is first a belief that man possesses a spirit (the unseen man) that is not bound by the limitation of the senses, but can see without using the bodily eye, hear when no sound is conveyed to the outward ear, and can travel without the body's organs of locomotion. Does man possess such a spirit? If he does, we may reasonably expect to find some evidence of it in the present condition of existence, as we see in the egg before it is hatched the undeveloped wings that are eventually to be used in flying. If man is to see in the future, when the eye has become dust, we may expect to find some indication of it while he is still in the body; and this we do.

The writers of the famous Atkinson and Martineau Letters (Dr. Atkinson and Harriet Martineau) fearlessly announce in them (and I admire their honesty and boldness), that they are atheists, and have no faith in man's existence after death; * and yet they present us with facts that establish, I think, the existence in man of something altogether distinct from the body, and that can obtain knowledge without using the ordinary senses. I quote from them, because testimony in reference to this question coming from such a source is particularly valuable; their opinions giving them no bias in the direction of belief in such facts, but rather the contrary.

Dr. Atkinson says, "I had once a very remarkable patient, a somnambule, who, with the eyes closed, could easily read any writing I gave her. She read it from the top of her head, or when placed in her hand, or, in fact, from any part of her body; and it was to be noticed, in this case, that, the more tightly you pressed upon her eyes, the more clearly she could see." Dr. Atkinson adds, "This was a young lady staying with my mother and sisters; and I may say, that no one, however scepti-

* I am glad to learn, since this was written, that Harriet Martineau has become convinced of man's future existence.

cal, doubted *clairvoyance* after seeing this case. The clear evidence and daylight facts were too strong for scepticism itself." *

Instead of seeing with her eyes, then, the more unfavorably her eyes were situated for seeing, and the more readily she could see.

So satisfied of clairvoyance had he become, that he says, "I have heard men say, 'We are men of facts, and do not believe in *clairvoyance*.' I have replied, 'You are not men of facts, or, at least, not of these facts. You are like machines which spin out only one kind of fabric. You are men of one language and one country; prisoners with a window to the north, and declare there is no moon.'" † A class of prisoners of which there are not a few in our own country.

This making the circle of a man's knowledge the boundary of the universe has been altogether too common; and even Carlyle and Emerson, men of uncommon ability in many directions, have shown themselves very circumscribed in this respect, sneering at that which they have never or very slightly investigated.

It is no wonder that Dr. Atkinson speaks so confidently on the subject of clairvoyance; for he is a clairvoyant himself. He says, "One evening, I saw very distinctly, when a few steps from my door, two letters on my table, and from the same person. 'Now,' I thought, 'this will show me that these perceptions are crude fancies;' for I had received a letter from the same person the day before, and it was out of all probability that there should be two more letters from the same person, by the same post. On entering the room,

* Atkinson and Martineau Letters, p. 104. † Ibid. p. p. 153.

there were the two letters, sure enough, and lying precisely as I had seen them; and I must say it made me start, for this I could not suppose to be a coincidence." *

What was this which saw the two letters on his table, when he was several steps from the door, so that he knew how they lay, and whom they were from? Certainly we have no knowledge of the bodily senses possessing such power. I think we shall see, in the light of accumulated facts, that, in this case, the spirit-eyes beheld the letters, — these eyes that can see through a brick wall as readily as through air, and a hundred miles off as distinctly as at twelve inches.

However unlikely that it should be, some would account for this by coincidence: "He happened to think of two letters from that person at that time, and it happened to be so; that is all." Such an explanation cannot, however, be given in the following cases: "Dr. Gregory, professor of chemistry in the University of Edinburgh, tells us that Major Buckley has produced conscious clairvoyance in eighty-nine persons; of whom forty-four have been able to read mottoes contained in nut-shells purchased by other parties for the experiment. The longest motto thus read contained ninety-eight words. Many subjects will read motto after motto without one mistake. In this way, the mottoes contained in four thousand eight hundred and sixty nut-shells have been read, some of them, indeed, by persons in the mesmeric sleep, but most of them by persons in the conscious state, many of whom have never been put to sleep. In boxes, upward

* Atkinson and Martineau Letters, p. 110.

of thirty-six thousand words have been read; in one paper, three hundred and seventy-one words. Including those who have read words contained in boxes when in the sleep, one hundred and forty-eight persons have thus read. In a few cases, the words may have been read by thought-reading, as the persons who put them in the boxes were present; but, in most cases, no one who knew the words has been present, and they must, therefore, have been read by direct clairvoyance. The nuts enclosing mottoes, for example, have been purchased of forty different confectioners, and have been sealed up till read." *

Dr. Ashburner of London, not trusting to the nutshells furnished by the major, purchased some himself, and these were read by the clairvoyants with accuracy. † He also says, "Delicately sensitive persons have, in my presence, read printed words and sentences on slips of paper, previously concealed from them carefully in another apartment, in the innermost of a nest of four silver boxes, all enclosed in a morocco case, or folded up in nutshells."

"All that is done by mind-reading," says one. But, where the mottoes were sealed up till read, this appears to be impossible; and, in the following case given by Dr. Gregory, it was manifestly impossible, for the individual who supposed he knew the word was mistaken, and the clairvoyant right.

"On one occasion, Sir T. Willshire took home a nest of boxes belonging to the major, and placed in the inner box a paper on which he had written a word. He sealed up the boxes in paper, and asked one of the

* Gregory's Letters on Animal Magnetism, p. 302.

† Ashburner's Animal Magnetism and Spiritualism, p. 271

clairvoyants to read it. She said she saw the word 'concert.' He declared that she was wrong, though right with regard to the first and last letters. She persisted that it was 'concert;' and, opening the boxes, it was found that she was correct, the baronet having forgotten the word." *

Rev. Chauncey H. Townshend tells us of a young man, E. A——, whom he mesmerized, and took into a perfectly dark closet, when, he says, "I drew a card at hazard from a pack with which I had provided myself, and presented to him. He said it was so and so. The admission of light established his correctness: it was the card he had named. The experiment repeated four times gave the same satisfactory result. He used to declare, that, the more complete the darkness was, the better he could exercise his new mode of perception." †

Such evidence as this might be considered sufficient to establish the fact of clairvoyance; but extraordinary evidence is needed to establish extraordinary facts.

In 1825, Dr. Foissac demanded of the Royal Academy of Medicine in Paris, that a commission should be appointed to examine the claims of animal magnetism. Nine men of learning, several of whom had European reputations, were appointed, and after five years published their report. In this report they state that animal magnetism may produce somnambulic sleep; that some sleepers can see with their eyes closed, can foretell accurately, even months in advance, the time of the access of epileptic fits, or the time of their cure;

* Gregory's Letters on Animal Magnetism, p. 272.
† Townshend's Facts in Animal Magnetism, p. 244.

and can discover the diseases of persons with whom they are placed in magnetic connection.*

Baron Reichenbach, the well-known chemist, and author of the "Dynamics of Magnetism," says that high sensitives in the somnambulic condition, when they have their eyes closed, perceive the forms and colors of the external world, and in the same manner they can look into the human body.

Dr. Colby of Stanstead, Canada, informed me that he had a patient who was so good a clairvoyant, that she read for him a paper just taken from the press, with her eyes bandaged, and a tea-tray between her eyes and the paper.

There are but few who have investigated mesmeric or psychometric phenomena, who have not had opportunities of seeing clairvoyant phenomena. "Vision," says M. Teste, "through the closed eyelids, and through opaque bodies, is not only a real fact, but a very *frequent* fact. There is no magnetizer who has not observed it twenty times; and I know at the present day, in Paris alone, a very great number of somnambulists who might furnish proofs of it." † I have had very frequent opportunities of observing the exercise of this power, both in mesmeric and psychometric subjects.

It is evident that the eye is not necessary to enable some persons to see; and the reason appears to be, that the indwelling spirit, although ordinarily dependent upon the senses for its knowledge of the exterior world, is not confined to them. It can see by other portions of the body as well as by the eyes, hear by the

* New American Cyclopædia, art. "Animal Magnetism."

† Quoted by Bush in Mesmer and Swedenborg, p. 107.

fingers as well as by the ears, and can both see and hear when it appears impossible that any portion of the body can be influenced by what is seen and heard.

Dr. Mayo, professor of comparative anatomy in the Royal College of Surgeons, London, relates several instances of such phenomena. He says, "The psychical phenomena exhibited by the patient when thus entranced are the following: The organs of sensation are deserted by their natural sensibility. The patient neither feels with the skin, nor sees with the eyes, nor hears with the ears, nor tastes with the mouth. All these senses, however, are not lost. Sight and hearing, if not smell and taste, re-appear in some other part, — at the pit of the stomach, for instance, or the tips of the fingers.

"The patient manifests new perceptive powers. She discerns objects all around her, and through any obstructions, partitions, walls, or houses, and at an indefinite distance. She sees her own inside, as it were, illuminated, and can tell what is wrong in the health of others." *

Dr. Gregory says, "The clairvoyant power has been observed to be located in the pit of the stomach, in the tips of the fingers, in the occiput as well as in the forehead, or on the top of the head. . . . In one form or other, the power of dispensing with the eyes, and yet perceiving color, &c., quite plainly, is found in every good subject.

"The same thing frequently happens in hearing. Thus E., when on her travelling state or stage, is utterly deaf to all sounds save those which are addressed

* Popular Superstitions, p. 121.

to her by speaking with the mouth in contact with the tips of her fingers. This fact I have myself verified." *

Dr. Mayo relates the following on the authority of Baron de Fortis. The patient had epilepsy, for the cure of which she went to Aix. "There she had all sorts of fits and day-somnambulism, during which she waited at table, with her eyes shut perfectly. She likewise saw alternately with her fingers, the palm of her hand, and her elbow, and would write with precision with the right hand, superintending the process with her left elbow." In explanation of such phenomena, Dr. Mayo says, "The possibility of an abnormal relation of the mind and body, allowing the former either to shift the place of its manifestations in the nervous system, or partially to energize as free spirit, is the only principle which at present offers any solution of the new powers displayed in catalepsy." † And I think this explanation is the true one.

"But is it not possible that the brain has the power of receiving sensations by other than the ordinary channels, and that it is the brain, after all, by which this is accomplished, and not a spirit behind or within the man ?"

It is well that this question should be asked, and the reasons given for regarding the spirit as the agent, and not the brain. "During sleep," says Dr. Hammond, "the brain is in a comparatively bloodless condition, and the blood in the encephalic vessels is not only diminished in quantity, but moves with diminished rapidity." ‡ If the brain is the agent concerned in

* Gregory's Letters on Animal Magnetism, p. 148.

† Popular Superstitions, p. 130.

‡ Sleep and its Derangements, p. 35.

clairvoyant and clairaudient phenomena, its power being very much reduced by sleep, we should naturally expect that sleep would decrease or destroy its ability in this direction: but the very opposite seems to be the case; for many who possess no clairvoyant power in the waking condition have, in sleep, a remarkable development of it.

William Howitt relates the following case, which is also given by Mayo. In December, 1848, Mr. Smith, gardener to Sir Clifford Constable, disappeared; but his hat and stick were found near the River Tees. The river was dragged daily, but to no purpose. One night, a person named Awde, living at Little Newsham, dreamed that Smith was laid under the ledge of a certain rock about three hundred yards below Whorlton Bridge, and that his right arm was broken. He got up early the next morning, and determined to search the river. On arriving at the boat-house, he told the boatman his object, on being asked for what purpose he wished the boat. He rowed to the spot he had seen in his dream, and pulled up the body of the man with the boat-hook, on the first trial, with his right arm actually broken.* There is no intimation given, that Mr. Awde possessed any clairvoyant power in his waking state.

Similar instances might be given, for they are by no means rare (some I shall give in another connection), that seem to prove that the brain, which, as is now well known, is contracted in sleep, and therefore less fitted for obtaining ideas, cannot be the agent in clairvoyance, but it must be the all-seeing spirit.

* Ennemoser's History of Magic, p. 417.

Mesmerism induces, generally, a state of still deeper sleep than the ordinary, and therefore less fitted for the action of the brain; and yet in just that proportion does it seem to be favorable for the exercise of clairvoyance and its accompanying phenomena; and when the deepest sleep is secured by magnetism, and the eye is no longer sensitive to light, the ear to sound, and the skin to touch, it is then that these peculiar powers are most frequently and clearly manifested, as nearly all writers on mesmerism testify.

When approaching death enfeebles all the body's powers, then the permeating spirit asserts its true nature, most strong when the body is most weak.

The Rev. Hare Townshend gives us an instance of this. Chevalier Filippi of Milan informed him of a patient of his who had an abscess, and whom, on visiting, he found had but a few hours to live. Leaving the sick-chamber, he shut the door, and passed through two other rooms, the doors of which he also carefully shut, and entered an apartment where some friends of the patient were assembled. To these he said, speaking in a low tone, "The Signor Valdrighi is much worse. He cannot possibly survive till morning." Scarcely had he uttered the words, when the patient's bell was heard to ring violently, and soon after a servant summoned the doctor back again. "Why did you deceive me?" exclaimed the dying man: "I heard every word you said just now in the farther apartment." He then repeated to the astonished physician the very words he had made use of.* How, otherwise, can such facts be explained, than as evidences of man's

* Townshend's Facts in Animal Magnetism, p. 321.

possession of a spirit whose powers are altogether superior to those of the body?

The fact that one person can read the thoughts of another, no word being spoken, and no communication given, most persons conversant with mesmerism are familiar with. I have sometimes heard people say, when attempting to explain remarkable mesmeric or spiritual phenomena, "Oh, well! that is thought-reading." But what, pray, is thought-reading? Can we imagine any thing more remarkable? In ordinary clairvoyance, objects that the eye might behold are seen; but in thought-reading that is done which no bodily sense can accomplish, unless it is some sense of which as yet we know nothing.

Dr. Mayo says, "Presently, if his trance-faculties continue to be developed, the entranced person enters into communication with the entire mind of the mesmerizer. His apprehension seems to penetrate the brain of the latter, and is capable of reading all his thoughts." *

Dr. Gregory says, "The sleeper, being placed *en rapport* with any person, can often describe with the greatest accuracy the subject that occupies the thoughts of that person. It may be an absent friend, or his own house, or that of another, or his drawing-room, bedroom, study, &c., — all these things the sleeper perceives as they pass through the mind of the experimenter, and describes with great minuteness and accuracy. . . . He perceives things once known to, and now forgotten by, the experimenter." †

Townshend relates that a lady, wishing to test a mes-

* Popular Superstitions, p. 177.

† Letters on Animal Magnetism, pp. 108, 109.

meric subject of his, was about to choose two cards from a number lying upon the table, and then ask him to discover which they were. She had chosen the cards by her eye only, in perfect silence, and standing behind the subject, when he exclaimed, "Why should I go through this farce? I know already the two cards which the lady thought of: they were so and so." He was perfectly right. *

But what is this that reads thoughts? Certainly not the eye, and assuredly no other known sense. Can it be the brain, destitute of all organs for that purpose? Can it be other than the spirit, exercising those powers which it will constantly employ when released from the body? Within us all these wondrous powers lie as

"The wings that form
The butterfly lie folded in the worm."

Were it not, however, for other and more convincing evidence of the spirit's existence and operation, we might still refer all these cases to the operation of some occult power in the body yet to be discovered. But the persons through whom such phenomena are manifested, frequently have the sensation of being distinct from the body, of even looking down upon it, of travelling to distant localities, and returning again to the body. All who have experimented much in mesmerism are familiar with this; and evidence on this subject is quite voluminous. Dr. Mayo says, "These more complicated cases prove that the clairvoyant actually pays a mental visit to the scene. But she can do more: she can pass on to other and remoter scenes

* Townshend's Facts in Animal Magnetism, p. 447.

and places of which her fellow-traveller has no cognizance." *

Thomas C. Hartshorn, a well-known magnetizer, writing many years ago for "The Providence Journal," says of a friend whom he had magnetized, "I can send him forth instantly through the thick darkness of night into distant lands, and cause him to bring us tidings of our absent friends. His spirit seems to delight in this activity: his intellectual countenance brightens up with various emotions. He glides along the surface of the earth and ocean as rapid as the lambent borealis; and ever and anon, as different scenes arrest his attention, he bursts out into involuntary exclamations of pleasure or surprise, of joy or sorrow." This is no exaggeration, as my own experience with clairvoyants has repeatedly demonstrated. Before the advent of modern Spiritualism, I had, on numerous occasions, sent mesmeric subjects on distant journeys, and obtained from them knowledge of events then transpiring, as subsequent inquiries proved, — events absolutely unknown to all others present, and of such a character that they could not be guessed.

Mr. Hartshorn again says, "That the human spirit hath power to leave the body, and take cognizance of things distant in space, is but an elementary truth in this branch of psychology."

Dr. Cleaveland of Providence gives the following statement, made to him by a carpenter, who fell from the staging of a building to the ground. "As I struck the ground," said he, "I suddenly bounded up, seeming to have a new body, and to be standing among the

* Popular Superstitions, p. 191.

spectators, looking at my old one. I saw them trying to bring it to. I made several fruitless efforts to re-enter my body, and finally succeeded."

Mr. Moore of Malden, an officer in the Charlestown navy-yard, informed me, that, when fifteen years of age, he fell in climbing a lamp-post; and his head struck the curb-stone of the street with such violence as to fracture his skull. He instantly found himself out of his body, and looking down upon it; but in a few minutes, with a struggle, was able to return to ordinary consciousness.

Sensations similar to these have been frequently experienced by intelligent and reliable persons with whom I have conversed; and I know of no way in which they can be accounted for save by acknowledging that man does possess a spirit having organs of sensation.

John O. Wattles of Kansas, well known in the West as one of the most eloquent and earnest laborers in the antislavery cause at a time when to be such was to be ostracised, informed me, that, on one occasion, he accidentally discovered that his spirit could leave the body, and return. He found, afterward, that this could be done at will; and he frequently looked down as a spectator upon his body lying in a death-like trance, and then roamed at pleasure over the earth, and returned again.

Psychometers have frequently the power to do this; yet the body, in their case, presents no apparent difference from its ordinary condition. Mrs. Cridge, Mrs. Denton, and my son Sherman, travel spiritually with great ease, and describe with great accuracy distant localities never visited by them, and sometimes unknown to all persons present. They describe themselves as being there, to all appearance, in the body, so that they can see its different parts; the spiritual body being as real to spiritual sight as the physical body is to the physical eye, and quite as much so to the touch. They can hear, see, feel, taste, smell, and, in short, exercise every sense, much more perfectly than if present in the body: and this I have known psychometers to express hundreds of times; several independent psychometers, knowing nothing of the experience of others, giving exactly similar statements.

Lydia Maria Child has just published the following statement regarding her deceased friend Henrietta Sargent. "One morning, she spoke of not feeling as well as usual; but it was regarded by herself and others as merely a slight deviation from her customary good health. But in the course of the day she suddenly fainted away. As the usual restoratives produced no effect, the family physician was summoned. No better success attended his efforts. The breath appeared to be entirely suspended, and the limbs remained rigid and cold. Her daughters feared she must be dead; and the doctor began to be doubtful whether animation would ever be restored. How long she continued in this state, I do not remember. But, while they were watching her with ever-deepening anxiety, she gasped feebly, and, after a while, opened her eyes. When she had completely recovered, she told her daughters she had been standing by them all the time, looking upon her lifeless body, and seeing all they did to resuscitate it; and she astonished them by repeating the minutest details of all that had been said or done by them and the doctor during her prolonged state of utter insensibility."

Dr. Kerner relates of the Seeress of Prevorst: "On the 28th of May, 1827, at midnight, when I was with her, she again saw herself sitting on a stool. . . . She tried to cry out, but could neither speak nor move. . . . The image ran towards her; and, just as it reached her, a sort of electric shock passed over her which I saw: she then uttered a scream, and related to me what she had seen." In this case, the body appears to have seen the spirit; in all cases with which I have been conversant, the spirit has seen the body or seen itself. All these facts, however, like converging rays, point to the grand luminous truth from which they proceed, — the possession by man of a spirit.

I have noticed that when persons in their ordinary condition have no belief in future existence, yet, when their spiritual faculties are awakened, they realize its truth, and rejoice in the satisfaction that it brings to the soul; and the more highly-developed mesmeric subjects frequently manifest this.

Townshend tells us of a materialistic young Frenchman whom he frequently mesmerized. In his waking condition, he had no faith in future existence, and was not at all backward in declaring it; but, "in sleep-walking," says Townshend, "all this was changed. His ideas of the mind were correct, and singularly opposed to the material views he took of all questions when in the waking state. . . . Beautiful are the things he has said to me respecting the soul's recognition of those it loved on earth, and of the privilege of departed friends to watch over the objects of their solicitude while toiling through the pilgrimage of life." *

* Townshend's Facts in Animal Magnetism, p. 163.

These facts are in no other way related to modern Spiritualism than as evidencesof the existence in Nature of that of which the facts of modern Spiritualism are more recent and fuller illustrations; most of them belong to a time previous to the first Rochester rap.

One or two such facts might be considered of little importance; but together they form a body of evidence that seems to me absolutely irresistible. And, if this is true, the foundation of Spiritualism is true. Man is not merely an animated clod, to lie down with his fellow-clods, and know no more than they. We do not see all there is of him: he has a wondrous body, but a vastly more wondrous spirit, to which no night is dark, no body opaque; no distance can baffle its gaze, no bodily sense limit its knowledge. It is the true man, and the body but its incasement, — the shell, only useful till the spirit is plumed for its flight.

Then the materialist and the adventist are alike wrong. The materialist sees but the surface of things, knows nothing of the all-controlling spirit within, yet makes his knowledge the boundary of the universe. The adventist calls in miracle where it is altogether unnecessary. Man *is* a spirit: he is not to become one. Nature knows no favored saints, who are to be spiritually created for the barbarous heaven of a half-Jewish, half-Christian mythology, while the rest are left to sink into nonentity; but she has given to all freely as life, light, and air, that spirit which can smile at death, and soar triumphant when the lifeless body sinks to the dust.

Spiritualism also includes the belief that *this spirit lives when the body dies.* Accept the first, and there is little difficulty in believing the second. If man has a spirit that can see without using the eyes of the body; see even when these eyes do not exist, or are incapable of vision, as in the case of blind somnambulists and clairvoyants,—it is not unreasonable to suppose that it may see when its connection with the body is entirely destroyed by death. If he has a spirit that can hear sounds that are made hundreds of miles away from the body, and thus independent of the body's ears, it is not unreasonable to suppose that it may continue to hear when the body and all its organs are abandoned by the spirit, and the dust claims its kindred dust. And why may not the spirit, which has demonstrated its independence so clearly of all the body's faculties, continue to manifest its powers, though the body be no more? Why should we possess faculties all but unused, or used by but one in ten thousand? Why these spiritual eyes, if we are never to use them? Why these ears that hear so little, and yet have such wonderful capacity? Why this ability to travel more rapidly than light, if death is to destroy it when it has so seldom been employed? There is a physical body, and there is a spiritual body; and, in the light of facts, it is most reasonable to believe that the spiritual body will live when the physical body dies.

I can imagine two worms just folded in their cocoon, arguing the question whether there is to be any future life for them. "I have an idea," says one, "that I shall fly when I have eaten my way out of this case in which I am enclosed." — "You fly!" says the other: "that is all nonsense. You are a worm; and your life has been spent in crawling on the ground, for which alone all your faculties are fitted. Whoever saw worms fly? Worms we are, and worms we must ever be, and are now shut up in what must, in the nature of things, be our grave." — "But what are these wings for? I can feel wings that are growing on my sides; and I am persuaded that they are to be used. I shall fly, and, in the summer's sun of another year, flit from flower to flower, and enjoy the beauty of the bright world." And the hopeful worm is right. And we say, "What are these spiritual faculties for? They are our wings; and there is a realm where they are to be exercised during a life that only truly commences after what we call death."

As an evidence of this, let us again refer to sleep. If the spirit ceases to exist when the body dies, it is but reasonable to suppose that it will be influenced by the condition of the body in life; so that, when the body is in the most unfavorable condition for receiving knowledge through the senses, the spirit will likewise be in an equally unfavorable condition for receiving knowledge: but if the spirit is to survive death, and exercise its powers when it is separated from the body, we may reasonably expect that it will be able to manifest these powers when the ordinary senses are locked in sleep; and this we find to be the case. Sleep closes the eye and prevents vision, contracts the brain, reduces the circulation, and deadens the general sensibility: and yet the spirit in this condition can see what the open eye could not perceive; it reveals what it has tortured the brain for days in vain to discover; it visits distant lands, and beholds the succession of passing events in which the individual is interested, and sometimes even those in which he takes no special interest.

Dr. Carpenter relates, that Condorcet saw in his dreams the final steps of a difficult calculation which had puzzled him during the day; and Condillac states, that, when engaged with his "Course of Study," he frequently developed and finished a subject in his dreams which he had broken off before retiring to rest. Can it be the brain that does this in sleep, when it has been unable to accomplish it in the waking state? We might as well suppose a man could run eight miles an hour with his feet shackled, while he could only run four when they were free.

Chambers, in an essay on sleep, says, "A distinguished divine of the present day, who in his college-days, was devoted to mathematical studies, was once baffled for several days by a difficult problem, which he finally solved in his sleep." If you say, all this, however, the brain might do, stimulated into unusual activity by the waking desires, there are numerous cases that cannot be so explained.

In "The Penny Encyclopædia," article "Dreams," I find the following, "In the night of the 11th of May, 1812, Mr. Williams of Scorrior House, near Redruth in Cornwall, awoke his wife, and, exceedingly agitated, told her that he had dreamed that he was in the lobby of the House of Commons, and saw a man shoot with a pistol a gentleman who had just entered the lobby, who was said to be the chancellor; to which Mrs. Williams replied, that it was only a dream, and recommended him to go to sleep as soon as he could. He did so; but, shortly after, he again awoke her, and said that he had a second time had the same dream. The same vision was repeated a third time; on which, notwithstanding his wife's entreaties that he would lie quiet, and endeavor to forget it, he arose (then between one and two o'clock) and dressed himself. At breakfast, the dreams were the sole subject of conversation; and in the forenoon Mr. Williams went to Falmouth, where he related the particulars of them to all of his acquaintances that he met. On the following day, Mr. Tucker of Trematon Castle, accompanied by his wife, (a daughter of Mr. Williams), went to Scorrior House on a visit. Mr. Williams related to Mr. Tucker the circumstance of his dreams; on which Mr. Tucker observed, that it would do very well for a dream to have the chancellor in the lobby of the House of Commons, but that he would not be found there in reality. Mr. Tucker then asked what sort of a man he appeared to be, when Mr. Williams described him minutely. Mr. Tucker replied, 'Your description is not at all that of the chancellor, but is very exactly that of Mr. Perceval, the chancellor of the exchequer.' He then inquired whether Mr. Williams had ever seen Mr. Perceval, and was told that he had never seen him, nor had he ever had any thing to do with him; and, further, that he had never been in the House of Commons in his life. At this moment they heard a horse gallop to the door of the house; and immediately after a son of Mr. Williams entered the room, and said that he had galloped out from Truro, having seen a gentleman there who had come by that evening's mail from town, and who had been in the lobby of the House of Commons on the evening of the 11th, when a man called Bellingham had shot Mr. Perceval (the chancellor of the exchequer). After the astonishment which this intelligence created had a little subsided, Mr. Williams described most minutely the appearance and dress of the man that he saw in his dream fire the pistol at the chancellor, as also of the chancellor. About six weeks after, Mr. Williams, having business in town, went, accompanied by a friend, to the House of Commons, where, as has been already observed, he had never before been. Immediately that he came to the steps at the entrance of the lobby, he said, 'This place is as distinctly within my recollection as any room in my house;' and he made the same observation when he entered the lobby. He then pointed out the exact spot where Bellingham stood when he fired, and which Mr. Perceval had reached when he was struck by the ball when he fell. The dress both of Mr. Perceval and Bellingham agreed with the description given by Mr. Williams, even to the minutest particulars. The dream is related by Dr. Abercrombie with some additional circumstances."

Mr. Williams obtained in sleep knowledge, that, even in the waking state, he could not have obtained; and sleep, instead of diminishing the spirit's power, vastly increased it, showing its independence of the body's condition.

"A respected correspondent of Mr. F.," says Chambers in his "Essay on Dreams," "was a man of exemplary piety and the strictest veracity. He was in the East-India Company's service, and, having served one and twenty years, was about to return to his native country on leave of absence for three years. Some nights before his departure from Calcutta, he had a dream that his father died. It was so vivid, and so minutely circumstantial, that it made a very deep impression on him; and he entered all the particulars and the date into his pocket-book. In about six months after, on his arrival in London, he found letters from Ireland, where his family resided, waiting for him.

They announced the death of his father, which had occurred on *the very night of his dream*. This was so singular, that, when he joined his sister a few days after, he desired her to enter into no particulars relative to his father's death till she should hear him. 'Sarah,' said he, 'I believe that my father did not die in his own room: his bed was in the parlor.' — 'It was, it was, indeed,' replied she: 'he had it brought down a short time after he was taken ill, to save him the fatigue of going up and down stairs.' — 'I will show you the spot where it was placed,' said Capt. F. He immediately pointed out the situation of the bed, exactly where it had been. He showed where the coffin had been laid. There was nothing connected with the melancholy event which he could not detail as minutely as those who had actually been present. Strange as all this may appear, it is nevertheless perfectly true. I have frequently heard it from Capt. F. himself, and from his wife and sister."

The Pacific Hotel in St. Louis was destroyed by fire in February, 1858, and twenty-one lives were lost. On the night of the fire, a little brother of Mr. Henry Rochester, living at home with his parents, near Avon, N.Y., awoke some time after midnight with screaming and tears, saying that the hotel in St. Louis was on fire, and that his brother Henry was burning to death. At noon on the following day, his parents received a telegram from St. Louis confirming his dream in every particular.*

There is no evidence that these individuals possessed any clairvoyant power in their waking state; but, as the bodily eye closes, the spiritual eye opens, and when

* Planchette; or, The Despair of Science, p. 168.

the brain and senses are in an eminently unfavorable condition for obtaining knowledge, then knowledge of even distant events is easily and readily obtained by the spirit.

In death-trance, when even the circulation is stopped, and respiration can no longer be perceived, when the pallor of death overspreads the countenance, and death itself is so well counterfeited that it is hardly possible to distinguish the one from the other, the spirit asserts its superiority and independence; it hears, sees, feels, and obtains knowledge, that, out of this trance-state, the individual is unable to obtain.

In "The American Phrenological Journal," I find the following. "A daughter of Mr. Hangley of Bangor, seven years of age, was taken sick of cholera, and, to all appearance, died, but in a few hours stretched forth her arms, and exclaimed, 'O father! I have been to heaven, and it is a beautiful place.' She stated that she saw her mother there, who had died but a few days before, and she was taking care of little children, among whom, she said, were 'four children of Uncle Hangley, and three children of Uncle Casey.' — 'But,' said an older sister, 'it cannot be so; for there are but two of Uncle Casey's children dead.' — 'Yes,' she replied, 'I saw three of them in heaven. All were dressed in white, and all were very happy, and the children playing.' Shortly after, a message came from Mr. Casey in Carmel, giving information of the death of another child, and inviting them to attend the funeral."

The spirit's powers are not weakened by sleep nor death-trance, but vastly increased; just what we should expect if the spirit is to survive death, but altogether inexplicable if death is to extinguish us.

What effect has the approach of death itself? In drowning, when the thread of life has been all but severed, and with the greatest difficulty animation has been restored to the apparently lifeless body, it is well known that the activity of the spirit has been by no means decreased, but often vastly increased.

From a letter by F. Beaufort to Dr. W. Hyde, published in "The American Phrenological Journal," I extract the following. He fell into the water, and says, "From the moment that all exertion had ceased, which, I imagine, was the immediate consequence of complete suffocation, a calm feeling of the most perfect tranquillity superseded the previous tumultuous sensations: it might be called apathy, certainly not resignation; for drowning no longer appeared to be an evil. I no longer thought of being rescued; nor was I in any bodily pain. The senses were deadened; but not so the mind. Its activity seemed to be invigorated in a ratio which defies all description; for thought rose after thought with a rapidity of succession that is not only indescribable, but probably inconceivable by any one who has not been himself in a similar situation. . . . Travelling backward, every past incident of my life seemed to glance at my recollection in retrograde succession; not, however, in mere outline, as here stated, but the picture filled up with every minute and collateral feature: in short, the whole period of my existence seemed to be placed before me in a kind of panoramic review, and each act of it seemed to be accompanied by a consciousness of right or wrong, or by some reflection on its cause or consequences; indeed, many trifling events that had long been forgotten then crowded into my imagination, and with the character of recent familiarity."

Could the man's body have been examined while this was going on, the surface would have been found cold, the whole of the arterial blood converted into black venous blood, and this distending the heart, the lungs, and the brain, rendering the whole physical man as unfit for action as a locomotive with the fire out, and the water in the boiler changed to ice. If we found a locomotive going at the rate of a thousand miles an hour under such circumstances, we should conclude that it ran by some other motive-power than steam. What remembered, thought, imagined, when the body was in this condition? That which will remember, think, and imagine when the body has returned to dust.

As an evidence of this extraordinary memory in drowning, I present the following, taken from "The Rome Daily Sentinel." A held a bond of B for several hundred dollars, having some time to run. At its maturity, he found that he had put it away so carefully that he could not find it. He called on B, related the circumstance, and proposed to give him a receipt; but B denied owing him any thing, and intimated that A wished to cheat him. Several years passed, when A, bathing in Charles River, sunk, and was completely unconscious before he was rescued. "On the first return of strength to walk, he left his bed, went to his book-case, took out a book, opened it, and handed his long-lost bond to a friend who was present. He then informed him, that when drowning and sinking, as he supposed, to rise no more, in a moment there stood out distinctly before him as a picture every act of his life, from the hour of childhood to the hour of sinking beneath the water; and among them the circumstance of putting the bond in the book, the book itself, and the place in which he had put it in the book-case."

The spirit apparently forgets nothing, and when released from the body all our past is present to us, — ours forever.

How exceedingly common it is for the dying to see and hear what those present are utterly unconscious of! It is easy to say that they are idle fancies clustering around the dying man, that reason is too weak to dispel. They should at least be in harmony with his previous ideas if this theory of their origin be granted.

A Methodist minister, Purcell P. Hamilton of Litchfield, Ill., near the close of a lingering illness, was entranced. His friends thought him gone; but he unexpectedly revived, and said to his wife, "I have not left you yet. I have been to see my heavenly home; but they told me I could not go until I came back and told you that the teachings of all these years from my pulpit are false. Our ideas of heaven are all wrong. I have taught and thought we would die and go straight to God and glory. All wrong. Tell all you meet my last words to them, — all wrong. The spirit-home is a beautiful land; but we must go up step by step, and work out our own salvation."

It is so common for the dying to be clairvoyant, that, in every age, it has been noticed by the intelligent. Plutarch says in reference to it, "It is not probable, that, in death, the soul gains new powers which it was not before possessed of when the heart was confined with the chains of the body: but it is much more probable that these powers were always in being, though dimmed and clogged by the body; and the soul is only then able to practise them when the corporeal bonds are loosened, and the drooping limbs and stagnant juices no longer oppress it."

Schiller's last words when dying were, "Many things are growing plain and clear to me." Is this the talk of an expiring soul going down to the grave to come up no more, the night of annihilation closing around it? It is the joyous exclamation of one long living in obscurity, who for the first time finds the windows ajar, and the light of a deathless morn looking in. We dwell in the twilight, and we pine for the glory of a day that must shine.

So far, then, from the approach of death weakening the soul as it does the body, and thus rendering probable its dissolution with the body, it develops its peculiar powers, and prepares the way for their manifestation, and thus gives us the assurance, that, when it is consummated, the spirit will be free to exercise those faculties untrammelled, which are manifested here in their greatest strength when the body is most weak.

If the spirit exists after death, what can be more reasonable than that it should desire to communicate with its friends still in the body? Can the mother forget the family from which death has torn her? the patriot the country for which his life has been spent? the youth the home around which all his associations are clustered? If the emigrant thinks of his country over the sea, and sends messages to those whom he never again expects to see, how much more shall those who have gone to the land of souls remember the loved ones remaining, and desire to give them tidings of their welfare!

Can it be done? Dr. Gregory says, "I can vouch for this fact, — that a magnetizer can strongly affect a person who is not only in another room, or another house, or many hundred yards off, but who is utterly unaware that any thing is to be done."

Dr. Foissac magnetized Paul Villagrand at the distance of three hundred miles. The doctor gave a note to his father, which he desired him to hand to Paul at half-past five, P.M. It read thus, "I am magnetizing you at this moment: I will awake you when you have had a quarter of an hour's sleep." But the father, to make the experiment decisive, never gave the letter to his son. "Nevertheless, at ten minutes before six, Paul, being in the midst of his family, experienced a sensation of heat, and considerable uneasiness. His shirt was wet through with perspiration; he wished to retire to his room: but they detained him. In a few minutes, he was entranced. In this state, he astonished the persons present, by reading, with his eyes shut, several lines of a book taken at hazard from the library, and by telling the hour upon a watch they held to him. He awoke in a quarter of an hour."

If the spirit while in the body can influence the spirits of others in the body, at a distance of hundreds of miles, it is surely not unreasonable to suppose, that, when the spirit has dropped the body, it can still influence them, and thus reveal its existence. Besides this, we have abundant evidence that the spirit does communicate with the living, thus establishing the third fundamental principle of Spiritualism.

On this subject we have the testimony of all ages. The sacred books of the Jews and Christians contain such accounts, and, although the fabulous character of portions of the Bible leads to suspicion of all its marvellous statements, yet many of its accounts of spiritual manifestations are in harmony with those of other peoples and all time.

It is noticeable, that, as people have become more intelligent, spiritual manifestations have increased in the same proportion. As chemistry became established, alchemy died out; as astronomy advanced, astrology retreated, and hides to-day only in the obscurest corners: but as a knowledge of man's true nature increases, so do the evidences of communication between the spirit-world and our own multiply around us. In the early history of the Jews, we find but few of them; they were more common in the time of Jesus and his immediate followers, and are most common in this the most intelligent age the world has seen.

In bringing forward testimony on this subject, the only difficulty is to choose out of the abundance presented. Do we desire the testimony of a scientific man, let us take that of Prof. Hare, the well-known chemist, who at one time maintained most earnestly the mechanical theory of Faraday, but abandoned it in consequence of the experiments undertaken to demonstrate it. He visited a medium, through whom communications were received by the tipping of a table. The alphabet was placed upon a table, and, when a pencil held by a gentleman at the foot of the table passed over it, the table tipped when the right letter was indicated. In this way, this message was spelled out, "Light is dawning on the mind of your friend; soon he will speak trumpet-tongued to the scientific world, and add a new link to that chain of evidence on which our hope of man's salvation is founded."

This appeared to him almost unaccountable; but he was resolved to prevent the possibility of deception. He made a disk of pasteboard about a foot in diameter, around which the letters of the alphabet were placed as much as possible out of their regular order. The disk was made to revolve upon an axis by a string which passed over a groove in the hub of the wheel; a weight being attached to each end of the string, — a large one on the ground, and a smaller suspended on the other side of the wheel. The medium was seated at the table with a screen between her eyes and the disk. The table was tilted, and thus the disk, which was on the axle attached to it, was made to revolve, and the letters of the alphabet were brought under a stationary index before it. Prof. Hare sat in front of it, and said, "If there be a spirit present, let the letter *y* be brought under the index." The disk revolved to the letter *y*. But I will let him tell the story in his own words. "'Will the spirit be so kind as to give his initials?' It revolved immediately to R. and to H. 'What,' said I, 'my father?' It revolved again to the letter *y*, indicating the affirmative. 'Will you arrange these letters in alphabetical order?' The disk again moved; and the letters were arranged as requested. 'Will you now spell the name of Washington?' It was spelled. 'Now,' said a bystander, 'you must give up. You made this instrument to disprove Spiritualism, and you see it confirms it.' I remarked that this was the most important experiment which I had ever performed, if viewed as proving that the shade of my honored father was there. I said, 'You must allow me time to deliberate, and to repeat the experiment, before ultimately deciding.'"

10

Subsequently he obtained analogous results by another medium, who had not previously seen his apparatus, and whom he had never seen before.

It was suggested that the medium might be clairvoyant, and thus see through the disk. To obviate this objection, Prof. Hare procured a brass ball, something like a billiard-ball, and placed upon it a smooth plate of metal on which the hands of the medium rested, so that she could not possibly control the movements of the table. His father communicating with him under these circumstances, the name of an uncle of his, who was killed by the Arabs seventy years ago, was spelled out. "Also the name of a partner who came out and took care of his affairs during the Revolution," nobody present knowing the name but himself. Then the names of some English relatives were given, the name of an aunt who died forty years ago, and the name of his English grandfather's partner. Cards were held up; and the spirits accurately described them when neither the medium nor himself knew what they were. Sitting with a medium who was not a Latin scholar, he asked his father to point out the words in Virgil which he admired as describing the beating which Entellus gave Dares; and he spelled out the words, "*pulsatque versatque.*"

No wonder that Prof. Hare became a Spiritualist, and announced it to the world, after such demonstrative tests as these; and so, I think, would every other scientist, had he an equal determination to know the truth, and as much courage to avow it.

Do we desire the testimony of a literary man, here is that of William Howitt, whose reputation is world-wide.

"More than six years ago, I began to examine the phenomena of Spiritualism. I did not go to paid or even to public mediums. I sat down at my own table with members of my own family, or with friends,—persons of high character, and serious as myself in the inquiry. I saw tables moved, rocked to and fro, and raised repeatedly into the air. I heard the raps, sometimes a hundred at once, in every imaginable part of the table, in all keys, and of various degrees of loudness. I examined the phenomena thoroughly. Silly but playful spirits came frequently. I heard accordions play wonderful music as they were held in one hand, often by a person who could not play at all. I heard and saw hand-bells carried about the room in the air; put first into one person's hand, and then into another's; taken away again by a strong pull, though you could not see the hand touching them. . . . As for communications professedly from spirits, they were of daily occurrence, and often wonderful. Our previous theological opinions were resisted and condemned when I and my wife were alone.

"I have seen spirit-hands moving about; I have felt them again and again. I have seen writing done by spirits, by laying a pencil and paper in the middle of the floor, and very good sense written too.

"I could give you a whole volume of the remarkable and even startling revelations made by our own departed friends at our own evening table; those friends coming at wholly unexpected times, and bringing messages of the most vital importance; carrying them on from period to period, sometimes at intervals of years, into a perfect history. But these things are too sacred for the public eye."

The testimony of Dr. Ashburner, a well-known London physician, is very satisfactory. "I have myself so often witnessed spiritual manifestations, that I could not, if I were inclined, put aside the evidences which have come before me. When Mr. Charles Foster was in London in 1863, he was often in my house; and numerous friends had opportunities of witnessing the phenomena which occurred in his presence. The second morning that he called on me was about two weeks after his arrival in England. Accidentally, at the same time arrived at my door, Lady C. H. and her aunt, wife of the Rev. A. E. I urged them to come in, and placed them on chairs at the sides of my dining-table. Their names had not been mentioned; Mr. Foster having retired to the farther extremity of the room, so as not to be able to see what the ladies wrote, I induced them each to write, upon separate slips of paper, six names of friends who had departed this world. These they folded into pellets, which were placed together.

"Mr. Foster, coming back to the table, immediately picked up a pellet, and addressing himself to Mrs. A. E., 'Alice,' he said, which made the lady start, and ask how he knew her name. He replied, 'Your cousin, John Whitney, whose name you wrote in that little piece of paper, stands by your side, and desires me to say, that he often watches over you, and reads your thoughts, which are always pure and good. He is delighted at the tenderness and care which you exhibit in the education of your children.' Then he turned towards me, and said, 'Alice's uncle is smiling benignantly as he is looking towards you. He says you and he were very intimate friends.' I said, 'I should like to know the name of my friend;' and Mr. Foster instantly replied, 'Gaven. His Christian name will appear on my right arm.'

"The arm was bared; and there appeared in red letters, fully one inch and a quarter long, the name William, raised on the skin of his arm. Certainly, William Gaven was my dear old friend, and the uncle of the lady whose name is Alice.

"Mr. Foster next addressed himself to Lady C., whom he had never seen before in his life. 'Your mother,' said he, 'the Marchioness of ——, stands by your side, and desires to give you her fond blessing and very affectionate love.' He added, 'Lady C., you wrote on a piece of paper I hold here the name of Miss Stuart. She stands by the side of your mother, and is beaming with delight at the sight of her pupil. She was your governess, and was much attached to you.' He added, 'That charming person, the marchioness, was a great friend of the doctor's. She is so pleased to find you all here! Her Christian name is to appear on my arm.' Mr. Foster drew up his sleeve, and there appeared in raised, red letters on the skin, the name Barbara." Dr. Ashburner adds, "Here were cases in which it was quite impossible that the medium could have known any single fact relating to the families, or to the intimacies, of any of the persons present. I had myself formed his acquaintance only two days before; and the ladies had arrived from a part of the country with which he could not possibly be acquainted."

If it is said that this might be accomplished by mind-reading, then the question arises, How does it happen that the medium has no knowledge of this? Can this, the most wonderful of all powers, be exercised unconsciously ? And why are such manifestations invariably attributed to spirits by the manifestations themselves ? Do mediums not only unconsciously read mind, move physical bodies, and write messages, but at the same time unconsciously lie regarding the cause of these varied phenomena ?

My own spiritual experience has been much like that of William Howitt. I commenced the investigation of Spiritualism at home, with the members of our own family; when we had raps, movement of tables, and, by these means, communications from unseen intelligences professing to be our departed friends, and giving us satisfactory evidence of this. After this, I saw remarkable physical manifestations through mediums in Ohio, Indiana, New York, and Canada,— such as the elevation of heavy tables and other bodies when no person was in contact with them, the rooms in which these took place being at the time well lighted. I have seen hands repeatedly, and felt them still more often, when the hands of the only person in the room beside myself lay upon the table before me; and this frequently in the broad daylight also. I have induced spirits to make for me impressions of their hands on plastic substances, such as putty and clay, and to draw their outlines with pencil on paper, which they have done repeatedly in my presence in a well-lighted room. On one occasion, I received in this way the outline of a hand larger than I ever saw; when the only person present beside myself was a lady of average size, and both her hands at the time were on the table before me.

I have frequently received communications in writing both on slate and paper; and in all cases this took place in the daytime, or in a lighted room, and under circumstances that rendered it utterly impossible for any person in the body to produce them. I desire no more evidence than I have had on this subject; for it leaves no room for question or doubt.

Those who can be satisfied by testimony upon this subject may certainly obtain all that is needed. If they desire personal experience, they need not go far to obtain that also, and know for themselves that Spiritualism is true, and rejoice in a knowledge of the most glorious gospel that was ever preached to mankind.

Our graveyards are not the dwelling-places of the departed; nor are their coffins the bedrooms in which they are to sleep till a trumpet-blast shall wake the dust, and call it forth to life again. There we lay away the shards, the cast-off cases of humanity, while the friends we mourn are sadly smiling at our sorrow, and longing to enlighten us, and bear up the load that presses the mourner's spirit down.

What we call death is but an epoch in the soul's history. Life here is the first act in the great drama of existence; and the curtain only falls to rise again, and show us a fairer scene, and introduce us to a better life. We mourn not the departure of our friends as those who are agonized with doubt as to whether they have gone to a heaven of pious bliss or a hell of abysmal despair; nor do we mourn as those who believe they are asleep, and that only a miracle can awake them. There is no gulf between us and them, that needs to be bridged; no wall that needs to be scaled; no vigilant gate-keepers to be eluded. In sorrow they are near to cheer us, in danger to warn, in temptation to strengthen. No selfish enjoyment eclipses their love or weakens their affection, and as surely as we part we shall meet again.

Tell it to the ocean, and let his deep voice repeat it to the thousand islands that lie upon his broad breast; tell it to the winds, and let its glad tidings be carried on their wings over the wide continents, and let earth's millions join in one grand hymn of praise.

Let the mourner's tears be dried, and bid the orphan smile: death is no longer man's enemy; by the angel of Spiritualism he swears eternal friendship to mankind.

Do I, then, indorse all that professes to come from the spirit-world? By no means. Some things attributed to this source are doubtless produced by fraud; though by no means as much as some would have us believe. The charge of fraud has been made against some of the best people that ever lived; and some timid ones have been broken down by it, who were as true and pure as Nature herself. Some phenomena attributed to spirits outside of the body are in reality produced by spirits still remaining in the body. These spirits, that are to do such wonderful things when they have left the body, possess the power, to a certain extent, now, and frequently exercise it; and multitudes innocently, because ignorantly, attribute to spirits what has no other source than themselves, it may be, in a peculiar condition.

Nor do I indorse as good or true all that in reality comes from the spirit-world. We are spirits incased in clay: they are spirits who have dropped the case, but, in other respects, are identically the same. Every second a human being becomes a spirit; and the spirit-world cannot but abound with ignorant, vicious, undeveloped spirits. Shall we submit to their dictation? Shall we give ourselves up to their influence regardless of their character? The consequences might be, as they have frequently been, most disastrous. We must stand by our own sense of what is true, right, and pure, and never move a step without good reason.

Prove to us that you are in communication with Franklin, Channing, Parker, George Fox, or Jesus, what then? We must still take what they say for what it seems to us to be worth when weighed in the scale of our judgment; for, if God spoke, we could do no other. Herein differs modern from ancient Spiritualism. Ancient Spiritualism—that which the Christian Church believes in and indorses to-day—overpowers the individual soul, robs it of its heritage, sets a master over it who graciously permits it to echo his voice. But we have learned that a man's soul is to him the highest tribunal in the universe; by that he must stand first, last, and always. All revelations must appeal to that, and nothing be accepted that it rejects; each for himself, making daily the heaven that he desires, and bearing it with him to the land of souls, whither Time bears us with rapid strides.

ORTHODOXY FALSE.

ORTHODOXY FALSE SINCE SPIRITUALISM IS TRUE.

EVERYBODY has heard of the witty saying of Sydney Smith, "Orthodoxy is my doxy, and heterodoxy the other man's doxy." But this is not what I mean by orthodoxy, when I say orthodoxy is false since spiritualism is true. I mean the peculiar religious doctrines taught by what are called the evangelical churches,—those who take the ground that the Bible is the inspired word of God; that man is totally depraved, and born to do evil continually, in consequence of Adam's transgression; who believe in the eternity of torment to which he thus became liable, and from which he can only be saved by belief in Jesus, the second person of the Trinity, through whose merits the true believer escapes the pit of woe, and passes through the pearly gates into the New Jerusalem, there to sing the praises of his Redeemer forever. The orthodox, therefore, include Catholics, Orthodox Quakers, Methodists, Baptists, Presbyterians, and a host of others.

We are in daily communication with the spirits of the departed, some of whom never belonged to any religious organization, never attended church, believed not in Jesus as a Son of God, and the Saviour, never professed to be born more than once, and were therefore orthodoxically wicked; yet we find they are in no hopeless prison, —

> "Where sinners must with devils dwell,
> In darkness, fire, and chains."

They are swimming in no shoreless brimstone lake, with waves of damnation rolling over their guilty souls; they are not crying for a drop of water to cool their scorched tongues; they are not even advising their friends who are still on earth to believe the doctrines of orthodoxy, and obey its requirements, that they may improve their condition when they pass to the land of souls.

But some of our departed friends were members of orthodox churches: they did believe in Jesus as their Saviour; they were baptized in his name; they believed themselves mysteriously born again, and died in the faith, with the full prospect of the heaven that had been preached to them, as a reward of the righteous, from their infancy. We now converse with them, and find them to be just such persons as we knew upon earth, save that their orthodoxy has been terribly shattered. They confess to us that the religious views that they held here were altogether contrary to the facts as they find them there, and that orthodoxy is as wrong as its name is right. They find no golden city with gates of pearl, no God seated upon a great white throne, no Jesus at his right hand, no twelve subordinate thrones upon which his fishermen disciples sit, judging the twelve tribes of Israel. There are no eye-full beasts guarding the throne, and crying, "Holy, holy, holy!" day and night; nor elders forever throwing down their crowns, while the crowd look on in holy admiration.

Thus we find that hell and heaven alike depart; and orthodoxy, dressed in crape, goes weeping after them. No more can the orthodox poet picture, as did Pollok in his "Course of Time," the sinners' abode: —

"Wide was the place,
And deep as wide, and ruinous as deep.
Beneath, I saw a lake of burning fire,
With tempest tossed perpetually; and still
The waves of fiery darkness [strange darkness that] 'gainst the rocks
Of dark damnation broke, and music made
Of melancholy sort; and overhead,
And all around, wind warred with wind, storm howled
To storm, and lightning, forkèd lightning, crossed,
And thunder answered thunder, muttering sounds
Of sullen wrath. And, far as sight could pierce,
Or down descend in caves of hopeless depth,
Through all that dungeon of unfading fire,
I saw most miserable beings walk;
Burning continually, yet unconsumed;
Forever wasting, yet enduring still;
Dying perpetually, yet never dead.
Some wandered lonely in the desert flames:
And some in fell encounter fiercely met,
With curses loud, and blasphemies that made
The cheek of darkness pale; and as they fought,
And cursed, and gnashed their teeth, and wished to die,
Their hollow eyes did utter streams of woe.
And there were groans that ended not, and sighs
That always sighed, and tears that ever wept
And ever fell, but not in mercy's sight."

This *was* the hell of orthodoxy. It has cooled down considerably since this was written. It was once as fiery as the primeval earth, when white-hot billows rolled along its breast; but it cools so much more rapidly, that our children may expect to find it a very comfortable place of abode. All will yet learn that no worse hell exists than earth makes: the soul's condition, wherever that soul may be, produces hell or heaven, if we still make use of the names. If any thing has been demonstrated by the unnumbered communications received from the spirit-world within the last twenty years, it is this.

Since the hell of orthodoxy is false, man was never in danger of it, and he never needed any Jesus to save him from what never had an existence. Jesus, then, is no Saviour in the orthodox sense: no salvation came by him. He was no more sent of God than Patrick's baby, born yesterday; for the necessity of his being sent did not exist. He was no more the Son of God than Socrates who preceded him, John Brown who came after him, or we who criticise him; no more a Saviour than Socrates and Plato who shine like stars in the pagan heavens, or Garrison and Phillips who shine in ours to-day,— all of these men far in advance of Jesus in many respects.

The whole plan of salvation indeed, as taught by orthodoxy, is essentially unreasonable, mean, and unmanly: it will not bear the light of rational investigation for a moment. The whole human race had become, by the sin of the first pair, exposed to eternal torments, and were of themselves utterly unable to do one good deed, or think one good thought. They had no power to elevate themselves from the horrible pit in which they are born, none to save themselves from the terrible consequences of their crimes. In this lost condition, God, in his great mercy, formed the plan to save us through the merits of his well-beloved Son, who knew no sin, but became a sin-offering for us, that we might be made the righteousness of God in him. He suffered in our room and stead. Our chastisement was laid upon him, God treating him as if he had been guilty of all human crime; and we, by faith in him, are treated by God as if we had lived his life of perfect goodness. We have no virtue; but the virtue of Jesus is attributed to us. We deserve nothing but hell, — even the best of us; but, by some godly hocus-pocus, we are to be conjured into heaven. We are filthy, vile, abominable; but, as the old Orthodox hymn says, —

"Jesus, thy blood and righteousness
My beauty are, my glorious dress:
Midst flaming worlds, in these arrayed,
With joy shall I lift up my head."

What a contemptible piece of business is this! Where is he, possessing the soul of a man, that would wish to sneak into heaven under the cloak of Jesus (and such a cloak!) when he knew in his own soul that he had no right to be there? Instead of lifting up his head with joy, a decent man would hang his head, and blush for shame. Suppose that robe of "blood and righteousness" should be torn from his back, and he revealed in his hideous nakedness!

The heaven of orthodoxy must be one of poltroons, and spiritless, fawning sycophants, who chant forever the praises of Him who cheated the Prince of Darkness of his due, and opened a palace of bliss for hell-deserving sinners, who, for the privilege of entering, must bow and sing glory to him who redeemed them forever. Such a scheme could never have been devised in America: it smacks of the despotism, the servility, and the meanness of the Old World of kings, my lords, serene highnesses, and grand seigniors. The true, unbiassed soul intuitively scorns it. It says, "If I have done deeds worthy of hell, then to hell I will go, and bear its penalties like a man, asking no odds of the torturing gods. Let me pass for what I am (cloaks for hypocrites and cowards): I desire no heaven that I have not won, and I fear no hell that I do not deserve." The man who deserves heaven will have it. He carries the key to its gate in his soul, and needs no Jesus to indorse him. Give us justice, and what more do we need in the universe? All the sin of all the men that ever lived never deserved the pain of an orthodox hell for a single day; and any being that could be unjust enough to make it should be the first to suffer in it.

Reason cannot but reject this whole "scheme" of salvation. Finite man is guilty of an infinite offence against God. He incurs by this means a debt that infinity alone can pay. All earth's treasures cast into the balance weigh not the millionth of a feather; the brightest jewels of heaven move not the balance one jot: only the exchequer of a God can furnish the means to pay the mighty debt we owe. What shall be done? If the debt is not paid, hell and its eternal torments await every sinful soul. At length, Jehovah plans the wondrous scheme: Jesus, one with the Father, "very God of very God," as the Athanasian Creed calls him, comes down to this abode of guilty wretches. He is born of a woman,—a pure and spotless virgin, lives a perfect life, preaches the gospel of the kingdom, works the most wonderful miracles, is despised and rejected of men, spat upon, buffeted, and is crucified, the just for the unjust. He bore man's sins, suffered in his stead, washed out with the blood of a God the damning spot of guilt in God's book of justice, paid the infinite debt we owed; and God can now be just, and the justifier of him that believeth in Jesus.

What a medley! — God is the creditor; yet God, in the person of his Son, pays the debt. Man is the debtor: the debtor is poor, and cannot pay one cent of the infinite amount he owes. God, in a voice of thunder, and with a look that strikes terror to the guilty sinner's heart, demands payment of the debt, and holds his glittering sword ready to cut him down unless the sum is paid. Man, in an agony, looks up, expecting the blow to descend. But now God's pity is moved for the trembling wretch. "You cannot pay, I know," says he; "but the debt *must* be paid to the uttermost farthing. How else can my justice be satisfied? Now I think of a plan;" and, taking a full purse from his pocket, he hands it to the sinner, who returns it to his creditor. God pockets it with a satisfied air. The debt is paid; justice is satisfied; and the sinner may now be justified. And this is the wonderful plan of salvation that angels desire to see into. Blind must that soul be that cannot see through it! Man was so wicked before Jesus came, that God could by no means pardon him; but he kills God, and thus crowns his wickedness, and God is graciously pleased, when he pleads the merits of Jesus, to forgive him, receives him into his house, and calls him his son! Yet, now that the debt is paid, and full satisfaction given, not one in ten receives the benefit: the great body of the human race must languish forever in hell, eternal prisoners for debt.

The God whom we are told declares that he will by no means clear the guilty, and that every man shall be rewarded according to his works, is, by this salvation, represented, not only as clearing the guilty, but predicating this clearance upon the sufferings of the innocent, and rewarding them, not according to their works, but their belief in the works of another.

The cruelty of God cannot be surpassed: he is, according to this salvation, the veriest Shylock: "I will have the due and forfeit of my bond, though every soul that I have made in deep damnation endless sink." At the same time, he has made them so beggarly poor, that they cannot pay. The sword of his justice, red-hot, can only be cooled in the blood of his innocent Son; and he is even yet to wreak his vengeance upon the great mass of mankind, who with good sense refuse to accept such a useless, contradictory, irrational, and unmanly system.

The God who made this plan must have less judgment than an intelligent school-boy, less conscience than a pettifogger, and less mercy than a Confederate prison-keeper. Hear what Watts, the orthodox poet, says of him,—

> "Our God appeared consuming fire;
> And Vengeance was his name.
> Rich were the drops of Jesus' blood
> That calmed his frowning face,
> That sprinkled o'er his burning throne,
> And turned the wrath to grace."

What a monster!

No wonder that men and women love Jesus, pray to Jesus, and sing, —

> "Jesus, lover of my soul,
> Let me to thy bosom fly."

God is furious as a chafed lion; Jesus, gentle as a turtle-dove: God is the jailer; Jesus, the deliverer of those that are bound: God is the heartless Jew, saying, "I stay here on my bond;" Jesus, the gentle Portia, suggesting to him, "Mercy is twice blessed: it blesseth him that gives, and him that takes." Yet both are, after all, the same individual. It would seem as if such a story could only have been received on the principle that it is right for God to do what would be infamous in a man; and that what in us would be utter folly may be in him superlative wisdom. And, when a man comes to that conclusion to-day, he will be prepared to kiss the pope's toe to-morrow. It needs but the fearless exercise of reason, and such gods will be speedily cast into the limbo where lie the defunct deities of Greece and Rome.

But, if Jesus is no Saviour, there is no forgiveness of sin to those who trust in him or pray to him. Put as much faith and trust in a rubber doll, and there is no doubt it would be equally efficacious in removing guilt, and sending the repenting sinner home rejoicing. "But I have felt it *here*," replies the Christian, placing his hand upon his breast. Yes, I have no doubt: that is just where I supposed you felt it. But the Mohammedan feels it *here;* and who saves him? The Catholic after confession, the Mormon, and the Buddhist, feel it *here;* and who saves all these? You ought to *know* it in your brain. The judgment is of infinitely more importance than the feelings in such matters, and, when properly cultivated and unbiassed, will lead you into truth.

The believer in Jesus is not saved from sin: he is not even saved from the filthy habit of tobacco-chewing, as any church-sexton will tell you; and, on communion-days, you may see those who have been cleansed in the blood of the Lamb take the quid out of their mouths, that they may put the body of Jesus in; and he then suffers a worse fate than he did on Calvary. The Christian believer is not saved from ignorance, bigotry, sickness, poverty, or, indeed, any evil; and all professions of this character result either from ignorance, or an intention to deceive. Salvation by Jesus is a delusion; and the sooner we see it and proclaim it, the better for mankind.

But if these orthodox doctrines are untrue, then the Bible, on which they rest, is untrue. It teaches the existence of an "everlasting fire prepared for the devil and his angels," — a "lake that burns with fire and brimstone;" and, if the Bible-writers had been acquainted with the article, it had doubtless burned with petroleum also. The orthodox heaven is the heaven of the Bible: its God-man is he who says, "Before Abraham was, I am," and, "He that hath seen me hath seen the Father." It is the Bible that represents Jesus as the Saviour; and by its texts, hammered like nails, every Sunday, into rickety souls, orthodoxy is still supported, and scares its victims from the exercise of their reason, or cajoles them into the support of its delusions.

Man does not go down to the grave at death to come up no more, as the Bible declares; neither does he sleep in the dust till awakened by a great trumpet-blast, as the Bible also declares. There will be no judgment-day, with a great king reviewing all nations, divided into the two classes, righteous and wicked; for there are no such persons, all people being partly good, and partly bad. Our friends that departed are neither dead nor asleep: they live and love, and come to us, teaching us that the life of the future is but a continuation of that of the present, and altogether different from the gloomy and unnatural views of it given in the Bible, which must cease, before long, to be regarded as authority by a single thinking soul.

You tell me that the Bible is the text-book of our churches; it is read in our schools, recognized in our courts of justice, and reverenced even by our men of science. Yes; and it was the text-book of all slaveholders from New Jersey to Texas; it was reverenced by Constantine, the bloody tyrant of the fourth century, and is reverenced to-day by nearly every criminal that our prisons hold. The less that is said about the reverence that men of science have for it, the better. The reverence that such men as Agassiz, Dana, Dawson, and others, have for it, is the fraternal greeting of Joab, who speaks peaceably to Abner, but smites him under the fifth rib, so that he dies: a kiss is on their lips, but a dagger in their hands.

We cannot do otherwise than discard the Bible as authority; and, should it be retranslated and amended a thousand times, it would still be the same. It abounds with the grossest fables; it tells the filthiest and bloodiest stories; it contains bad grammar, bad logic, innumerable contradictions, bad science, and, what is worse, bad morality. It has been the bulwark of slavery, woman's degradation, bigotry, and religious persecution, in every age, and blasts every soul that submits with unquestioning reverence to its teachings. Under the direction of orthodoxy, it has made Jesus a highwayman, who clutches men by the throat, and demands, " Your soul's life, or belief in my doctrine." And we have been so cowardly as to allow him to parade our highways, and throttle our citizens, almost without expostulation, because he lets loose the hound of public opinion upon those who refuse to yield to his outrageous demand.

Jesus must come to us as a philosopher does, and present his reasons for the faith that he demands ; he must place his doctrine before us as a merchant does his wares, and we must judge for ourselves whether they are worthy of our acceptance. What should we think of the merchant who demanded that we should close our eyes before we purchased his goods? We should naturally conclude that they would not bear examination, and that he wished to cheat us. When a man says to us, " He that believeth not what I teach shall be damned," he is attempting to close the eyes of our reason ; and we need to be doubly cautious in receiving what he presents. " So much of your doctrine as appears to us to be reasonable, Jesus, we will accept; and, if you are a sensible man, this is all you can desire: if you are otherwise, we are not to be troubled by you."

The day of unquestioning acceptance, of childish, gaping belief, is forever over. We say to Moses, " Come with your old stories of God-planted gardens; of God-created innocent people, who did not know good or evil till they had partaken of a mysterious and forbidden fruit; of wonderful walking and talking snakes; of the ark that saved ten times as many as could get into it: we will receive you as we do the Arab with his " Nights' Entertainments," and Swift with his stories of the Liliputians and Brobdingnagians.

One is as reasonable as the other. Men are as likely to be forty feet high as to be nine hundred and sixty-nine years old. You are just as welcome as they. Your tales can go with those of "Sinbad the Sailor," the "Wonderful Lamp," and the "Forty Thieves," — no worse thieves than the Israelites after they had been forty years under your tuition. You saw God as Aladdin saw the enchanted garden. You talked with him as really as Aladdin with the geni, and received the tables of stone from him just as truly as Sinbad picked up the precious stones in the Valley of Diamonds. But you must not expect of us any more than this. You cannot make us believe that you talked with the Universal Soul; that he engaged you to make the fantastic fooleries for your tabernacle, and sat upon a shittim-wood box, and chatted with you by the hour,* and permitted impertinences from you that a king would not permit from his prime-minister. We tell you plainly that you state, what, in the nature of things, must be false, and what, if any man should declare to-day, his neighbors would consider him in consequence deranged or an infamous liar."

We will give the Bible a place with the Koran, the Talmud, the Book of Mormon, the Vedas and Shasters, Swedenborg's works, and Davis's Divine Revelations,— no more from God than they, and no more to be taken as authority than they.

But if the Bible of orthodoxy is false, so is the God that it reveals,— Jehovah, the great object of religious worship in the churches all over this broad land. The Jewish Jehovah is no less an idol than the Beelzebub of the Philistine, or the Jove of the Roman. The one

* Exodus xxv. 10, 22.

is just as blessed as the other; the one is just as much our Maker as the other. If the man who worships Jupiter is an idolater, the man who worships Jehovah is equally so. If the temples of Jupiter were the fanes of an idolatrous people, then the steeple-crowned churches of orthodoxy are the temples of idolatrous worship; and the ministers who officiate in their pulpits are but priests at the altar of the one great idol. A prayer offered to Jupiter is just as good as a prayer offered to Jehovah: "O Jupiter! father of the gods, and lord of lords; thou who created the heavens and the earth, and man to dwell upon it: we beseech thee to hear our prayer, and give heed to the voice of our supplication. Thou wert the god of Remus and Romulus, the god of Cæsar and Seneca, and thou art our god, and we will worship thee. Thou wert with thy people, the Romans, and subdued all nations upon earth to their sway; thou gavest them dominion from sea to sea, and from Rome to the ends of the earth. O Jupiter! be with us as thou wert with them; subdue our enemies before us; let thy spirit, and the spirit of thy wife Juno, descend, and dwell in our hearts, and abide with us forever. Hear us and help us. Give us of thy light, thy wisdom, and thy power, that we may serve thee with our whole souls while here, and be fitted to enjoy the heaven of the gods hereafter." Why is not that as good as ninety-nine hundredths of the prayers offered in our orthodox churches? It will ascend just as high, and be just as effectual in bringing a blessing down. Jove is as nigh to them that call upon him as Jehovah; and we are as much his offspring as we are the children of Him whom Paul calls the God and Father of our Lord Jesus Christ.

What has the Soul of the universe to do with that being who cursed Adam and Eve, and Eve more than Adam, for doing what, with the nature he had given them, they could not help doing? — a being who curses on account of them every child born into the world. Is the Soul of the universe related to Him who walked about in a garden, and, like children playing at hide-and-seek, called out, "Adam, where art thou? To Him who wrestled with a tricky Jewish stock-breeder for a whole night, and only escaped from his hands by putting his thigh out of joint?

What have we to do with a being that turned water into blood, made lice out of dust, filled the land of Egypt with flies and frogs, and at length murdered more than a million people, because Pharaoh did what he had predetermined that he should do, and so hardened his heart that he could not avoid doing? — a being who gave a country already occupied to a nation who had no right to a foot of it, and made every man in that nation a murderer that they might conquer and possess it?

Was it the Soul of the universe that tempted Abraham to slay his cherished son, and, when the infatuated patriarch took up the knife to perform the dreadful deed, sent his angel to stay the murderous hand, and said, "In blessing I will bless thee, and in multiplying I will multiply thy seed as the stars of heaven, and as the sand which is upon the seashore. . . . And in thy seed shall all the nations of the earth be blessed because thou hast obeyed my voice"?

What a pious old saint to be sure! — ready to commit a murder because a voice commanded him. Human nature, and the God within, should have led him to reply, "I won't touch the lad for you nor the universe; and I despise you for asking me to do such an infamous deed." When men set up such a great bloody idol as this for a God, it is our duty, as recipients of clearer light, to overthrow it, and deliver the world from its curse.

Neither Elohim nor Jehovah created the earth and the heavens in six days, nor in sixty millions. He did not make man about six thousand years ago; for man has been here a hundred times as long. He did not curse man with death; for death was in the world ages before man made his appearance. In short, he never did any thing, for he is not; and his worshippers are as truly idolaters as those whose condition they deplore.

But I am asked, "How is it that men of well-developed minds and cultivated intellects have bowed down to this God, and accepted the religion that inculcates his worship? Why is it, that, among the most intelligent people of this planet, Jesus is regarded as the Saviour, and Jehovah as the God and Father, of all?"

The mass of the people ask only that a thing shall be popular. If they find a faith in existence in their country when they arrive, — and where is the country destitute of one? — ninety-nine out of every hundred draw it in as they do their mother's milk. When grown to the age of understanding, how difficult to deliver ourselves from the influence of early training, and still more, perhaps, to resist the psychologic influence of the masses surrounding us! As the magnetism of the earth causes every poised needle to point to the north; so the influence of a people's faith bears on every individual, and tends to bring each to the same opinion. But few are able to withstand its power. Of a thousand born in Arabia, there is not, probably, more than one who thinks of questioning the popular faith,—"There is one God, and Mohammed is his prophet." Tell them that Mohammed was like other men, except that he was more shrewd and more fanatical, and they exclaim at once, "You infidel dog!" The more intelligent say, "If you have no respect for our prophet, have some for these indisputable facts: Mohammedans number to-day one hundred and thirty millions. Established six hundred years after Christianity, our religion has supplanted it in its original home. It has overspread, not only Arabia, but Persia, Turkey, Palestine, a large portion of South-eastern Asia, and half of Africa. When all Christian countries were buried in the ignorance of the dark ages, then science flourished only where our religion fostered it. Can you not see the hand of God in such a career? and is it not evident that Mohammed was indeed what he proclaimed,—the prophet of God?" *We* cannot see this, of course. Neither can I see the hand of God in the career of Jesus, nor in Christianity since his death. When Christianity was first taught, Jesus was expected to be seen "coming in the clouds" every day, to reward those who believed in him, and punish all who rejected his gospel. What more natural than for the multitude, who desire to be on what seems the safe side, to accept this simple faith in Jesus, which promises such unspeakable blessings here and hereafter, and deliverance from the terrible woes denounced against the unbeliever? When the multitude have accepted a certain religion, how few, even of men of science, have backbone enough to reject it, when at heart they despise the creed that cramps them! Humboldt is content privately to sneer at orthodoxy, but never publicly attacks it. Agassiz states what falsifies the Mosaic story, and evidently disbelieves it, and yet so writes as to lead people to think that he credits its fables. Müller, the linguist, shows conclusively, that he has outgrown all faith in the miraculous inspiration of the Bible; but his position keeps him from boldly declaring the fact. It is not bearing false witness to say, that at least three-fourths of the scientific professors in England and America have no faith in Christianity as a miraculous religion; but their position is such, that very *few* dare to be true to their inward convictions.

But I am asked, "How could Jesus have attained the lofty position that he at present occupies, how could he have commanded the veneration of the wisest and the best for nearly two thousand years, if he was not indeed the Son of God, and the Saviour of mankind?"

The time in which he was born was one of ignorance and superstition; faith in miracles was almost universal; and but little knowledge existed of the operations of natural law. The whole Jewish nation was looking for the Messiah; and this was just the soil in which he might be expected to spring up. How many who believe in Jesus in America would accept as a Son of God, and a miraculous Saviour, the man who could present no better credentials than Jesus did? — his mother denying that he was his reputed father's son, the only evidence to show that he was not illegitimate being such as dreams furnish. He lives for thirty years, but does scarcely any thing worthy of record: he picks out for his disciples twelve illiterate and superstitious fishermen, who appear, from the record, to have been ready to believe any thing that their master told them. When the sceptical very properly ask him for a sign, he abuses them by calling them an evil and adulterous generation. Should a man perform all the miracles that Jesus is *said* to have performed, how many believers would he have now? — not one-half of those who saw him do them. Circumstances favored the claim of Jesus, just as they favored Mohammed, and as they favored Gautama. Jesus was not the first, by a hundred, who had called himself the Christ, or was so considered by others; and, after his time, there were "Christs many." How could Gautama be the centre of attraction to thousands of millions (four hundred millions now living), if he was not what the Buddhists believe him to have been, — a god, and the savior of mankind? How came such gods as Zeus, Jove, Hercules, Bacchus, and Esculapius, to be worshipped by the master-intellects of Greece and Rome for ages? — beings that never existed at all, yet commanded the heart's adoration of thousands of millions of the wisest and best of their time. Do you, Protestant, suppose that Mary, the mother of Jesus, was any more than a dark-eyed, chatty Jewish maiden, who, going barefoot to the well at Nazareth, captivated the mechanic, Joseph, as he worked on the roof of a neighboring house? Yet read the Catholic prayer-book, and see the adoration paid to their queen of heaven, the mother of God, whom millions beg to intercede for them.

When a man asks me to accept Christianity because

of its widespread power and influence, I say to him, Why not turn Buddhist? Christianity numbers two hundred millions of believers; but Buddhism has a list of four hundred millions. If the fact contained in the first figures makes Christianity the true religion, and Jesus the Son of God, then Buddhism must be doubly true, and Gautama twice as much God's son.

Jesus was a man who taught many beautiful and excellent lessons; a man who sympathized with the poor, and denounced their tyrants, but at the same time taught many lessons that were neither true nor beautiful; a man who displayed overweening self-esteem, and who was much more desirous that men should believe in him than that they should be true to themselves. He is no more our master than George Fox, John Wesley, or Joseph Smith. We do not therefore exhort men to "stand up for Jesus," but to stand up for humanity that needs it. Man has been trampled upon, his reason denounced, his selfhood cast down, that an idol might be elevated upon it. Jesus is the Christian Juggernaut. In India, the devotees throw their bodies before the idol: in Christian countries, they prostrate their souls before theirs; and Jesus in his triumphal car, drawn by his blinded followers, encouraged by his priests, rides ever over them. Let a man offer his reasonable protest against this idolatry, and he is at once denounced as the vilest criminal; the orthodox bloodhounds are put upon his track, and their bayings tell how gladly they would hunt the heretic to death if they only had the power, as they had before intelligence muzzled them.

All these false, then is orthodoxy false. These churches of the living God, so called, are shams every one; and the ceremonies performed in them the veriest child's play. What has the Soul of the universe to do with their pompous prayers, their silly rituals, their sprinklings, dippings, and port-wine sippings, called holy sacraments? what to do with their begging, beseeching, sometimes howling prayer-meetings? their mesmeric revivals, in which the hallucination of one is communicated to the many, and a foolish consistency leads men to cling to it for life? God has no more to do with all this than he has with the shoe-shops of Massachusetts, or the printing-offices; and it would be just as proper to call a ball-club the club of God as a hundred ignorant orthodox believers God's church. It is high time that the pretensions of the high priests of a no better than pagan mythology were scouted, and a true estimate made of their sanctity, knowledge, and power. Professing to know God, they are the most ignorant of him, for they do not study Nature by science, which alone reveals him; pretending to teach men the way to heaven, they close the door against the very angels who come to reveal it.

Spiritualism is to aid greatly in delivering us from orthodox tyranny and idolatrous man-worship, leading men to the God and Saviour within that each possesses, to the salvation that comes by the exercise of our own powers, and to the heaven for all, of which no Peter keeps the key, and to which the name of Jesus is no "*Open, sesame.*" Think of the time and energy wasted in praising Jesus, praying to Jesus, preaching Jesus, and the labor and money squandered in spreading abroad fantastic statements concerning this man, over the world, instead of giving people a knowledge of themselves and the laws of the universe, — knowledge that concerns us every day.

But orthodoxy has seen its greatest triumphs; and its day of prosperity is over. Its feeble stars are paling in the light of the new morn that greets humanity. It is already ashamed of its hell, — a phantom conjured up in the days of ignorance by some undeveloped soul, who, in deep malignity, wished that those who had offended him here might be infinitely tortured hereafter. The brimstone and the smoke are indeed gone; the Devil, the dusky jailer of the pit, is dead. And what becomes of orthodoxy then? Hell has been the fire whose heat created nine-tenths of the steam that ran the machinery. Take the fire of hell out of a revival, and then try to keep it up! You might as well think of running a locomotive by crowding the fire-box with ice-blocks. No fire, no steam; no steam, no motion; the orthodox train at a dead stand-still. How many missionaries would wander into foreign lands to preach the story of the cross, if Jesus does not save his believers from hell? How long would Christian churches be crowded to listen to dry-as-dust sermons, and nod over mile-long prayers, if the hearers did not imagine, that, in some way, this helps them "to escape the jaws of hell"?

Orthodoxy is doomed, and is powerless as its God to avert its doom. And why should we mourn? It scatters its hymn-books, pious tracts, and Bibles, but stands at the door of our public library, and refuses on its market-day (Sunday) to open, and admit the hungry souls; for that might diminish the attendance at its temples. It would thus stand at the door of heaven, if it had the power, and admit none but the bigots who can pronounce its shibboleth. It would "circumnavigate the globe to disturb the creed of a single beggar;" but it would not stir a step to break the chains of four million slaves, and cursed, in the name of Jehovah, all who did: but, when infidel abolitionists made antislavery popular, it joined in the cry for freedom, and now demands that all the credit of the slave's freedom shall be given to the "church of the Lord Jesus Christ." It imprisoned Galileo; it murdered Bruno; it slandered and belied Thomas Paine, and still repeats its calumnies and lies; it burned Michael Servetus; it hung the Quakers, who were less orthodox than its creed; it imprisoned Abner Kneeland, and compels our children to listen daily to the reading of its Jewish story-book, that it claims contains the will of "God Most High." If its prayers had been of any avail, it would have murdered Theodore Parker: it did its best, and now sits, and gnashes its teeth at those it is no longer able to tear. It dooms Dickens to damnation, because his heart was too large, and his intellect too clear, to accept its dogmas, and by his presence there makes its hell so much more attractive than its heaven. He had his faults, who is without them? but none one-half as bad as the bigotry of the reverend Maw worms that anathematize him. "He was no Christian," say the bigots. Let us hope that he was not. He was something very much superior,— a man of surpassing genius and world-wide humanity, whose name will be blessed when orthodoxy will be a by-word among all people.

What, then, have we to do with orthodoxy? Shall we give our money to raise its proud steeples? shall we send our children to its Sunday schools to have fetters fastened upon their limbs that it will take years to break? shall we pay for pews in its heathen temples, and reverence its false gods? If all who are reformers at heart would assert their individuality, we should soon see the good time that we hope for. Don't go ducking and bowing, cringing and crawling, through the world; believing in Nature, and sacrificing to Jehovah; believing in individuality, and yet paying priests, and building their "joss-houses!" We can do infinitely better.

Our God is Nature — father, mother. As near to thy child, hard-handed mechanic, and thy child as dear to God, as the infant Jesus was when he lay on the breast of Mary. On his broad bosom we shall be borne beyond death to the glorious world of the hereafter, — life there a continuance of life here, a spiritual blossoming of what this life has been but the bud.

We can make no compromise with orthodoxy henceforth and forever. Ours is a new religion, a new God, a new heaven, and a gospel which is destined to make a new earth. We do not blame the people who have accepted the old (they probably did the best they could); but these old skeletons shall not reach their bony hands out of their mouldy sepulchres, and drag us in to chatter with them. Ours the living present; ours the sunshine and the song of birds, the sound of purling brooks, the joy of the living world ripening in God's smile, — the vestibule of heaven.

WHAT IS RIGHT?

WHAT IS RIGHT?

It is Friday, the Mussulman's holy day. The cry of the muezzin has stirred the sultry air, and thousands are flowing through the streets to the stately mosque. Let us follow. The swelling dome is over our heads, the marble pavement beneath our feet, and around us a host of bended worshippers, their hands clasped in the fervor of devotion. Listen to the voice of this kneeling supplicant by our side: "O Allah! I am weak, but thou art all-strong; strengthen me to do the right, that I may enjoy hereafter the bliss of Paradise."

As he rises from his knees, we accost him, and say, "Friend, you have been praying to Allah, or God, to strengthen you to do right: will you please to tell us what you mean by right?" — "Certainly," replies the Mussulman, with a look of sorrow for our ignorance of so simple yet important a subject. "There is one God, and Mohammed is his prophet. This God has graciously revealed his will to us, by his prophet, in his holy word the Koran, — a book superior to every other book in the world. To obey the commands of

God, as given in this book, is to do right; and to disobey them is to do wrong. Cast away this precious volume, and we have no guiding star by which to regulate our wanderings: we cannot tell what is right, or what is wrong, and are the slaves of ignorance and vice."

It is Saturday, the Jewish holy day. There stands the gorgeous temple, little less beautiful than the pride of Jerusalem on Mount Moriah, so silently erected in the days of Solomon. In the pulpit behold the venerable rabbi, his white beard resting upon his breast. Around him are the sons of Israel, and above in the gallery the daughters, assembled to worship the God of their fathers. From the ark he has taken the sacred parchment; and, reverentially unrolling it, he reads a portion of the law of Moses, and then addresses the assembled congregation: "Men and brethren, children of our father Jacob, I beseech you, do right; then shall ye be blessed in your basket and in your store, in your going-out, and in your coming-in. Do right at all times, and the blessing of Jehovah out of Zion will descend and rest upon you."

As the aged rabbi descends from the pulpit, we accost him, "You have been advising your brethren to do right: will you please to tell us what you mean by right?" — "Certainly, my son," replies the rabbi. "The Almighty God, who made the heavens and the earth, has revealed himself to mankind by his servant Moses, and the prophets: they have written his holy law; and that law is contained in a book that Christians call the Old Testament (the New Testament is but a record of fables, and unworthy of credence from any rational mind). To obey God's law as thus revealed, is to do right; to violate it is to do wrong: and under heaven there is no other way by which a man can tell what is right or what is wrong, but by studying this word of Jehovah."

It is Sunday, the Christian's holy day; and from a hundred steeples floats the music of a thousand bells; and through the streets of the city pass multitudes, dressed in their gayest attire, to their respective places of worship. There stands the grand cathedral, with its cloud-reaching spire. We enter, and admire the stateliness and beauty of this "God's house."

The organ's peal sweeps through the aisle
In tones would make an angel smile;
Now soft, as is a fairy strain,
Then "groaning like a god in pain."

Slowly a head rises from behind a tasselled desk, and the minister reads, "He that doeth righteousness is righteous, even as he is righteous;" and from this text he preaches. "Friends," he exclaims, as he proceeds with his discourse, "to be happy here and hereafter, we must obey the will of God; in other words, do right. He who does the right has God for his father, Jesus for his friend, and heaven for his home; but to the wrong-doer there is misery in this world, and a fearful looking-for of fiery indignation in the next."

When the congregation is dismissed, we approach the minister, and inquire what he means by the word "right," which he has so frequently used in his discourse. "To do right, sir," he replies, "is to do as God commands us. He has revealed his will to us by his word, contained in the Old and New Testaments, where we find 'truth without any mixture of error.' To obey his will, as thus revealed, is to do right: to violate that will is to do wrong; and the wrong-doer, unless he applies to the Friend of sinners for pardon, will be cast into outer darkness, where there is weeping and wailing, and gnashing of teeth."

We have, then, already three rules of right,—the Mohammedan, Jewish, and Christian. "How do you know," we say to the Mohammedan, "that yours is *the* rule of right?"—"There can be no doubt of it," he replies. "Did not the angel Gabriel appear to our prophet, and cause the Koran, that holy volume written on a table, by the throne of God himself, to descend on his heart for a direction and good-tidings to the faithful? No unassisted human being could ever have written such a wonderful book, every page of which bears the impress of a hand divine. See the rapid advance of our religion, which, in a few years, overspread the world, and now comprises so large a portion of its population. Besides, I *know* that the Koran is divine, and the only rule of right. Obeying its precepts, I have fasted and prayed, with my face towards Mecca, groaning under the weight of my sins, when the prophet (glory to his name!) has taken away my guilt, revealed himself to my soul, and I have gone on my way rejoicing."

To the Jew we say, "How do you know that you are right?"—"Nothing can be more certain," replies the Jew. "God appeared to Moses, our lawgiver, on Mount Sinai, and amid thunders and lightnings delivered to him our holy law, and instituted his everlasting ordinances. Through the Red Sea he brought our fathers by the strength of his own right arm, fed them with angels' food, and delivered their enemies into their hands. And in the day of atonement have I gone to our synagogue, bowed down with guilt, where the rabbi has interceded for us, and I have returned rejoicing in the God of my salvation; for my sins, which were heavy as a mountain, he lifted off, and removed far from me."

To the Christian we say, "Are you sure that yours is the rule of right? May you not be mistaken?" "Never," he replies: "it is impossible. The Bible is God's holy word, confirmed by miracles, prophecies, and a morality pure as the light of day. It is a sun without a spot, a fountain of eternal truth, of which he that drinks shall live forever. Besides, I *know* that it is true. Burdened with guilt, I came to the foot of the cross, as this book teaches; I cast my sins on my Saviour, and rose a new creature in Christ Jesus. I carry about with me, therefore, continually the evidence, — God's seal set to his own word."

Which of these is right? Each seems to be satisfied with his own side, says he knows he is right; and, of course, if one is right, the rest are wrong.

Suppose we take up some practical questions that are likely to come before us in daily life, and observe how these various rules of right deal with them. "Is it right to drink intoxicating drinks?" we say to the Mohammedan. "No, certainly not," he replies, turning over the leaves of the Koran, and reading to us the following passage: 'O true believers! surely wine and lots and images and divining arrows are an abomination, and of the work of Satan; therefore avoid them that ye may prosper.'

"That is sufficient," he says. "God, by his holy prophet, has forbidden wine, which includes every thing that intoxicates; and no true believer can use it."

"What do you think on that subject, Jew?"—"I cannot learn that there is any thing wrong in the moderate use of intoxicating drinks, though drunkenness is of course a great crime, and forbidden by our holy law."

"What is your opinion upon that subject?" we say to the Christian. "Wrong, sir, wrong decidedly, and contrary to the uniform tenor of God's word, from Genesis to Revelations, which expressly declares that we must touch not, taste not, handle not, the unclean thing."

"That is not so," says a gentleman standing by his side, who overhears our conversation. "Pray, what are you, sir?"—"I am a believer in the Bible: and I say that the whole Bible, from Genesis to Revelations, sanctions the moderate use of intoxicating drinks; and it is only their abuse that is forbidden."—"What shall we do in this case?" I say. "Go to the Bible," replies the abstaining Christian. "To the law and to the testimony," says the little-drop brother: "if they speak not according to this rule, it is because there is no light in them." So to the Bible we go; and, after turning over several of its pages, we at length come to a passage referring to the subject that we are considering: "And Noah began to be a husbandman; and he planted a vineyard; and he drank of the wine, and was drunken." (Gen. ix. 20.) Within his tent the old man lay uncovered; while in this condition, his younger son found him, and, as it appears, made sport of his father, who, learning the fact, on awaking, cursed his offspring most bitterly. And some pious divines see in the dark faces of the negroes, "the servile progeny of Ham," the consequence of this black curse of Noah to this day. The Bible does not, however, inform us whether Noah did right or wrong in getting drunk or in drinking; and the question is left very much as we found it.

We proceed, and our little-drop friend points significantly to the case of Lot as one having some bearing upon the question. We find, on reading, that, before the "fire-shower of ruin" descended on the doomed cities of the plain, Lot and his family fled from Sodom, his wife being turned into a statue of salt on the way; and he and his two daughters dwelt in a cave in the mountain. Having made their father drunk with wine, he committed incest with one of his daughters, and on the next evening did the same thing with the other. (Gen. xix. 30–38.) Yet not a word of condemnation is uttered, either of the man, or the liquor that was the means of placing him in such a disgraceful position: he is styled emphatically "just Lot," and a "righteous man." (2 Pet. ii. 7, 8.)

"If," says the moderate-drinking Christian, "God had not intended man to use the article, this was just the very time to forbid its use, and preach your temperance doctrine. Before you reply to my remarks," turning to his temperance brother, "let me refer you to one express passage upon the subject, that ought to set the question at rest forever. It reads thus: 'Thou shalt bestow that money for whatsoever thy soul lusteth after: for oxen, or for sheep, or for wine, or for strong drink.' (Deut. xiv. 26.) Now, if a man may spend his money for these articles, he certainly would be at liberty to drink them after so doing: it is absurd to think otherwise."

"My dear sir," replies the temperance man, "you must never build up a doctrine on an isolated passage of Scripture: after that fashion, a man may prove any thing from the Bible. You must take the whole tenor of the Scriptures, from one end to the other, and, comparing passage with passage, thus learn what the will of the Lord is. Let me refer you to some parts of the Bible having an important bearing on this question. Take, for instance, the case of Samson, recorded in the 13th chapter of Judges. The children of Israel had been in bondage to the Philistines for forty years, and the Lord sought a deliverer for them. For this purpose he needed a strong man,—for God works, you know, by instruments: he desired to put the strength of a hundred men's arms into one man's arm,—a shepherd of might, that could rescue his sheep from the jaws of the devouring lion. Now, mark how he does this: the angel of the Lord—that is, the Lord's messenger—appears to Samson's mother, and says to her, 'Thou shalt conceive and bear a son. Now, therefore, beware, I pray thee, and drink not wine nor strong drink.' And to her husband he says, 'She may not eat of any thing that cometh of the vine; neither let her drink wine nor strong drink.' Why these stringent prohibitions? Evidently that the child might be free from alcoholic taint, he being also a Nazarite from the womb to the day of his death. Thus did God accomplish his purposes by the strength of this mighty abstainer, and deliver the Israelites from the hand of their oppressors. Nor is this all: God's word abounds with passages condemning the use of intoxicating drinks. Let us hear what Solomon, the king of wise men, says, 'Who hath woe? who hath sorrow? who hath contentions? who hath babbling? who hath wounds without cause? who hath redness of eyes? They that tarry long at the wine, they that go to seek mixed wine. Look not thou upon the wine when it is red, when it giveth its color in the cup, when it moveth itself aright: at the last, it biteth like a serpent, and stingeth like an adder.' (Prov. xxiii. 29.) What can be plainer than this? No abstainer could write a passage more strongly forbidding the use of intoxicating drinks. You must not even look at the tempter, lest you be poisoned by its deadly venom."

"Stop, stop!" says the moderate drinker. "I cannot allow you to rattle along in that way. You must remember it will never do to build up a doctrine on an isolated passage of Scripture; you must take the whole tenor of God's Word, from one end to the other: that's the way to arrive at truth. Solomon certainly never meant what you want to wrest from his words; for, turn to the last chapter of Proverbs and read: 'It is not for kings, O Lemuel! it is not for kings, to drink wine; nor for princes strong drink. Give strong drink unto him that is ready to perish, and wine unto those that be of heavy hearts. Let him drink, and forget his poverty, and remember his misery no more.' (Prov. xxxi. 4–7.) That is the doctrine. You see it is kings and princes that are not to look on the wine; those are the men that are not to drink: but, for such men as we, there is no such command. When our hearts are heavy, we may drink, and forget our poverty, and remember our misery no more. When you come to read the Bible understandingly, you will find this to be its tenor throughout."

"The passage that you appeal to," says his opponent, "only refers to criminals condemned to die, who drank till they were stupid, in order to drown the sense of their miseries. God's holy word is guilty of no such contradictions as you seem to make it. Allow me to refer you to the case of Daniel and the three Hebrew children, as one bearing out the glorious doctrine of abstinence from all intoxicating drinks. The children of Israel were carried off captives to Babylon. Nebuchadnezzar, desirous of having the most beautiful and intelligent of them instructed in the language and learning of the Chaldæans, commands the master of the eunuchs to search them out. He does so, and Daniel and the three Hebrew children are chosen. The king appoints them a certain portion of meat from his table, and of the wine that he drank; but they refuse the king's wine, and eat not his meat: but pulse had they for food, and water for drink.

> 'Yet they were fatter and far more fair
> Than any among their fellows there,
> And surpassed in learning and wisdom, too,
> Each proud Chaldæan and boastful Jew.'

"See how the blessing of God followed these temperate young men! Daniel is saved from the hungry lions; for God shut their mouths. The Hebrew children walk unhurt in the fiery furnace heated seven times hotter than it was wont to be; not even the smell of fire upon their garments. What better evidence can we have of God's blessing crowning the temperance cause?"

"Allow me to ask you a question," says the drinking Christian. "Was not Jesus Christ a greater person than Daniel?"—"Oh, certainly! he was God Almighty, who came down from heaven."—"Very well, then, the example of Jesus must be as much more important than Daniel's as God is greater than man. Now, let us look at his example (John ii. 1–10.) There was a marriage in Cana of Galilee, and Jesus and his disciples were invited to the wedding. The tables are spread for the feast, and the guests sit down to partake: the wine is handed round, and, before the feast is over, it is all gone (not many of your kind of people there, you see). The mother of Jesus whispers to him, 'They have no wine.' There were set there six water-pots, holding, say the commentators, about a hundred and twenty gallons. Jesus says, 'Fill them with water.' They fill them to the brim. 'Now bear out to the governor of the feast.' They do so, and the governor proclaims it good wine.

> 'The conscious water saw its God,
> And, blushing, turned to generous wine.'

Had you temperance men had his power, you would have turned all the wine provided for the feast to water; but "he, the gracious Lord divine, turns simple water into wine," and by so doing places the force of his holy example on the side of those who believe in using with moderation the gifts of God's bounty. When about to leave his disciples, they took a last supper together; at that supper they had bread and wine. Taking the cup in his hand, and offering it to them, he said, 'Drink ye all of it.' (Matt. xxvi. 27.) 'And as oft as ye do it, do it in remembrance of me.' (1 Cor. xi. 25.) And I never take a glass of wine without remembering the dying Saviour. But you temperance men, by your doctrines, cast discredit on the Saviour of the world; and, if he were here now, you would look down upon him with scorn and contempt: and how must he look upon you in the last great day? Paul, who followed in the footsteps of his Master, when writing to Timothy, one of your cold-water men, says (1 Tim. v. 23), 'Drink no longer water, but use a little wine for thy stomach's sake and thine often infirmities.'"

After these two Christians have thus fought their way through the Bible, can any man tell on which side of the question the Bible stands? Is it not on both sides? It is a witness as ready to swear for plaintiff as defendant; a guide pointing east and west at the same time, to the great astonishment of the bewildered traveller. Right and wrong are alternately on the sides of drinking and abstaining; and a man who seeks for information in the Bible on this subject is farther off when done than when he began. And what is true in reference to the use of intoxicating drinks is equally true in reference to every other practical question that can come before us.

"Is there any day holier than another?" I say to the Mohammedan. "Most assuredly," he replies "What day is it?" — "Friday, of course: every child knows that." — "What makes Friday so much better than other days?" — "What a question, O infidel, to ask! Friday is the day on which God ended his labors, and rested after he had made the heavens and the earth. Friday is the day on which our holy prophet (blessed be his name!) fled from Mecca to Medina; it is the day set apart by the Koran as the sabbath, and has been observed by our Church from the earliest times: the man who labors on that day is accursed of God."

I turn to the Jew. "What do you think upon that subject?" — "There is no holy day," he replies, "but Saturday. Fridays are no better than Sundays; but Saturday, the seventh day, is the sabbath of the Lord our God, on which no manner of work may be done." "What makes Saturday so much better than other days?" — "Do you not know that in six days the Lord made heaven and earth, and rested on the seventh, wherefore he blessed and hallowed it? In his law, delivered to Moses on Mount Sinai, he gave the command to observe this day as a holy day forever. (Ex. xxxi. 13–16.) And what God commands, man must do."

"What do you think about that, Christian?"—"Well, sir, of keeping Fridays and Saturdays I know nothing. They are no better than other days of the week; but Sunday is the Lord's Day: and whoever breaks the sabbath, by work or play, does it at the peril of his soul; for all sabbath-breakers shall have their portion in the lake that burns with fire and brimstone." — "But wherein lies the peculiar sanctity of the Sunday?" "Have you not read the Bible, sir, God's holy word of truth? 'Remember the sabbath day to keep it holy.'" — "Yes; but that is Saturday." — "No, it is Sunday; for the day has been changed by the resurrection of Jesus Christ from the dead, on the first day of the week." — "But, as he rested in the grave on Saturday, the Jewish sabbath might very well have been retained." — "The Church, sir, from the earliest times, observed the first day of the week. On that day the disciples met to break bread; and, from those earliest times to the present, the Sunday has been observed as a day of rest, and a peculiarly holy day, by all classes of Christians everywhere. John, in the Revelation, evidently refers to it when he speaks of 'the Lord's Day.'"

"Is thee not somewhat mistaken there?" says an old gentleman with a broad-brimmed hat, who had entered during our conversation. "I am a Christian, and a believer in that book to which thee has been appealing, and I find no such doctrine in it as thee sets forth. I find Jesus setting at nought the sabbath by selecting it for the performance of his most notable miracles; and, when chided by the Pharisees, he says, 'The sabbath was made for man, and not man for the sabbath. The Son of man is Lord also of the sabbath day.' (Mark ii. 27.) He never commanded his followers to observe holy days, but nailed all their ceremonial observances to his cross; for they were only a shadow of good things to come. Paul says, 'One man esteemeth one day above another; another regardeth every day alike: let every man be fully persuaded in his own mind.' (Rom. xiv. 5.) And, writing to the Colossians, in the spirit of his Master, he says, 'Let no man, therefore, judge you in meat or in drink, or in respect of an holy day, or of the new moon, or of the sabbath, which are a shadow of things to come; but the body is of Christ.' (Col.

ii. 16.) Now, when a man has his body, he never troubles himself to look after his shadow; and when Jesus, the body, came in his light and glory, the Jewish types and shadows disappeared, lost in his resplendent brightness. In writing to the Galatians, Paul says, 'Ye observe days and months and times: I am afraid of you lest I have bestowed upon you labor in vain.' (Gal. iv. 10–11.) There are multitudes living now that Paul would be afraid of if he were here; for they have departed from the simplicity of the gospel of Jesus, and are bowing to the idols that men have set up." So says this Quaker of the old school.

If these men are to be believed, the Bible is a guide-board pointing in three different directions, for the same place, at the same time. Saturday is the holy day, and no other; Sunday is the holy day, and must be observed; and no day is holier than another, but all are alike good. What shall the traveller do who finds these contradictory directions? Is this the road that is so plain that a wayfaring man, though a fool, need not err therein?

If we take any other practical question, we find the same difficulty in deciding what is right or wrong by any sacred book that may have been adopted as a standard. Should a man have more wives than one? The Mohammedan replies yes, at once: his prophet had, and his holy book permits polygamy. The Jew says it was allowed by God at one time, but is no longer permitted. We ask the Christian; but he stares with astonishment that we should ask him such a question. "One man and one woman united together for life is the doctrine of the Bible, taught most explicitly throughout the pages of that blessed book; and no Christian for a moment doubts it."

"You are mistaken, sir," exclaims the Mormon: "on the contrary, polygamy is plainly taught in the Scriptures, as practised in our Church at the present time." — "How can you say so?" replies the Monogamist. "The Bible is opposed to such a doctrine from Genesis to Revelation. Just turn to the account of creation as given in Genesis, and what can be plainer than the dual relation between the sexes there declared, as established by God himself? Adam being created, and placed in Eden's flowery garden, the beasts were brought to him to name; and, as they marched before him, from the mouse to the monkey, he gave them appropriate names, but sought in vain for a companion. God, compassionating Adam in his lonely condition, cast him into a deep sleep, extracted *one* of his ribs, and of this made a woman, and brought her unto Adam. Had polygamy been right for man, then was the time for it to be made manifest. God could just as easily have taken out two or three ribs, and made as many women of them, as to take one; but, in his infinite wisdom and goodness, he makes of *one* rib *one* woman, a companion for Adam for life. By what sophistries can you set aside these explicit revelations?"

"You don't understand the Bible, sir: you are blind to the beauty of its glorious teachings. Do you not know, sir, that, through all Nature, every thing has a small beginning, however mighty it may become? First we have the germ peeping above the ground, then the sapling, and in the end the giant oak. First the spring, then the rill, the streamlet, and the river.

This is God's method of working; and it is not surprising that the statements of the Bible, God's holy word, should harmonize with it. Adam had one wife by God's appointment: that is true, and what we should reasonably expect. God could not have given him less, and, in accordance with his natural law, we could not expect him to give more. But mark, as we advance along the line of the eminent worthies whom God has chosen to honor in his sacred word, how the stream widens and deepens. Abraham, who was 'the father of the faithful, and the friend of God,' had one wife Sarah, and another Hagar. (Gen. xvi. 3.) And, when Sarah died, he took another (Keturah), so as to keep up his number, two. (Gen. xxv. 1.) Jacob, farther along the line, married two wives, his own first cousins, daughters of his Uncle Laban; and then had children by their two handmaids, making his number four. Gideon, a man of the Lord, by whom he delivered Israel, and one of Paul's cloud of witnesses, must have had at least ten wives; for the Bible informs us that he had many wives and seventy sons. (Judg. viii. 30.) Then David, the 'man after God's own heart,' the man who, we are told by God himself, never did wrong in his life but once (and that was in the matter of Uriah), takes to himself a number of wives; and, when Saul dies, the blessed Bible declares that 'God gave to him the wives of his master Saul into his bosom.' (2 Sam. xii. 8.) Do not you begin to see how naturally and beautifully this blessed system of polygamy grows? — Adam one, Abraham two, Jacob four, Gideon ten, David twenty or thirty, and, lastly, Solomon, the wisest man that ever lived or ever shall live, with his seven hundred wives and three hundred concubines. In him humanity culminated; and from that time men went downward and backward, till Joseph Smith, the prophet of the Lord, arose and brought in the glory of the latter day. The Bible is full of beauty when properly understood, but in the hands of the wilful and ignorant is like a sharp sword, that cuts the hand of him who knows not how to wield it."

"Filthy wretches! to pervert the word of God in order to pander to your depraved appetites," says a tall, pale, overcoated, broad-brimmed-hatted gentleman, who has been listening attentively to the discussion. "Who are you?" exclaim both with one breath. "I am a Shaker, gentlemen, and a devout believer in the truths of that blessed volume that you wrest to your own destruction: and I say that the Bible teaches, by example and precept, that marriage is one of the most prolific sources of evil; and that, as God's children, we should abstain from it. Go to the garden of Eden, and what do you find? A paradise of delights. Every thing that is pleasant to the eye and useful for food is there. No earthquake heaves the ground, no volcano opens its fiery mouth; but the angel of peace holds dominion over the world. The lion and the tiger, the lamb and the kid, lie side by side together, and there is nothing to hurt or destroy. But mark the change! Adam, dissatisfied, desires a helpmeet; and no sooner does she come than misery comes as her companion. When woman came, the Devil came; and then came death and all our woe. The fair face of Nature became seamed with yawning chasms, earthquakes shook the world, and volcanoes poured out desolating floods; the lion fleshed his teeth in the innocent lamb, and the tiger, seizing the kid, rent it in pieces; the soul of man was dyed by sin as black as hell, and nothing but the blood of God could wash it out. Abraham has two wives; but their quarrels imbitter his existence: and, for the sake of peace, he is compelled to turn one of them with her child out of doors into the wilderness. Jacob the shepherd, keeping the sheep of his uncle Laban, is a lovely character, dreaming of heaven and angels, and communing with God; but with his marriage commences his misery. His wives quarrel; his children are robbers and murderers, and even conspire against the life of their brother, till the old man, in the anguish of his heart, exclaims, 'Ye will bring down my gray hairs with sorrow to the grave.' David's wives vex his righteous soul, and Bathsheba leads him to the commission of that terrible crime that blots his whole life. His beloved son makes war against his father, and is slain; David, in his soul's agony, exclaiming, 'O Absalom! my son, my son! Would God I had died for thee, O Absalom, my son!' Even Solomon, the wisest man, is dragged down from the throne of his glory by his wives and concubines, who turned his heart from the Lord; and he gives us the result of his wide experience in the mournful words, 'A man in a thousand have I found, but a woman in a thousand have I not found.' 'Vanity of vanities; all is vanity, and vexation of spirit.' Come down to the New Testament; and Jesus our Lord and Master, who set us an example that we should tread in his steps, was never married; and he says, (oh that mankind would read and understand!) 'He that looketh on a woman to lust after her hath committed adultery with her already in his heart.' Paul, who trod in the footsteps of his divine Master, was no husband to any woman, no father to any child, and desired others to follow him, as he followed Jesus. When John the revelator had those sublime visions in the Isle of Patmos, he saw a hundred and forty-four thousand around the throne of God, who were singing day and night unto him. John inquires who these favored few are, who thus approach the throne, and on whom God's smile rests continually; and the answer is,— mark it,—'These are they that were not defiled with women.' (Rev. xvi. 4.) In other words, they were Shakers; and we shall bask in the sunshine of God's glory, when filthy sinners like you will be compelled to stand afar off."

So argue Bible believers; and no wonder, while they follow such a guide, who stands at life's cross-roads, with as many hands as a Hindoo god; his fingers directing to every point of the compass, while he exclaims, "*That* is the way to life!"

Does it point slavery-ward? "No such thing," said the North, and shouted itself hoarse in repeating, "'Do unto another as ye would that another should do unto you.' 'Call no man master; for one is your master, even Christ, and all ye are brethren.' 'Woe unto him that useth his neighbor's service without wages, and giveth him not for his work.' 'The stranger that dwelleth with you shall be unto you as one born among you, and thou shalt love him as thyself.'" "How plain!" said the antislavery minister. "None but those blinded by avarice can help seeing how God frowns upon the damnable traffic in the souls of human beings, and how his Word is laid like an axe at the root of this tree of misery."

"The Almighty Maker of the universe," said the Southern slaveholder, "is ever the same. He never commands in one age what he forbids in another, nor blesses at one time what he curses and denounces at other times; and he has said in his Word, 'Both thy bondmen and bondmaids which thou shalt have shall be of the heathen that are round about you; of them shall ye buy bondmen and bondmaids, and ye shall take them as an inheritance for your children after you, to inherit them for a possession: they shall be your bondmen forever.' (Lev. xxv. 44–46.) None of your antislavery and abolition in the Bible, but there we have God's charter, signed, sealed, and delivered; our rights guaranteed by the great *I Am* forever. Abraham the friend of God, Jacob his intimate companion, and David his beloved, all held slaves; and Jesus, finding the institution of slavery everywhere through Palestine, never said one word against its continuance. Paul not only recognizes slavery, but regulates it, when he says, 'Servants, obey in all things your masters, according to the flesh; not with eye-service, as men-pleasers, but in singleness of heart, fearing God.' Masters are to give unto their servants what is just and equal. No word of denunciation of the institution, nothing of abolition; but the right of the master is recognized, and the duty of the servant prescribed."

On this, as on all practical questions, the Bible is double-tongued, and is therefore no true moral guide.

What, then, shall the traveller do? Is there no pole-star in the heavens, fixed immovably, while around the shifting lights revolve? Is man left to tread the wilderness in midnight darkness, with nothing to dispel the gloom around his tortuous pathway but the flash of a meteor, or the uncertain light of the *ignis fatuis?* There is a pole-star for the mariner, a highway for the traveller, with daylight to guide him, and men need not drive on shoals, flounder in bogs, or move slowly in darkness with fear and trembling. THAT IS RIGHT WHICH IS FOR HUMANITY'S BENEFIT; THAT IS WRONG WHICH IS OPPOSED TO THE WELFARE OF THE HUMAN RACE. It is not presumable that we can add to the happiness or diminish the enjoyment of God; but our deeds constantly influence ourselves and our fellows for good and evil. To know what actions are productive of good or evil, we need to use our judgment, aided by all the light that science can bestow.

Let us try by this rule the various questions that have come before us. Is it right or wrong to use intoxicating drinks? The basis of all intoxicating drinks is alcohol: it is this in them that makes them intoxicating. Rum and brandy contain a large quantity, while beer and hard cider contain but little. What is this alcohol? we inquire of science; and the answer is, an acrid poison. Then intoxicating liquors are poisonous in proportion to the alcohol that they contain, and as such are at war with the healthy operations of the human system. The man in health who uses them violates the law that governs his physical organism; and no amount of prayer or Bible reading can absolve the sinner from the consequences of his deeds. The headache that admonishes the moderate drinker, the diseased body that the drunkard carries with him continually, are much more effectual texts than "Thus saith the Lord," in Bible or in Koran.

Texts are they written in an ever-living language, understood by men of every tongue.

Intoxicating drinks are injurious to those who use them; at war with the health of the body and strength of the mind; stimulating to physical and mental activity for a time, it is true, but using the strength of to-morrow to-day, and demanding for its use a fearful interest, that soon bankrupts the foolish borrower. Hence we apply our rule, and decide that it is not right to use intoxicating drinks. "But your rule," says an objector, "leads no more to unanimity of opinion than the Bible. Men who do not make the Bible their guide differ in opinion on this subject as much as those who do." To those who are governed by it, it does. Multitudes never investigate the subject: some who do have a strong appetite for intoxicating drinks that hinders clear vision. As people become intelligent, opinion on this subject becomes more unanimous, and there is no doubt, that, eventually, the use of these drinks will be abandoned.

Is one day holier than another? The conflicting testimony of so-called holy books can never give a reasonable answer to this question; but Nature's ample and consistent page contains a satisfactory reply. I work for six or eight hours daily on my farm, and note carefully the condition of my system on the various days of the week. I do this for a whole year; and I find that labor agrees with my physical and mental constitution on every day of the week. Fridays are no more consecrated to rest by Nature than Saturdays; Sundays than Mondays. The corn I plant on Sunday grows as well as that planted on Monday; the rains refuse not to fall upon it, nor the sun to shine upon it. On every day the grass grows, the water flows, gayly blows the breeze, the sap climbs up the trees. Sunday puts no brake on the world's wheels; but the sound of the rushing sphere comes humming into the church on Sunday, as into the synagogue on Saturday. Nature knows no red-letter days.

The man who invented the sabbath evidently supposed the world to be flat. When the sun went down, it was night all over the world; and, when he rose, day was everywhere. Not otherwise could all the people of the world observe the same portion of time. At six o'clock on Sunday evening, the Christian minister in this country gives out his text, "Remember the sabbath day to keep it holy," and solemnly denounces the violators of the holy day who do their own work, and obey not the divine record; and at the very same time his Christian brethren in China are swinging their axes, driving their planes, and wielding their hammers, for it is Monday morning with them. If we would but climb the mountain, sun ourselves in the daylight, and let the wind blow the cobwebs out of our eyes, we might read this truthful Scripture, "All days are thine, man: use them for thy good." No tyrannical monarch sits in state, watching with scowling brow the little boys who play on Sunday, striking one with lightning, and drowning another.

There is a time of rest marked by Nature, which none can disregard with impunity. It is when the sun sinks, and the curtain of night is drawn around the world; when

> "The daisies have shut up their sleepy red eyes,
> And the bees and the birds are at rest."

Then sleep, like an angel, closes the laborer's eyes, and his soul wanders off into heaven. Abstain from sleep to-night, and to-morrow you feel faint and languid. Try it to-morrow night, and the pain you will suffer will teach you the necessity of obeying the laws that Nature makes. It is said that Napoleon's soldiers, in the retreat from Moscow, slept on the march. So well does Nature provide for obedience to her commands, that disobedience is almost impossible. This is the only sabbath that Nature imposes: all others are of man's manufacture.

Indiscriminate intercourse between the sexes produces the foulest diseases, and its mental and moral effects are most disastrous. Polygamy debases woman, and degrades and brutalizes man. If one man appropriates to himself a dozen wives, he is a tyrant, and they his slaves. If many men were to do it, many of their brethren would be robbed of the happiness that flows from congenial companionship with woman. Monogamy is evidently the law of Nature; and when two congenial souls are truly united theirs is the kingdom of heaven.

What are the effects of slavery? Does it elevate mankind? Is it a blessing to the race? Its very defenders acknowledge that it is a curse. In consequence of it, comes to the white man idleness, that eats away his manhood like a canker-worm; cruelty, that enthrones the beast in his soul; and fear, that holds a dagger before his eyes continually: to the colored man, a prison-house for his mind, from which the light of knowledge is carefully excluded; a stagnation of soul that breeds pestilence and crime. It is accursed, let it die, says Nature; and die it will.

For want of this principle by which to distinguish right from wrong, the world is most sadly cursed. We have artificial virtues and artificial vices without number. Men are trained to believe that certain actions are right, nay, imperative, that have no tendency to benefit the doer or his neighbors; while they are trained to carefully abstain from doing what would be of decided benefit.

The faculty of conscience is blind, and never enables a man to know whether actions are right or wrong: it only induces us to do that which the judgment has decided to be right. The Hindoo devotee holds his closed hand above his head in a fixed position till the nails grow through his hand, and the muscles of his arm become so rigid that it is impossible to bend it. The torture thus inflicted upon the body he is taught to believe is so much virtue placed to the account of his soul; and his conscience assists him in bearing the pain. The Mohammedan dervise dances and howls by the hour, not because his dancing and howling benefit either himself or others, but to propitiate God, and obtain favors from him. We need not travel far to find instances of a somewhat similar kind in what we are pleased to call an "enlightened land."

Here is a baby held in the arms of a gentleman, who utters some words over it, as if for a charm, and then sprinkles water in its face till it cries; all parties looking on with the greatest seriousness.

It is winter, and cold in the extreme. A hole has been cut in the ice, and in the water stands another gentleman, a crowd of lookers-on surrounding the spot, attracted by the singular spectacle. He dips overhead twenty or thirty people, two-thirds of them women or girls; and with stiffened clothes and chattering teeth they make their way to some neighboring house. Who is benefited? The water is no purer, the people no cleaner, the gentleman no warmer, the world no wiser.

A hundred people are gathered in a Christian place of worship. It is communion-day. The minister discourses about a young man who was put to death more than eighteen centuries ago, who, he says, was God. He then hands to them cups filled with wine, and plates containing pieces of bread, and tells them to eat and drink; assuring them, as they do, that they are eating the flesh and drinking the blood of this young man who died so long ago, though the bread was made by the baker, and the wine is generally some villanous compound concocted by the wine-merchant.

Artificial virtues that are no virtues, that make no soul wiser or better, purer or happier, take the place of manliness, intelligence, and use. Human beings meet by thousands, and cry to deaf gods; they build sumptuous temples, and employ men to retail to them ancient fables, while they sternly reject living and important facts.

Artificial vices go side by side with artificial virtues. Your hired man is a Catholic. It is Friday, and the church says no meat shall be eaten. A round of beef is on the table; Patrick has been laboring hard, and hunger has shortened his memory; cut after cut disappears, till the thought flashes like lightning into his mind, — it is Friday! Down drop knife and fork, and remorse of conscience supplies the remainder of the meal. On Sunday he is off to confessional. He kneels, "O father, I have committed a great sin." — "What is it, my son?" says the priest, who thinks of nothing less than murder. "I ate some beef on Friday." The priest prescribes a light penance, and away goes Patrick rejoicing, while he rolls over a large quid of tobacco, and chews with double force for joy. It is all right to chew tobacco; but to eat meat on Friday — what a deadly sin!

A company of Methodists have met in the basement of the church at class-meeting. The leader asks them one by one how it is with their souls, till he arrives at a poor widow, left with four young children and a heritage of woe. She tells with trembling voice of her many shortcomings: she does the things she ought not to do, and leaves undone the things she ought to do; she begs an interest in their prayers, that she may grieve her God no more by wandering from him, but move steadily on to Zion with her face thitherward. What has this poor soul done? What are the sins that she has committed, the remembrance of which overwhelms her like a flood? Fatigued with hard labor for herself and darlings, she slept without first praying, and thought of her children in the morning before she thought of her God. She heard a dull, prosy sermon last Sunday, and went to sleep (the best possible thing she could do under the circumstances); and, bearing the burden of such artificial sins as these, she goes mourning all her days.

Thousands are made miserable by their violation of commands that they were never under any obligation to obey, and, on the other hand, are ruined by disobeying what Nature commands, of which they are generally ignorant.

Let us study the effect of our actions upon ourselves and our neighbors; and what conduces to true permanent happiness let us perform. Here are the ignorant; let us enlighten them by all the means in our power. Here are our neighbors, suffering, dying; let us assist and relieve them. Man needs our assistance, and all that we can give. Blessed is he that applies his life to this work! In this world he has peace and joy, and in the world to come the happiness that legitimately springs from well-doing, and that cannot be separated from it.

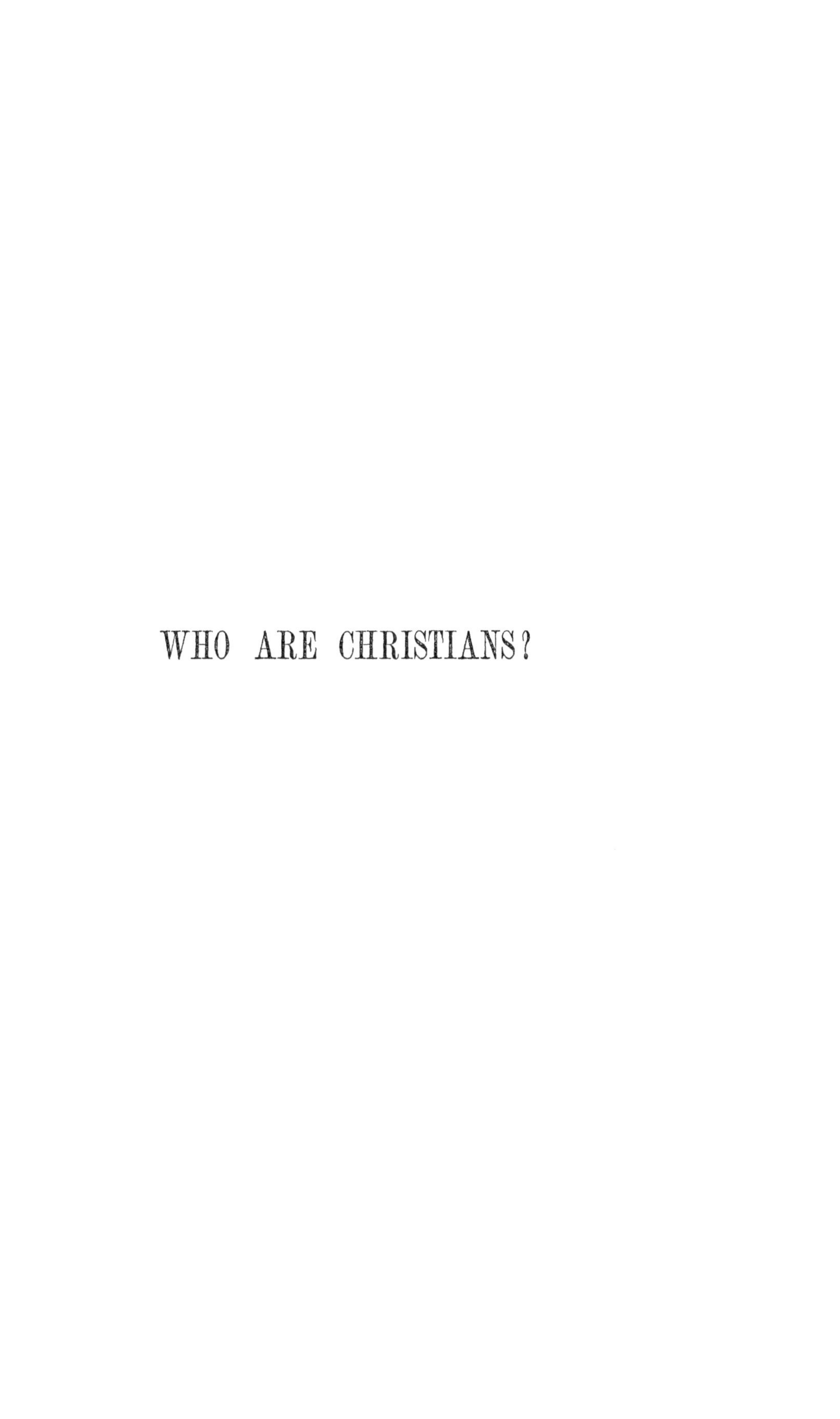

WHO ARE CHRISTIANS?

WHO ARE CHRISTIANS?

If Christianity, as taught in our evangelical churches, is true, the most important question that one man can ask another is, Are you a Christian? Next to this in importance must be the question, What constitutes a Christian?

Noah Webster says that a Christian is one who believes in Christ, and "especially one whose inward and outward life is conformed to the doctrines of Christ." According to this, there are two classes of Christians, — a general class who believe, and a special class who believe, and whose life accords with, the doctrines or teachings of Jesus. To the first class belong, probably, three-fourths of all the people of Christian countries, — England, France, Germany, Spain, Italy, indeed, of Europe generally, and the United States. They regard Jesus as the Messiah, the sent of God, the Christ, and think that salvation can only come by him. They are Christians, as Turks are Mohammedans.

Christians, then, fill our prisons, almshouses, lunatic-asylums, and houses of prostitution. Our thieves are Christian thieves, and our murderers Christian murderers. How rare it is for infidels to be convicted of theft, or hung for murder! On the gallows it is the name of Jesus the Christ that gives consolation to the dying criminal; and he expects, with the repentant thief, to be with him in Paradise. The late riots in New York were Christian riots. Our rowdies swear Christian oaths; and, when the death-angel appears to call them, they send for a Christian priest to prepare them for their departure.

Constantine the Great was a Christian, — he who murdered his son Crispus and his nephew Licinus, and suffocated his wife Faustus in a bath: he may be regarded, indeed, as the founder of our present Christian sabbath. Theodosius I., another Roman emperor, who murdered in cold blood seven thousand of the inhabitants of Thessalonica, without distinction of age, was a zealous and orthodox Christian; and so was Leo III., who commanded every person in his dominions to be baptized, under pain of banishment, and sentenced those to death who relapsed into idolatry after the ceremony.

Those men of Alexandria who murdered Hypatia were Christians to a man. Though she gave public lectures on philosophy, and proved herself to be one of the most noble women of her time, yet the Christian monks and rowdies, headed by a Christian priest, seized her in the street, dragged her into a Christian Church, stripped her naked, whipped her, cut her in pieces, and burned her mangled remains in the market-place.

Peter the Hermit was a famous Christian: clad in rags, and bare-footed, he wandered up and down

Europe, stirring up his fellow-Christians to rescue the Holy Land from the hands of the infidel Turks. Millions rallied to his call. "Their track," says Draper, "was marked by robbery, bloodshed, and fire." When they captured Jerusalem, "the brains of young children were dashed out against the walls; infants were pitched over the battlements; every woman that could be seized was violated; men were roasted at fires; some ripped up to see if they had swallowed gold. The Jews were driven into their synagogues, and burned; and nearly seventy thousand persons were massacred."

Father Dominic, who founded the Spanish Inquisition, was a Christian; and so were the wretches who applied its tortures. Torquemada, during his tenure of office as inquisitor-general, burned thousands, most of them fellow-Christians, who differed from him on some unimportant trifles. In less than three hundred years, the Spanish and Christian Inquisition burned alive more than thirty thousand persons, and condemned to various terms of imprisonment nearly three hundred thousand.

The Massacre of St. Bartholomew, in which sixty-six thousand persons were murdered for daring to be Protestants, was performed by Christians. In Rome, the papal Christians fired cannon and kindled bonfires, and Pope Gregory assisted at the celebration of a solemn mass, as a thanksgiving to God for his help in butchering their fellow-Christians. Indeed, to-day Christian Germans and Christian French are fighting; and the victories are duly celebrated by thanks to the Christian's God in the name of Jesus, the object of the Christian's faith.

"I deny that these were Christians," says one. "Think of Christian thieves, murderers, and prostitutes! Why, the statement is its own sufficient refutation." — "Who, then, are Christians?" I inquire. "Those only who obey the doctrines of Christ, and live the life of which he set a perfect example." This must be the second class of Christians to whom Webster refers. Where are we to find the doctrines of Jesus? In the New Testament, and especially in the Gospels, which are supposed to contain the commands that he gave in the very words in which they were uttered, infallibly reported by the inspired evangelists. Let us examine these, and compare them with the conduct of those who claim the Christian name, that we may discover who are the genuine Christians, and separate them from the miserable pretenders whom we have been considering.

Commencing with Matthew, who gives us a report of a famous sermon by Jesus himself, we find one of his commands to be, "Swear not at all . . . let your communication be, Yea, yea; Nay, nay: for whatsoever is more than these cometh of evil" (Matt. v. 34). And James, one of his disciples, who is supposed to have heard the discourse, reiterates the command, and even strengthens it: "Above all things, my brethren, swear not, neither by heaven, neither by the earth, neither by any other oath: but let your yea be yea; and your nay nay; lest ye fall into condemnation" (James v. 12). "Above all things," — above lying, then, above stealing, drunkenness, and even murder; and he who swears must, according to this, be the most guilty of all criminals.

Now, walk into one of our courts of justice. Hear what the judge says to a number of men who stand before him: "You solemnly swear, in the presence of Almighty God, that you will speak the truth, the whole truth, and nothing but the truth: so help you God." And the men hold up their right hands, and swear. Who can those men be? Are they Mohammedans, or ignorant pagans? One is a Catholic, another a Methodist, a third a Presbyterian, and all professing Christians; and there are none out of the millions professing the Christian name who regard these commands, except a handful of Quakers and Moravians. Can we consider those men Christians of the second class, who so grossly neglect such a plain and positive command of Christ as this?

In the same sermon, Jesus said, "Resist not evil; but whosoever shall smite thee on thy right cheek, turn to him the other also. And if any man will sue thee at the law, and take away thy coat, let him have thy cloak also. And whosoever shall compel thee to go a mile, go with him twain" (Matt. v. 39–41). In a report by Luke of the same discourse, we have these commands in a still stronger form: "Unto him that smiteth thee on the one cheek, offer also the other; and him that taketh away thy cloak forbid not to take thy coat also" (Luke vi. 29). Again he says, "Love your enemies; do good to them which hate you." These commands are plain; their meaning is evident: but who obeys them? Not the policeman who knocks down the man that strikes him, and takes him off to jail. Not the member of a Christian church who employs the policeman to resist the man whom he is unable or unwilling to resist himself. No policeman can be a true Christian: his business is to resist evil; and, when he ceases to do that, his work as a policeman is at an end. If a policeman could be a Christian, a man who lives by stealing could be an honest man. Our jailers, magistrates, judges, and attorneys, are constantly engaged in resisting evil, and even boast of what they accomplish in this way. They seem to have agreed to treat Jesus as we treat the insane, saying, Yes, yes, to all he utters, but never for a moment intending to obey his commands. From the decreasing ranks of our genuine Christians we must then take jailers, magistrates, judges, attorneys and justices: they not only disobey these commands of Jesus, but they live by their disobedience of them, and are constantly engaged in encouraging others to disobey them. Soldiers, from the man in the ranks to the general, must be counted out. They may plunder their enemies, shoot them, stab them; but, if they love them, they are spoiled for soldiers. What would a captain say to the man in his company who allowed the enemy to strike him, and never attempted to return the blow, but allowed him to strike the second time, and still made no resistance? A Christian soldier would be more useless than an idiotic school-teacher; and a musket is as much out of place in a Christian's hands as a telescope is at the eye of a blind man.

But the whole frame-work of our government rests on the soldier. Disobey the law, and the constable serves a warrant on you; resist the constable, and the general police are called out, or special constables sworn in; successfully resist these, and the State militia are employed; and if they should be too feeble to overcome the resistance, then the soldiers employed by the general government become the last resort: if they fail, the government is gone, and the successful resisters establish theirs in its place. Since soldiers cannot be Christians, all government officers who hold their situations by the soldiers' resistance share in their guilt, and must be counted unworthy of the Christian name.

But Christians everywhere act as if these commands of Jesus had never been given, or, being given, that they mean the very contrary of what they say. Joseph Smith, the Mormon prophet, was once asked what he thought of that passage of Scripture which says, "Whosoever shall smite thee on thy right cheek, turn to him the other also." — "Ah!" said Joseph, "Jesus Christ was a smart man, the wisest of men: he knew that a man might hit you accidentally or playfully, and, before resisting it, he wished you to make sure that he was in earnest, and that he meant you, by turning to him the other; but, if he hits you then, go into him like a thousand of brick." By the way that Christians generally act, one might suppose that they held a similar opinion with regard to its meaning.

Again Jesus says, "When thou prayest, enter into thy closet; and, when thou hast shut thy door, pray to thy Father which is in secret." Some Christians' praying is doubtless done after this fashion; but a large proportion of it is done in a very different way. Christian closets are very large in these days, and are generally furnished with steeples. The pompous clergyman in his sable robe, prayer-book before him, in stereotyped phrases offers his supplications in the presence of the assembled congregation. Another, before five hundred people, closes his eyes, lifts up his hands, and proceeds to inform God what he is, what he has done, and advise him for half an hour as to what he had better do. Not content with setting the commandments of Jesus at defiance themselves, these professed Christians establish meetings for public prayer, where men, and recently women, are encouraged to set the teachings of Jesus at defiance; and that is actually called a "Christian duty," which is in direct opposition to the teaching and practice of Jesus.

What sermon did he ever commence with a prayer? How many prayer-meetings did he establish or attend? Had he been like our modern Christians, we should have had some such record as this in the New Testament: "Now there was a prayer-meeting in Cana of Galilee, and Jesus and his disciples were there. Jesus opened the meeting by giving out one of the Psalms of David, and then called upon brother Simon Peter to pray, which he did in a voice of thunder, and with the unction of the Holy One: he was followed by brothers James and John, and all the disciples; and the power of the Lord was felt in their midst, so that the scribes and Pharisees marvelled, and a revival broke out, and many hundred souls were soundly converted to God." The difference between this and the statements made in the Gospels respecting the methods of Jesus represents the difference between Christianity and what passes for it at the present day. Had Jesus been like our present Christian ministers, he would have paid but little attention to men's bodies, he would have wasted but little time in curing their diseases: he would have established prayer-meetings, and formed societies from Nazareth to Jericho, and got up camp-meetings on the shores of Gennesaret, where he and his disciples would have prayed, and preached damnation to all unrepenting sinners, and salvation to all who should believe on a to-be-crucified Redeemer.

In the famous Sermon on the Mount, Jesus also says, "Give to him that asketh of thee, and from him that would borrow of thee turn not thou away" (Matt. v. 42). Luke's report also adds, "Of him that taketh away thy goods, ask them not again;" for, he says, "if ye lend to them of whom ye hope to receive, what thank have ye? for sinners also lend to sinners, to receive as much again. But love your enemies, and do good, and lend, hoping for nothing again, and your reward shall be great" (Luke vi. 30–34). This is also very plain: the disciples of Jesus are to be as widely different from sinners, and as easily distinguished, as sheep are from goats. But is this the case? Where are the men or women who obey these commands, or even try to obey them? It would only be necessary for the beggars to stand at the doors of our churches, to render themselves independently rich in a twelvemonth, if the professed Christians who worship in them were obedient to the commands of their Master. Where are the Christians, if those only are such who obey these commands? Are there any among the brokers of Wall Street or State Street? How many can Beacon Street show, or even Washington or Tremont Streets? It would require something brighter than Diogenes' lantern to find them. How do Christians lend? I find they are not averse to six per cent; nor do they often object to eight, even when the usury laws forbid it. Nor will they lend then without the best of security. They do not consider two per cent a month extravagant, if a man's necessities compel him to pay it; and they have no compunctions of conscience when they foreclose a mortgage, turn a man's family out, and take from them a five-thousand-dollar house on which they had lent but five hundred. A poor Christian wants to save his home from the clutches of some legal freebooter. Will his brother Christian lend him the money without interest, even if he has a million, and could do it as well as not? So seldom is it done, that such cases are almost unknown.

Had these commands of Jesus been the very opposite of what they are, the conduct of professing Christians would be almost in exact harmony with them. "Give nothing to him that asketh of thee, and from him that would borrow of thee turn thou away." "If any man take away thy goods, place him where there will be no opportunity to do it again." "Lend only to those of whom ye hope to receive, and where principal and interest are secured, then your reward shall be great." Read the passages thus, and I will find you obedient disciples in every church of the land.

I read also in this mountain sermon, "Lay not up for yourselves treasures upon earth, where moth and rust doth corrupt, and where thieves break through and steal." How many Christians obey this command? Few besides those who are so poor that they have nothing to lay up. If those only are Christians who obey the teachings of Jesus, all depositors in banks must be counted out, all holders of stocks and bonds. No free-mason can be a Christian, no odd-fellow, or son of temperance. All these have laid up for themselves treasures on earth, and have thereby forfeited all right to the treasures of heaven.

"*But Jesus never meant what you suppose.*" Who informed thee that Jesus did not mean what he said? Dost thou know better how to embody his meaning in words than He whom thou believest to be Lord of all the earth? It is passing strange, if he did not mean what he said, that he did not say what he meant.

"*But to obey such commands would make all Christians poor.*" Certainly; and this is just what is needed: Jesus evidently intended his disciples to be poor, and very poor. Nothing shows more clearly how the Christian standard has been lowered than the fact that rich men frequently claim to be Christians. The very first sentence that Jesus uttered in his Sermon on the Mount, according to Luke, was, "Blessed be ye poor; for yours is the kingdom of God." "Wha!" I hear some poverty-stricken wretch say, "is there any such passage as that in the Bible? Did the dear Jesus say that we the poor are blessed, and that ours is the kingdom of God?" I don't wonder that you ask the question. It is one of those passages that no minister chooses for a text, and that one never hears quoted from the pulpit; but here it is (Luke vi. 20): "Blessed be ye poor," — p-o-o-r, poor. More than that, he says, "Woe unto you that are rich, for ye have received your consolation" (Luke vi. 24). He declares that "it is easier for a camel to go through the eye of a needle than for a rich man to enter into the kingdom of God." Either the needle must be larger than needle ever was, or the camel smaller than camel ever can be ; or no rich man can be a Christian, if this statement of Jesus is correct. Of course, Christians must be poor; and Jesus, in insisting upon poverty, did the greatest service to mankind, if his fearful statements are true. I am here this afternoon to preach — what has never before been heard in Boston — the genuine gospel of Jesus ; not the emasculated gospel of the fashionable churches, but that of the homeless, bedless wanderer of Nazareth. You never heard it before, and never would hear it in any ecclesiastical edifice ; for they are built by the very men whom that gospel declares woe against, and for whom the fire of its hell is prepared.

Read the parable of the rich man and Lazarus (Luke xvi. 19) : "There was a certain rich man, which was clothed in purple and fine linen, and fared sumptuously every day." No intimation that he was either a drunkard, or licentious, dishonest, or even niggardly ; but he was rich. And there was a beggar laid at his gate, so poor that he desired to be fed with the crumbs that fell from the rich man's table. No intimation that he was conscientious, truthful, or even pious ; but he was poor, — one of those whose is the kingdom of God. The beggar died, and was carried by angels into Abraham's bosom : the rich man also died, and was buried ; but in hell he lifted up his eyes, being in torment ; nor could all his entreaties procure a drop of water to cool his parched tongue while tormented in the scorching flame. Here is the woe denounced upon the rich, here the terrible fate that awaits them. No wonder that James said, "Go to now, ye rich men, weep and howl for your miseries that shall come upon you." When the rich man in the parable asks Abraham that Lazarus may dip the tip of his finger in water and cool his tongue, the answer of Abraham is, "Son, remember that thou in thy lifetime receivedst thy good things, and likewise Lazarus evil things; but now he is comforted, and thou art tormented." The hungry are to rejoice, for by and by they will be fed; the mourners, for they will be comforted; and the miserably poor, for the joys of heaven await them. But this hell-tortured sinner, who might not have the slightest mitigation of his penalty, was guilty of the crime of being rich: he had had his good things, and now it is turn about; and in his fate all rich men may see the doom that awaits them: the smoke of their torment must ascend forever. Nor is it a donation of a hundred dollars to foreign missions that will save you, or two hundred to the Rev. Theophilus Hardshell's salary: your only chance for salvation is to become poor.

A young man comes running to Jesus: he is evidently in earnest, and says, "Good Master, what good thing shall I do, that I may have eternal life?" Suppose the answer of Jesus had never been recorded, and the professing Christians of the various sects had been left to fill in the answer, each according to his notion. "I have no doubt," says one, "that he told him there was nothing to do but to exercise saving faith in him as the Messiah." "He must have commanded him," says another, "to pray at least three times a day, to attend divine service every sabbath, and live a Christian life." "I can tell you just what he told the young man," a third would have confidentially exclaimed; "and that is, simply to believe in him as the Christ, and be immersed in his name." Very fortunately, the answer of Jesus has been recorded; and it is such a one as no member of the three hundred Christian sects would ever have supposed. He first tells him that he must keep the commandments; but this the young man declares he has done from his youth up: and then he asks the all-important question, "What lack I yet?" Now we shall have the very essence of Christianity: keeping the commandments was Jewish, and men had practised it for centuries before Jesus came. If Christianity is true, from the lips of the Master of life is about to fall the words that contain the key to bliss eternal. "Sell that thou hast, and give to the poor, and come and follow me." Imagine how chop-fallen the young man looked! How many young men who compose our Christian associations would have looked otherwise? Only those that had nothing to sell. "He went away sorrowful; for he had great possessions." Had Jesus tried the solid men of Boston, how many would have obeyed him? Not a soul. The difference between them and the young man would have been, that they would have gone away angry instead of sorrowful. If the Christian missionaries of to-day preached such a gospel as Jesus did, their disciples would be as few.

"*But Christianity does not require that a man should strip himself in that way.*" The sham Christianity of the churches does not; but the Christianity of Jesus does. His commands are, "Sell that ye have, and give alms" (Luke xii. 33). "Take no thought for your life, what ye shall eat, nor yet for your body, what ye shall put on." "Take no thought for the morrow" (Matt. vi. 25, 34). Jesus and his disciples wandered about Galilee, sleeping on the ground or in a fishing-boat, knowing not to-day how to-morrow's dinner would be obtained. Jesus appears to have been as regardless of to-morrow as the birds, whose practice he recommends. The members of the earliest Christian Church appear to have understood the commands of Jesus literally, and they acted accordingly. They sold their possessions, and laid the money at the apostles' feet; and distribution was made to every one according to his need (Acts ii. 45).

Let men obey the teachings of Jesus, and how long would they be rich, or have possessions? Let the strongest bank in Boston put out a sign, "Here we lend, hoping for nothing in return; we give to all who ask of us, and of those who take our goods we ask them not again." Though the parties were rich as the Rothschilds in the morning, and as sure of hell as Dives, they would be stripped as bare as Lazarus before night, and be just as certain of a place in Abraham's capacious bosom.

Where is the church that demands of its members obedience to these vital Christian duties? Jesus says, "Believe in me." They do it, and are not at all backward in saying so. Christianity is now a fashionable religion; and nothing can be easier than to be a floating chip on the current of public opinion. Jesus says, "When ye pray, say, Our Father:" and this how ready all are to perform, from the Unitarians to the ranters, from the prattling babe to the gray-haired sinner of ninety; and ask for their daily bread as if the breakfast-loaf depended on their morning petition. This also costs nothing. Jesus says, handing the wine-cup to his disciples, "Do this, as oft as ye do it, in remembrance of me;" and, although there is no positive command, they are eager to attend to the slightest hint of their Master, and down goes the poisonous alcoholic compound as the mystical blood of Jesus. He also says, "He that believeth, and is baptized, shall be saved." "Then we must be baptized," say the Baptists. "Yes, our little ones," say the pedo-Baptists; and up come the little children in the arms of their parents, and are sprinkled in the name of the triune Jehovah; and down go the children of a larger growth in the arms of the priest, to be dipped in the same name. This also costs next to nothing, and is often a passport into what is called good society. But when Jesus says, "Lend, hoping for nothing again," "Give to him that asketh of thee," "Sell that ye have, and give alms," all are stone-deaf; or, if they hear, they are quite sure that he does not mean what he says. Jesus may beckon for them to tread the path that he has trod; but they are all blind. This costs something; this strips them and tries them; this tests their faith. Jesus is reported as saying, "When the Son of man cometh, shall he find faith on the earth?" and I think, if he should come now, he would find the pretending members of his church to be infidels to a man: there is no faith in Jesus in the land. Let millionnaires distribute what they have robbed from the poor, when they take the Christian name; let them sell their mansions to-day, and distribute to the necessitous, and know not where they shall lay their heads to-morrow; let those Christian ministers who denounce all who do not accept their standard of Christianity set the example by reducing themselves to abject poverty, and then we shall have evidence of their sincerity at least.

Who are genuine Christians? They cannot be those lords over God's heritage, who pocket from five to fifteen thousand dollars a year for preaching a gospel scarcely an item of which Jesus could recognize. They cannot be among those sleek church-goers who pay from a hundred to a thousand dollars a year for the privilege of sitting in a cushioned pew, and listening to Rev. Silver-Tongue as he proves how easy it is for a camel to go through a needle's eye. Boston, among its regiment of preachers, cannot find a single man; and the New-York and Brooklyn pounders, expounders, and ten-pounders, are not a whit more Christian than their Boston brethren. If the Christians only are sheep, they are left-hand goats, to a man; and the Judge's fatal "Depart!" must ring through their guilty souls in "the last great day." Nor are the members of our so-called Christian churches in a much more hopeful condition. Not only is it impossible to find a man who obeys the commands of Jesus, we cannot even find one who tries to obey them; and, if we did, his Christian brethren would be among the first to conclude that he had taken leave of his senses.

If any of you still think that you are Christians, and that, on account of this, Jesus will save you from the curses pronounced on the disobedient, let me refer you to the sixteenth chapter of Mark. I read, "He that believeth and is baptized shall be saved; but he that believeth not shall be damned." Now comes the question of questions: Are you a believer? for, if you are not, damnation is yours. Jesus himself gives the test by which you may decide: "These signs shall follow them that believe: in my name shall they cast out devils; they shall speak with new tongues; they shall take up serpents; and, if they drink any deadly thing, it shall not hurt them; they shall lay hands on the sick, and they shall recover." Can you cast out devils in the name of Jesus? Can you speak with new tongues? It may be difficult to tell when the devils are in, and perhaps still more to tell when they are out; it may be impossible for us to tell whether any peculiar speech that you may utter is a veritable language or not: but can you handle serpents with impunity, say rattlesnakes, vipers, or copperheads? Can you drink any deadly thing without injury? — a dose of arsenic, for instance, a few grains of corrosive sublimate, or half a pint of sulphuric-acid? Can a man be found among the millions professing the Christian name that would submit to the test, to say nothing about being unharmed afterward? Or can you lay your hands on the sick, and they recover? I hear of Spiritualists doing this at times; but where are the Christians that can do it? And yet it is evident, if Jesus states what is true, that those who cannot do these things will be damned. Out of the way, you shams! — you Roman Catholic, with your seven sacraments, your holy water, your Latin gabble, your fantastic dresses! Away with you, monks, priests, cardinals, and infatuated popes, and take your *Pater-Nosters* and *Ave-Marias*, your litanies and your solemn masses, with you! What are they good for? The whole pile of your mummery never made a single Christian, and cannot save from damnation one guilty soul. You need not come, Episcopalian, to take his place. What better is your prayer-book than his mass-book? Are your two sacraments any more efficacious than his seven? your damnatory creed any more soul-saving than his? You can make Episcopalians by the million; but there is not a Christian among them; and, if Jesus speaks what is true, they will every one be damned with the common herd. Here come the Presbyterians. "We are *the* Christians, orthodox, evangelical. We have thrown overboard unscriptural Popery, unchristian Episcopalianism; and we are the true followers of the Saviour." You, with your cloud-cleaving spires, your velvet cushioned pews and your tasselled pulpits, your ten-thousand-dollar ministers and millionnaire members, — you Christians? Then are misers generous, drunkards temperate, and Hottentots the most beautiful of mankind. You need not crowd in, Methodist, Baptist, Quaker, Shaker, Unitarian, Universalist, and Adventist, — shams, every one. Jesus can only say to you all, "Depart from me: I never knew you!" You have built on the sand, and your structure must fall when the wrath of God is revealed on those who obey not the gospel of his Son.

If none are to be saved but Christians, where, my professing brother, will you appear?

I can see the last great day, "the day for which all other days were made." Down from heaven descends the Master, surrounded with the shining host; and at the sound of that trumpet whose call the very dead hear, up come earth's buried hosts. I behold all the Christians sects, marshalled by their leaders and under their respective banners, come before the throne of Him whose name had been their boast. The Roman Catholics, a myriad-membered throng, approach; and a venerable prelate stands as their mouthpiece before the "dread tribunal." "On what grounds do ye claim the Christian name, and a place in my kingdom?" said the once meek Nazarene, but now the lion of the tribe of Judah, with flaming vengeance in his eye and a dagger in every word. "Thou gavest to Peter the keys of the kingdom of heaven; and we have faithfully obeyed his successors, and proclaimed their decisions infallible. We have styled the holy Mary, thy mother, Mother of God, and given to her all but divine homage. We have built the most magnificent cathedrals, and drained from the poor more money for thy cause than any other people on earth. We have persecuted to death, wherever we have had the power, all who would not bow down to thy name, as our church directed: we burnt them at the stake, racked them on the wheel, hung them on the gibbet, and tortured them in all ways that our ingenuity could devise, to drive their heresies from them, and save precious souls. Surely we are thy people, and shall be allowed to enter into thy kingdom, and sit down with thee."

"Did you not know," and his voice sounded like thunder, "that Peter was he to whom I said, 'Get thee behind me, Satan!' and that he denied me with oaths and curses? What authority had you from me to call his pretended successors infallible? When I was on earth, my disciples wished to call down fire from heaven on those who rejected me; but I replied, as you know, 'The Son of man came not to destroy men's lives, but to save them.' Was it for you, then, in my name, to torture and burn men because they would not submit to a tyrannical church, — the most infernal that was ever established among men? My mother did no more than any other woman might have done in her place, and was no more divine than the mothers of my poor, whom you robbed to build your pompous piles, and feed your pampered church. Traitors to humanity, lovers of darkness, torturers of the conscientious, plunderers of the poor, depart from me!" Then the banners drooped, the proud prelates hung their heads, and the duped multitude blushed for shame as they moved on, and made room for the Presbyterians, who came boldly, in no degree disconcerted by the fate of the Romanists that had preceded them. "We are Christians," said they, "and we claim the kingdom which is ours by faith." — "What have ye done to deserve it?" said He on the throne. They answered, "We rescued thy Church and thy Word from the hands of the polluted wretches that preceded us, and uplifted thy banner, that had been trampled in the dust, and made it sacred in the eyes of the respectable in all Christian lands. We built the best of churches, paid millions for home and foreign missions, and made thy name to be honored by the rich and influential everywhere. We erected colleges for training young men to preach thy Word; and our doctors of divinity were renowned throughout the civilized world."

"Is this what I commanded you to do?" and his eye blazed like lightning; and a shudder ran through the multitude, so that they trembled, as he spoke, like a leaf on an aspen-tree. "You rescued my Church and my Bible? You never did either. My Church exists alone in the hearts of those who obey my instructions; and from whom did my Word need to be rescued more than from you who denied its meaning, and by every deed of your lives set at nought its requirements? You made my name honored by misrepresenting my character, and belying my gospel; and in my kingdom there is no place for such as you." And I saw the sad, solemn multitude depart like a funeral procession, to make room for the next claimants of the Christian's reward.

Confidently came a greater host, a host no man might number: a million columns filed before the throne, and they looked as if they might, in case of refusal, take heaven itself by storm. They were the Methodists. "We are thine," said they, "the children of the King; and we come to thee for our crown and our kingdom." —"Why should I give crowns to you? What proofs can you present of your relationship to me?" said the Judge. "Like thee we went among the poor and the lowly, we formed prayer-meetings, established class-meetings, got up revivals, and swept millions into thy Church and thy fold. We, too, have built churches in thy name; in thy name have founded colleges, and sent out preachers to the remotest bounds of the earth." — "I know you," said the Judge; and, as he said it, I saw darkness upon their faces like the shadow of a cloud on a mountain-side. "You went among the poor and lowly: ye did well; but did you go to distribute all that you had? Did you give to those who asked you? Did you lend, hoping for nothing? Did you denounce the tyrant lordlings who held my people in bondage, and wrung from them the fruits of their labor to pamper their pride? Who told you to form prayer-meetings and class-meetings? Who commanded you to get up revivals, build churches, and send preachers to declare a gospel which they preached, instead of my gospel, scarcely a word of which they ever uttered? My crowns are not for such as you, and my heaven cannot reward pretenders, or their dupes." And the weeping Methodists followed the Presbyterians and the Romanists, as all other Christian sects followed them; for in the heaven of Jesus the Christ there was no place found by them.

Where, then, shall we find the true Christians? I will give you the gospel-marks by which they may be distinguished; and, when you find one, you cannot be mistaken. They never swear, not even in a court of justice; they do not resist evil, and, if any man hits them on one cheek, they turn the other; they lend, hoping for nothing again; they give to all who ask of them; they sell what they have, and give alms; they take no thought for the morrow; they take no thought about what they shall eat, drink, or wear; they wash one another's feet. When they make a feast, they do not invite their friends nor their acquaintances nor their rich neighbors, but the poor, the halt, and the blind. They love their enemies; but they hate their fathers, mothers, sisters, brothers, husbands or wives, their children, and their own lives: for all these Jesus commanded. Should there be any doubt still remaining, you will know them by this: they can cast out devils, speak with new tongues, handle serpents, drink deadly poison with impunity, and heal the sick by laying their hands upon them. "But there are no such people," I think I hear you say. Certainly not; and hence there are no Christians in your sense, — none who obey the commands of Jesus; and indeed Jesus himself was no Christian, if this alone constitutes one. Like all other men, his ideal was different from his actual life. He says, "Whosoever calleth his brother a fool is in danger of hell-fire;" yet he repeatedly calls the Pharisees "fools and blind." He says, "Resist not evil," yet with a scourge drives the traffickers out of the temple, and overturns the tables of the money-changers. He tells men to be perfect, as their Father in heaven is perfect; and yet says there is but One good, that is God. He says, "Take no thought for the morrow." Hear him in the Garden of Gethsemane, as he prays, "O my Father, if it it be possible, let this cup pass from me." What cup? The cup of sorrow that he was to drink on the morrow. If none get to heaven but those who obey the commandments of Jesus, then Jesus himself will be absent: he too will be cast into outer darkness, where there is weeping, wailing, and teeth-gnashing. If Jesus was not a genuine Christian, what chance has any one else to be?

I do not, of course, blame any one for failing to be a

Christian. It is not in the power of humanity to be; and for men even to try to be would be most disastrous. It was this that made a eunuch of Origen, filled the Church with idle nuns and beggarly monks, and to-day makes celibates of hundreds of Shakers, who, but for their unfortunate faith, might be exemplary parents, and leave the world better than they found it. It has made multitudes fools for Christ's sake, who might have been intelligent and happy men and women. Let those who desire to become Christians give to those who ask of them, and lend, hoping for nothing again, and the list of paupers would soon be largely increased, and the idle and the industrious would be equally cursed. There is often no better way to cure a man of Christianity than to induce him to try to live his faith. These members of Christian churches, then, — these Christian ministers too, who "deal damnation round the land," — are Christians in no other sense than the mass of believers in Jesus outside of the Church; and, if their Master is to be believed, their damnation is as certain as that of those they denounce. They are Christian ministers, as our thieves are Christian thieves; and the churches in which they preach are Christian churches, as our jails are Christian jails, and our drink-houses, Christian grog-shops. They have taken just as much of the doctrine of Jesus as they pleased, mixed it with a set of monstrous fables of their own, or of other pretended Christians, from Paul down; and, having baptized this as Christianity, they curse every one who will not bow down to the idol that they have set up.

There are multitudes of well-meaning people, who

have been educated in the Christian faith, or what goes by that name, who are sincerely desirous to obey the teachings of Jesus, because they believe it to be their duty. Many such are made unhappy by their inability to live the life that their faith demands. What a satisfaction it must be to know that there is not the least necessity for any one to be a Christian! our welfare in this life or the next does not in the slightest degree depend upon it. You can be a philosopher, as Humboldt was, and be no Christian, as he was none; you may be a poet, with Shelley; a philanthropist with Henry C. Wright, who had long cast off the Christian name and the Christian pretence; you can be a good father or mother, a good citizen, a lover of man, and a doer of right, a practiser of temperance and every virtue, and yet be no Christian. And a man may be a thief, drunkard, murderer, adulterer, hypocrite, and brute, and yet be a Christian in the only sense in which any man can be a Christian.

Think of the time, labor, and energy wasted in the attempt to make men Christians. Think of the thousands of missionaries roaming over the world, and spending their lives in converting men from one form of superstition to another. Think of the millions spent in Massachusetts to convert men to the dogmas of twenty contending sects, that are no more Christian than the Roman Church is catholic. Instead of Bible-classes, where our young people are taught what the Bible means, and often what it does not mean, let us have classes of physiology, phrenology, geology, and astronomy; schools for adults, in which grammar, elocution, music, and drawing will be taught, and where instruction can be obtained in the moral duties which grow out of our relations to each other and to nature. Then every member will learn something useful, not only for this life, but that will be capital with which to start in the next. Instead of Christians, let us have whole-souled, well-developed men and women, who will do right because right-doing is best for humanity. Instead of Christian ministers, let us have human ministers, — men bound by no creed, tied to no church, cursed by no Bible; men who will simply ask, What does Nature teach? and, having learned this, seek to impress the truth on the minds of their fellows.

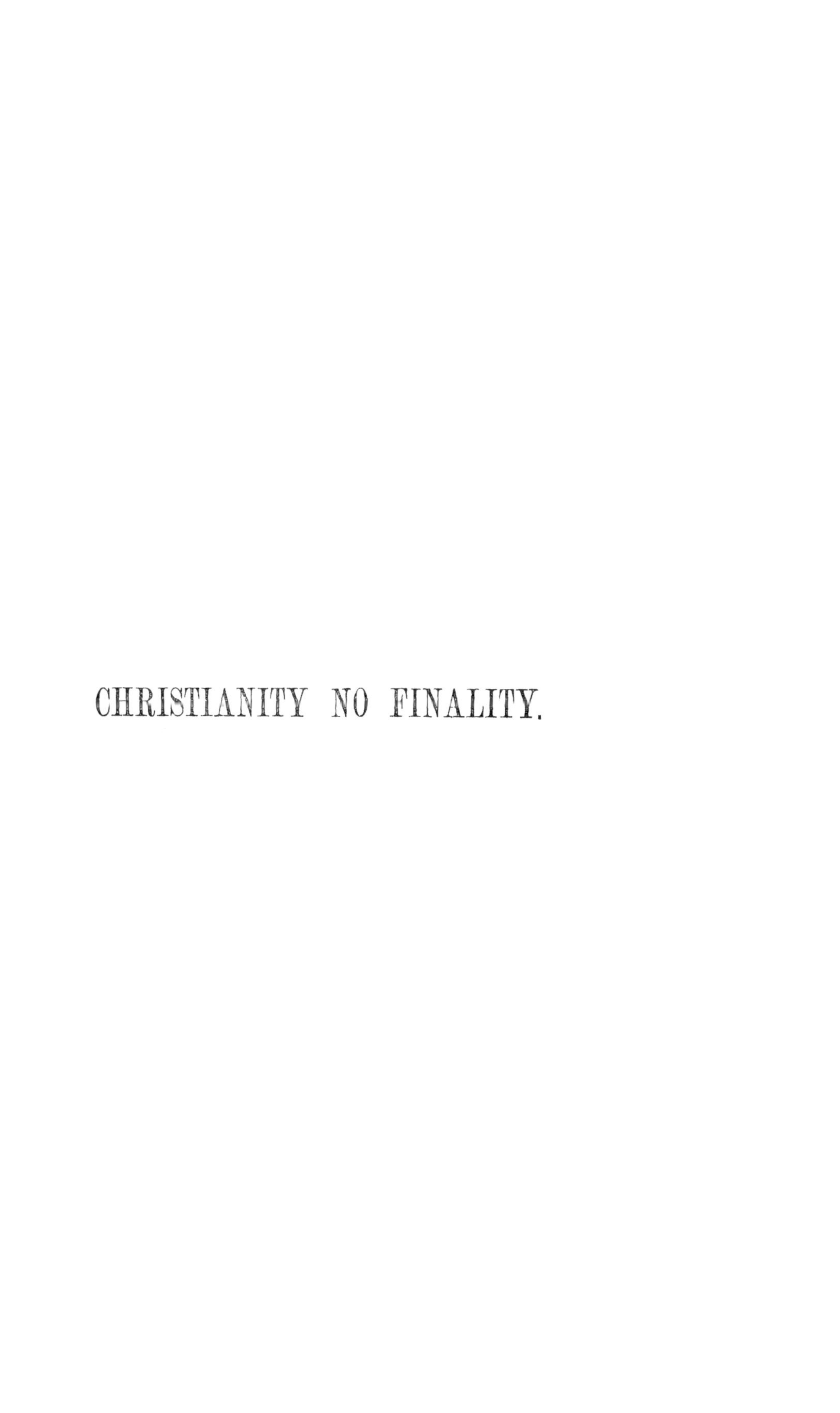

CHRISTIANITY NO FINALITY.

CHRISTIANITY NO FINALITY.

WE surpass the ancients in almost every department of literature, science, mechanics, and art. Among the Greeks and Romans, not more than one in a hundred could read and write, and among the ancient Jews still fewer. Charlemagne of France, the greatest of Christian kings, about a thousand years ago, never knew how to write. Very few of the French clergy knew how to read, and scarcely any to write; and, in England, the condition of the people was no better. Now a man so ignorant in this country is a rarity. Where there was one author two thousand years ago, there are a hundred now; and our schools and colleges contain thousands in the embryo. Then a book as large as Shakspeare's works could only be written by the unremitting labor of a year; now a dozen men will turn out a thousand in a day. Six hundred and fifty thousand "New-York Tribunes" are printed every week; each containing as much matter as the New Testament: to write them as they did then would require the labor of a thousand men for twelve years. It took a fortune in those days to buy a few manuscripts; now a peasant has a library that a Roman emperor would have envied.

In astronomy, we have advanced from the childish guesses of the Hebrews, and the only less wild conjectures of the Greeks, to the magnificent works of the Herschels, and the splendid and all but demonstrated theories of La Place. The little world made by the Jewish Jehovah in six days; that had ends, and was flat; that rested on pillars, and was established so that it could not be moved, — is gone; and in its place we have the grand old earth, born of the sun in the eternity of the past, rushing through space sixty times faster than a ball from the mouth of a cannon. In place of the stars that were made on the fourth day after the creation of the earth, to assist in giving light upon it, and that occasionally fell when Jehovah shook the heavens, we have millions of blazing suns, some of them a thousand times larger than the centre of our system; and, compared with them, we find our planet to be but a drop in an infinite ocean. We have deciphered the hieroglyphics on the rocks, in which the history of our planet is inscribed (a history all unknown to the men of the past); have called up from their long sleep the hosts of organic forms which flourished during the geologic ages; and wrested from Nature her deep secrets, hidden for so long from the most scrutinizing gaze. Physiology, phrenology, chemistry, sciences unknown to the world two thousand years ago, are blessing us daily with their beautiful and useful revelations; and the future is big with promise of new sciences to be born, new realms yet to be discovered, explored, and appropriated.

I am told that the Pyramids of Egypt are superior to all modern structures, and that they demonstrate how much the art of the ancients was superior to that of the moderns. But let a hundred thousand men be employed for thirty years, as they were to make the great Pyramid, with the appliances of modern mechanics and art, and they would pile up a mountain like Chimborazo, whose giant crest the traveller views at a distance of a hundred miles. For every art supposed to be lost, we have made a hundred; and new ones are starting up daily.

We have to-day better houses, better heads, consequently better brains and better minds, better books, better governments, than the ancients, and why not a better religion? Having advanced in every other direction, why not in this? Are we to march forward in science with *excelsior* for our motto, looking upward, and ever climbing to the untrodden heights; and, in religion, are we to be constantly looking over our shoulders, or groping in some mummy-pit over the musty records of the past, deciphering mouldy parchments, and mourning over mutilated manuscripts, as if God had left his word to the mercy of some spreading fungus or nibbling rat?

"Why should we see with dead men's eyes,
Looking at *Was* from morn till night?
When the beauteous *Now*, the divine *To be*,
Woo with their charms the living sight?"

As the race has advanced from its primitive barbarism, it has made for itself better and better religious forms, corresponding with its advancement. Fetichism was once the best form of religion, when men worshipped trees, stones, beetles, snakes, and more disgusting objects still.

"Then a crocodile served as a reverend lord,
And the leeks that we eat were the gods they adored."

The soul of man could not always thus grovel: some primitive Moses, Jesus, or Luther, denounced, doubtless, as a heretic and infidel, scouted the snaky gods, and turned men's attention to the heavens. "There," said he, "is the beautiful sun: what more glorious object of worship can you have? This makes our day; its absence, gloomy night; under its benignant reign spring up grasses, flowers, fruits, and all hearts are cheered." Listening to him, they abandoned the old gods, danced in circles at early morn, and chanted hymns of praise to the god of day. Heroes who had slain wild beasts, and destroyed neighboring tribes who were their enemies, in turn also became gods to be adored: their deeds were emulated by their worshippers; and the exaggerated stories of their exploits were handed down from generation to generation.

Judaism at length became possible, better than some of its predecessors; for it gave to its adherents the unseen God, "the Creator of the heavens and earth," in whose name a valuable moral code was inculcated, and the more flagrant crimes sternly denounced. But this God, though invisible, was in human shape; stern, revengeful, passionate, and, at times, terribly cruel. The Jews were his children beloved; the Gentiles, his illegitimate offspring, whom the Jews were commissioned by him to destroy whenever they interfered with their convenience or pleasure.

As men's minds expanded, the Jewish God, and the ritual founded in his name, could no longer command their respect. Jesus inaugurates a new era, and supersedes Judaism, as the dawn does the light of the stars. God is the Father of the human race: the sun that shines on all, the rain that drops so impartially on all, are the fit emblems of his unbiassed love. The burden of superstitious rites and ceremonies, the offering of sacrifices, the sabbaths, and the yearly pilgrimages, are abolished. Faith in Jesus, and obedience to his simple doctrine, are all that the new religion demands.

But is Christianity, even as Jesus taught it, a finality? Did this Galilean mechanic exhaust the Infinite? Has Nature no deeper secrets than he revealed? Did he climb higher than mortal can ever again rise? Did he alone know the way of life, and are we doomed to walk implicitly in his footsteps, or forever go astray? So thought the Jew of Moses; so thinks the Turk of Mohammed, and the Mormon of Joseph Smith.

We dream not that we have approached the Infinite in any other direction. Ask the best musician if he has exhausted the possibilities of his science and art, and he will tell you that we have but ascended to the clouds; and the infinite heaven of harmony lies beyond, yet to be scaled, and yet to be enjoyed. The geologist knows that we have but deciphered a few torn leaves of a mighty volume, whose unread lore will feast explorers for ages to come. Ask the astronomer if the last star in the firmament has yielded to him its secrets, and the heavens have no more to reveal, and he will tell you that he is but a babe, who has made the acquaintance of a few pebbles on the shore of the ocean, whose unfathomable waters spread illimitably around him. What would be thought of the man who should attempt to anchor us where our present attainments are in these sciences? He would be justly regarded as a foe to the human race. Was Jesus greater in religion than Newton and Herschel in astronomy, than Lyell in geology, or Humboldt in general science? We certainly have no evidence of it. If we are to rely upon the New-Testament record, and we have no other, his deficiencies, and that of his religion, are most manifest.

It is, in the first place, most sadly deficient in the ability to give to the sceptic any evidence of life beyond the grave. Judaism, it is true, was more deficient: it lacked even hope. Job says (Job vii. 9), "As the cloud is consumed and vanisheth away, so he that goeth down to the grave shall come up no more;" and certainly, if man does go down to the grave, he comes up no more: but man does no such thing. And David (Ps. cxlvi. 4): "His breath goeth forth, he returneth to his earth; in that very day his thoughts perish." And Solomon (Eccl. iii. 18–22): "I said in my heart concerning the estate of the sons of men, that God might manifest them, and that they might see that they themselves are beasts. For that which befalleth the sons of men befalleth the beasts; even one thing befalleth them: as the one dieth, so dieth the other; yea, they have all one breath; so that a man hath no pre-eminence above a beast: for all is vanity. All go unto one place; all are of the dust, and all turn to dust again. Who knoweth the spirit of man that goeth upward, and the spirit of the beast that goeth downward to the earth? Wherefore I perceive that there is nothing better than that a man should rejoice in his own works; for that is his portion: for who shall bring him to see what shall be after him ?" So said the grossly material Solomon, who drank the cup of pleasure to the dregs, and then called it bitter. I suppose it was in this spirit that he married seven hundred wives, and took three hundred concubines, the result of which he gives us in his despairing words, "All is vanity."

Christianity, it must be acknowledged, is far in advance of this. By the mouth of Jesus, it exclaims, "In my Father's house are many mansions: I go to prepare a place for you, that, where I am, there ye may be also." Abraham, Isaac, and Jacob still live, and Moses and Elias appear on the mountain, and talk. Paul says, "To be absent from the body is to be present with the Lord," and "If our earthly house of this tabernacle were dissolved, we have a building of God, a house not made with hands, eternal in the heavens." Blessed words! — how many sinking souls they have buoyed when the billows had well-nigh gone over them! What hosts of hearts they have gladdened, as they trod the dark valley, with no light but the star of Christianity to cheer them! Let us thankfully acknowledge the good of the old, though we prefer the new: the light of the stars is joyously accepted before the morning breaks.

But how little comfort the doubter obtains from these! How meagre the evidence of future existence which the Christian can give to those who dispute it! "How know you, my brother, that you will live when this body dies; that there is a bridge that spans the broad, dark chasm of death?" We pause for his reply. "Jesus died, and rose again triumphant; and, because he lives, we shall live also." — "But how do you know that Jesus rose from the dead?" — "We have the testimony of those who saw him after his resurrection, — the disciples with whom he brake bread after he rose, who saw, conversed with, and even handled him; the five hundred brethren who saw him at once, and never doubted his triumph over death and the grave." — "But where do you find all this?" — "In the New Testament." In vain the sceptic looks for what would justify such an extravagant statement. Here are accounts by Matthew, Mark, Luke, and John, and the merest mention in the Epistle of Peter, and, besides this, absolutely nothing from any one pretending to be an eye-witness of these occurrences. Let us examine what we possess. How much of it would be taken in a court of justice?

Mark's Gospel appears to have been transcribed from previous records; and we have no evidence that the writer ever saw Jesus, either after his death or before. Even Orthodox commentators do not pretend to know when his Gospel was written, or what Mark wrote it. "Of Mark, little, certainly, is known," says Albert Barnes the Orthodox commentator. Again: he says, "He was not an apostle or companion of the Lord Jesus during his ministry." We cannot, therefore, accept his statement: it would be ruled out of court at once.

Luke does not profess to have been an eye-witness of any of the events that he relates: he merely professes (Luke i. 1) to set forth, in order, a declaration of what was most surely believed among the Christians of that time; and his statement can do but little more in establishing the resurrection of Jesus than the statement of a Christian's belief in it at this day.

The Gospels of Matthew and John are, however,

believed by most Christians to have been written by the men whose names they bear, who saw Jesus before his death, and after he rose from the dead; and who are, in every respect, competent witnesses. This can never be proved; but, for the sake of the argument, we will grant it.

Let Matthew be examined. "Matthew, did you see Jesus of Nazareth die?" — "I did not: when the multitude came with swords and staves to take Jesus, we all forsook him, and fled." — "What was done with his body?" — "Joseph of Arimathea buried it in a new sepulchre in his garden." — "Who went to the sepulchre on the first day of the week?" — "Mary Magdalene and the other Mary" (Matt. xxviii. 1). "What did they see?" — "An angel, who said, Fear not ye; for I know that ye seek Jesus, which was crucified. He is not here; for he is risen, as he said. Go quickly, and tell his disciples that he is risen from the dead; and, behold, he goeth before you into Galilee; there shall ye see him: lo, I have told you!" — "Did these women see Jesus on that occasion?" — "They did: as they were going to tell the disciples, they saw him, held him by the feet, and worshipped him; and he said, 'Go tell my brethren that they go into Galilee, and there they shall see me.'" — "What then?" — "Then the eleven disciples went away into Galilee into a mountain where Jesus had appointed them; and, when they saw him, they worshipped him: but some doubted" (Matt. xxviii. 16, 17).

Let us look at Matthew's testimony for a moment. An angel tells the two women to go quickly and tell the disciples of Jesus that he is risen from the dead, and goes before them into Galilee, and that they shall see him there; and, on their seeing Jesus, he adds, "Go tell my brethren that they go into Galilee, and there they shall see me." What was meant to be conveyed by these commands? That Jesus was on his way to Galilee, and that he did not intend to see them till he should see them there; then that the disciples went at once to Galilee, and there first saw Jesus. Nothing else can be fairly gathered from them.

"Now, John, let us hear your testimony. Did you see Jesus of Nazareth die?" — "I did: I was standing near his mother, looking on at the time."

"Who went to the sepulchre on the first day of the week?" — "Mary Magdalene." — "What did she see?" — "She saw no one, but found that the body of Jesus was gone." — "What did she do?" — "She ran and told Peter and me; and we ran to the sepulchre, and found it to be as she had told us; and then we went home." — "What became of her?" — "She remained there weeping; and, looking into the sepulchre, she saw two angels who asked her why she wept; and, after telling them, she turned and saw Jesus, but thought he was the gardener, but, on his speaking, recognized him. He said, 'Touch me not, for I am not yet ascended to my Father; but go to my brethren, and say unto them, I ascend unto my Father and your Father, and to my God and your God.'" — "What did the disciples do?" — "They remained in Jerusalem; and the same day, at evening, all but Thomas being in an upper room for fear of the Jews, Jesus appeared to them and made them glad. Eight days afterwards, he appeared to them again in the same place; and, Thomas being present, satisfied him also of his resurrection from the dead."

From John, then, we learn that Jesus appeared to his disciples in Jerusalem on the same day that he rose from the dead, and satisfied all but Thomas of his resurrection; but, according to Matthew, when the eleven disciples saw him in Galilee, *some* doubted. This must, therefore, have been before he was seen in Jerusalem; for they could not have doubted in Galilee if they had previously been satisfied in Jerusalem. To make Matthew's statement and John's even appear to agree, the disciples must have first seen Jesus on the mountain at Galilee, and then at Jerusalem: but, to do this, they must, when Mary Magdalene and the other Mary gave them the imperative word of Jesus, have gone at once to Galilee, and returned to Jerusalem in time for the evening's appearance on the same day; which would involve a journey of at least a hundred and twenty miles, to say nothing of climbing the mountain. But those were not days of railroads, steamboats, nor even stage-coaches; and we see at once, if their other discrepancies had not satisfied us, that these pretended eye-witnesses are deceiving us. In court, they would be in danger of trial for perjury.

Although we have granted that Matthew wrote the gospel attributed to him, there is good reason to believe that he never did write a word of it. Could he have seen Jesus, as John represents, on the very day that he rose from the dead, in an upper room at Jerusalem, and yet have represented that Jesus was first seen at Galilee, at least sixty miles off, and never have said a word about his appearance at Jerusalem? It is impossible.

"What have we left, then?" — "The five hundred who saw Jesus at once." — "Who are they? Where is their testimony?"—"Nowhere: Paul *says* that five hundred brethren saw him at once." Very different, indeed, from the testimony of these five hundred, no name even of one being given.

We have, beside this, the testimony of Peter, who is supposed to have been an eye-witness; but it amounts to little. All that he says is, God "hath begotten us again to a lively hope by the resurrection of Jesus Christ from the dead;" and "God raised him up from the dead." And this is absolutely all from those pretending to have known Jesus when alive. Paul evidently knew nothing of him personally. If some of those who saw Jesus doubted,—the very disciples, while looking upon the face of their risen Master,—well may the sceptic doubt to-day, with nothing but such meagre and contradictory evidence before him as this. On what a slender thread this momentous doctrine has hung! Man's strong desire for immortality has led him to clutch at any straw to save him from the abyss of nothingness in which death threatened to plunge him, or such testimony as this never could have been accepted.

But suppose that Jesus did rise from the dead: he rose with his flesh, blood, and bones,—a proper physical man. He says, "A spirit hath not flesh and bones, as ye see me have." He ate broiled fish and honeycomb; showing that he was actually the same being after death as before. But we can never rise in this way: our friends have perished, if this is the only resurrection possible. Some lie in trenches in the bloody fields of the South, and their decomposing remains give verdure to the palmetto that waves over them: some sank into the turbid Mississippi, with the vessels they bravely defended: others were lost at sea, and sharks became their living sepulchres; or were burned up in houses and ships, and the particles of their bodies have been wafted over the globe on the wings of a thousand winds. They have become parts of other human bodies; and how can these ever be recovered and re-animated? It cannot be, in the nature of things. If we had no other evidence than this, well might we weep on the death of our friends, as those who have no hope! Christianity, then, utterly fails to give to the sceptic any evidence of life beyond the grave. When he asks for evidence on the most important question that the soul of man can consider, it is silent as a skeleton, or chatters but to reveal its imbecility.

Spiritualism is, in this respect, almost infinitely superior. Christianity rests on faith, spiritualism on knowledge. The one is a historical statement, the other a living fact. Christianity says, "Blessed are they who have not seen, and yet believed;" thus offering a premium for blind faith. Spiritualism says, "Come hither, ye sceptics: hear, see, feel, and know that your departed friends still live; and, because they live, receive the assurance that ye shall live also."

The riddle of the universe is read, the mystery of ages is revealed; the question that we have been asking with tearful eyes for long millenniums is answered in the affirmative, and we are men for the ages to come. Tell the Indian it was not all a delusion that his medicine-man taught him: the Indian lives where the pale-face interferes not with his domain, and the hell of the Christian is unknown. There is a paradise for the Mohammedan better suited to his soul's needs than the one promised by Mohammed to the faithful.

What Socrates hoped for, Jesus taught, and Paul believed, we know. Death is swallowed up in life, joyful life.

Who are the witnesses? No long-dead Peter, Matthew, or John, but living men and women, who can be questioned. Not three or four, of whom some may have been doubters; but unnumbered thousands, spread over the broad land, some of whom may be met and cross-questioned every day. Not merely the ignorant and superstitious, like the fishermen of Galilee, who seem to have been prepared for any story, however marvellous, but sceptics like the Owens, Hare, and Elliotson; such men and women as Thackeray, the Howitts and Halls, Dr. Ashburner, Lord Lyndhurst, Alfred R. Wallace, Epes Sargent, Prof. Gunning, Prof. Mapes, Drs. Hallock and Brittan, William Lloyd Garrison, Archbishop Whately and hosts of others, many of whom were convinced notwithstanding the strongest prejudice against it. Ministers in Orthodox pulpits have seen and believed, and preach now with a power on the subject of future life such as Christianity never could give. Sceptics the most determined have found their scepticism melting like snow before the sun of this truth.

Intelligent witnesses indeed we have, numbering hundreds of thousands, whose word upon any ordinary subject would be taken at once; and, if the fact of spiritual intercourse cannot be established, it is in vain to attempt to establish any very remarkable fact by human testimony.

Christianity is a miraculous religion. The earth and man are miraculously created; the earth will be miraculously destroyed; and man will miraculously die, since the constitution of man at first was such that he would not have died if God had not cursed him. He is to be miraculously raised from the dead by the miraculously begotten and resurrected Jesus. Future life is consequently miraculous: "It is the gift of God;" and those only can live to whom it is given.

All this is sadly out of joint: it fails to harmonize with what we know of Nature in the past, and hence we may fairly presume that it does with what is to be in the future. Men are learning that the earth came to be as it is by the operation of law, and man came in like manner. As his life here came naturally, so comes his life hereafter. The spirit lives when the body dies, by virtue of its nature: it cannot do otherwise. Immortality is not the gift of a jealous Jehovah, who may, in a fit of anger, withhold it, and drop us into nonentity: we live as the sun shines, because it is its nature.

It is no wonder that a religion so interwoven with miracle miraculously changes all persons at death, so as to destroy their individuality, and give future existence not to the same individuals, but to the beings into whom they have been thus changed. Heaven is the miraculous home of the righteous few, hell the miraculous prison for the wicked many. The good alone are to be admitted to heaven; no unclean thing can enter it: but, since all men are partly good and partly bad, all who enter there must be so changed as to be quite different individuals. What wife would recognize her quick-tempered husband, what husband would know his fretful wife, when two immaculate angels had taken their places? Where are the good fit for the heaven of the New Testament? From Abel, who was slain because he was more righteous than his brother, to Washington, the patron saint of America, there never was a good man, — never a man who did not lie, who did not at some time become angry, who was not envious or jealous or mean. If none but the good go to heaven, then it is as empty as an Orthodox church on week-days, and God is a king without a subject. Nor are there any bad men: from Cain, who murdered his brother, to Arnold, who tried to murder his country, there never was a man all bad, — one in whose heart pity never dwelt, from whose purse charity never drew a cent, nor pity from his eye a tear; who never spoke the truth when it was possible to lie, nor said a kind word or did a good deed during his miserable life. If none but the bad are sent to hell, that is just as empty as heaven.

A religion that teaches such a doctrine as this cannot be a finality. Science in this nineteenth century says to Miracle, "Away, hag of the night!" and she hides her deformed countenance. We have rent the veil of miracle that hid from us the orderly operations of Nature, and everywhere we see law and its manifestations; and, in harmony with that, we also see that men must be themselves, if there is to be any future life for them. All human beings are mixed: the sheep are not destitute of hair and beard, and might be at times mistaken for goats; the goats are not without wool, and some have a striking resemblance to sheep. From the best man to the worst, there is an infinite gradation; and Omnipotence itself can draw no line between the bad to be doomed to a Christian hell, and the good doomed to a Christian heaven. The natural consequences of our misdeeds, in a realm without miracle, cling to us, — as much a part of us as our memory ; and not even God can rob us of the fruit of our good actions, ours to enjoy while life endures. At one blow, away go the Christian's hell and heaven : they are foreign to the universe ; and in their place we have a spiritual realm for all, where the good-doer can rejoice in the society of the philanthropic, and with them lay plans for humanity's benefit, and where the evil-doer may learn the folly of his ways, cease to do evil, learn to do well, and reap the reward of well-doing.

The temporary nature of Christianity is plainly indicated by *its indorsement of the Old Testament.* Jesus was never able entirely to outgrow the prejudices of his Jewish education. " One jot or one tittle," says he, " shall in no wise pass from the law, till all be fulfilled." " The scribes and Pharisees sit in Moses' seat : all, therefore, whatsoever they bid you observe, that observe and do." As if the doctrine of these Jewish law-expounders was all divine ! Jesus refers to the old stories of the Jewish Bible as if he believed them ; and he evidently did : and even takes the marvellous tale of Jonah for true, and refers to prophecies of himself in the Old Testament which certainly have no existence. It is no wonder, when Swedenborg, in many respects a superior man to Jesus, was never able to shake off the biblical shackles in which his sectarian education had bound him.

Christianity, therefore, indorses the Old Testament, and drags around this shockingly offensive corpse, that is a stench in the nostrils of all intelligent and unprejudiced people. It takes this old bottle of Judaism, and puts into it the new, and in some respects better, religion of Jesus, and, in consequence, destroys its flavor, and renders it unfit for our acceptance.

Following in their Master's footsteps, the Christians of the present day not only indorse the Old Testament and its absurdities, but also the New Testament, with some absurdities greater than the writers of the Old ever dreamed of. To be wiser than the Bible is to the true Christian impossible: to teach that it can ever be superseded is blasphemy. It is his chart; and by it he will be guided, though his judgment tells him that it is wrong a thousand times a day.

What would be thought of the geographer who should found a class in geography based upon the old atlas of Ptolemy; every one of the class signing a declaration that Ptolemy's atlas was constructed by God himself, and contained all of geography that it was necessary for man to know? What progress could they ever make? How they would fight against every new geographical discovery, and denounce every discoverer as a heretic! What an arch infidel Columbus would have been regarded by such a class in his day! Thus it was, in the time of Galileo, with the Bible believers. No sooner did he discover in the heavens what could not be found in the Bible, than he was cast into prison as a reward for his superior knowledge. To-day, such men as Darwin, Vogt, Huxley, and Spencer are looked upon with suspicion, and denounced, because they have discovered new realms that the Bible does not describe, and that make it evident that a great deal which the Bible does describe is false. They have learned that Nature is infinitely wider than the Bible writers ever dreamed, and exceedingly different from their representations; and they may expect to be cursed by all who have sworn to be no wiser than the men of two thousand years ago.

We must say to the Bible, "Henceforth you take your place by the side of all other books. We are not to be deceived by your expanded size, your embossed covers, nor your gilded leaves. You must be content to be treated as we treat Milton's 'Paradise Lost,' Shakspeare's 'Plays,' and Bunyan's 'Pilgrim's Progress.'" And to Jesus, "You can no longer be our master. We do not object to you as a brother or a teacher: as such we will place you with Socrates, Plato, and Confucius, — just as good men in their way as you were in yours. You must not come between us and Nature, our mother, — just as much ours as yours. The man who pretends to possess a monopoly of Heaven's favors, and, in the name of God, lords it over his fellows, is either self-deceived or an impostor; and in either case is a very poor guide." To the Jewish Jehovah, "You are as truly an idol as the gods denounced in your name: they were the work of men's hands, and you of men's brains. You never made the world, or you could have informed us how you made it. Neither you nor your Son ever redeemed the world, for it is not redeemed; and the deliverance that has come to it has come in a very different channel from yours. You have long enough been a stumbling-block in the world's pathway: we move you to one side, that the car of progress may advance."

The indorsement of the divinity of the old Jewish records has been the curse of Christianity from its commencement. It prevented the disciples of Jesus from preaching it among the Samaritans and Gentiles during the lifetime of its founder; and, had it not been for the partial emancipation of Paul, it would have strangled it at its birth. It has produced a continual warfare between it and science, which will without doubt end in its death. It curses Unitarianism and Universalism to-day. They are trying to run with heavy Jewish shackles on their legs and this ponderous Bible on their backs. Brethren, drop your Bibles; if they cannot go alone, leave them behind: snap your Jewish shackles; unite with all who are laboring to benefit humanity, taking and giving the utmost freedom: then failure will be as impossible as success is now.

With the indorsement of the Old Testament comes the acceptance by Christianity of the Jewish Divinity; and I know of no worse feature of it than this. Originally the idol of a petty tribe of sheep and cattle breeders of Judea, Jehovah became the God of Abraham, Isaac, and Jacob, and their descendants. As they extended their domain by force of arms, so extended the kingdom of their Divinity, and his name became a terror to the nations round about; while the Jews credited him with all that their superior knowledge, craft, and cruelty enabled them to accomplish. The common sentiment of the Jewish nation at an early period is well exemplified in a song attributed to Moses, and which occurs in the fifteenth chapter of Exodus: "He is my God, and I will prepare him a habitation; my father's God, and I will exalt him. The Lord is a man of war: the Lord is his name." In accordance with this, they called him "the Lord of hosts," or, in other words, the Lord of armies, and the "Lord mighty in battle." A similar sentiment was shared in by the nations round about them, who had each divinities that they worshipped and prayed to, and to whom all their victories were ascribed.

What has the soul of the universe to do with this petty, jealous, vacillating, malignant, cruel idol of the Jews? The spirit that shines in the sun; that throbs in the heart of the distant nebula to form solar systems, as it does in that of the unborn child to form the man; that, out of the fiery hell of the world primeval, has developed plant, fish, reptile, brute, and man, and is urging the world on in that grand career of progress whose magnificent future may be estimated by its mighty past, — what relation is the sacrifice-loving, roasted-oxen-smelling deity of the Jews to this spirit? No more than Jupiter or Juno.

Jehovah is a being who cursed the earth and the entire race because the first pair fell, when he knew beforehand that they had not the ability to stand; he found the world of one language and of one speech, and, in a fit of jealousy lest they should build a tower to heaven and invade his domain, cursed them with a thousand different tongues, so that they could not understand each other's speech; he tempted Abraham to murder his own son, and, when he showed his readiness to commit the infamous crime, he blessed him, and represents him as the best man upon earth, because he was most willing to do the worst deed. He is a God that transmuted a woman into a pillar of salt, because she looked back upon her burning home, and lingeringly left her friends to perish; who hardened Pharoah's heart so that he should not let the people of Israel go, and then slew millions of innocent Egyptians because he was so hard-hearted that he would not let them go; he gave to the Jews the grand charter of death, — no Camanche chief's war-speech was ever worse, — "Thou shalt save alive nothing that breatheth." He has sent all mankind into the world with a strong disposition to do evil; he allows the Devil and his agents to tempt men, and thus make them worse than they are naturally, and then has so arranged matters, that, if they persist in doing what he calls evil, he will plunge them into a den of woe, from which there is no escape, but from which the smoke of their torment is to ascend for ever and ever. And we are told that it is our duty to love this monster that the Jew made and the Christian has remodelled. Tell the captive pining in his dungeon to love the tyrant that placed him there; tell the slave to love the master who has robbed him of his rights since he began to breathe, and whose back is yet bloody from the blows of his lash; tell the mother to love the fiend who has slain her darling, and now gloats over her agony. As impossible is it for us to love this Devil-creator, this plaguer of the human race, this framer and jailer of hell, and tormentor of the damned. Reason will not, cannot, call him father; Love shrinks with terror from his presence; and Justice says, "Let him die, for he is unworthy to live." The gods of silver and gold, of iron and brass, will perish; the gods of wood and stone shall be no more, and their worshippers shall be ashamed of their folly: and so shall this grim, blood-besprinkled, eternally hating and torturing Jehovah die, and a million ransomed souls join in swelling to heaven his funeral-hymn.

The transient character of the Christian religion is clearly manifested by *its intolerance.* Jesus said, "He that believeth and is baptized shall be saved: he that believeth not shall be damned;" and, so saying, he opened the doors of persecution as wide as the Christian faith. He sowed the seed that fruited in creeds and curses, prisons, chains, blazing fagots, and all the horrors of the Inquisition; he created hell, and placed it in the hands of priests to curse the world for ages. "If men are to be damned for a wrong faith," says the conscientious Christian, "we must do our best to provide them with a right faith, and to prevent the spread of what may damn them; and, since persecution will do this, we must persecute. Better by far to burn one man here, than that a thousand should burn hereafter." Calvin, who burnt Servetus, acted most conscientiously, I have no doubt; for his course was in perfect harmony with his faith. If the apostles had possessed the power, they would, doubtless, have exercised it in a similar manner. Hear Paul: "If any man love not *the Lord Jesus Christ, let him be anathema maranatha.*" Behind that lie thumb-screw, rack, and gibbet. Again: "If any man preach any other gospel unto you than that ye have received, let him be accursed." In other words, "Damn every man that preaches not our gospel;" which is a literal translation of his curse. Even the gentle John, the preacher of love, says, "If there come any unto you, and bring not this doctrine, receive him not into your house, neither bid him God speed." And the next step is easily taken, and legitimately follows: "Take him into your prison, and thus prevent the dissemination of his 'damnable heresies,'" — a New-Testament phrase, born of intolerance. As Christianity denounces the most fearful penalties for unbelief, so has it been the most persecuting and intolerant of all religions; and those among Christians who are farthest from this, as the Unitarians and Universalists, are farthest from primitive, genuine Christianity.

As soon as Christianity became strong enough to wield the sword, in harmony with its faith, it commenced a crusade against philosophy, and established a reign of terror over all who dared to think otherwise than as the church directed. Draper says of the Christian Church in the reign of Constantine, "They denounced as magic, or the sinful pursuit of vain trifling, all the learning that stood in the way. It was intended to cut off every philosopher. Every manuscript that could be seized was forthwith burned. Throughout the East, men, in terror, destroyed their libraries, for fear that some unfortunate sentence contained in any of the books should involve them and their families in destruction. The universal opinion was, that it was right to compel men to believe what the majority of society had now accepted as the truth; and, if they refused, it was right to punish them. No one was heard in the dominating party to raise his voice in behalf of intellectual liberty." Certainly not: this would be to tolerate another gospel, and open the door to all heresy, which might be the cause of eternal misery to millions. The belief that our future destiny is to be decided by our faith, so strenuously insisted upon by Christianity, has made Christians the most relentless persecutors the world has known. The pagan Romans, who never supposed that a false faith would damn men, were tolerant of all religions that did not interfere with the State. Since the religion that denounces most vehemently and threatens the most terrible tortures has the greatest advantage among the ignorant, who can fear when they cannot reason, Christianity spread, crowded out and destroyed paganism and philosophy, set up its tortures, and for centuries applied them. It is true that Christians do not so persecute to-day: but the reason is evident; they are more intelligent, and have less power. By the operation of irresistible law, the world has advanced, and superstition has been left behind in the march; and thus Christianity and its intolerant spirit are fast being superseded, and they shall rule the world no more.

Christianity favors sectarianism and priestcraft. In Judaism, the priest is the most imposing figure: dressed in his sacerdotal robes, he is the visible manifestation of the deity, and commands the reverence of all worshippers. Jesus called himself Lord and Master, and his followers have not been slow to imitate him; and, if the priest is not the great I AM, he is the little I am, and heathen all who reject the gospel he preaches. He prays in the name of the congregation, whom he calls "my people:" "We thank thee, O God," "we beseech thee;" and most of his people think that he is much nearer to God than themselves, so that, when sick, they send for him to pray, his prayers are so much more potent than their own. A man in the Christian church is a man bound to be no wiser than its creed, no broader than its intolerant spirit, no better than its impractical founder. As soon as he attempts to be any of these, the church's anathema is fulminated against him: he has committed the sin unpardonable.

I hail spiritualism as a deliverer from this priestcraft, this ecclesiastical bondage, an opener of prison-doors to the captives, and the usherer in of a new era for humanity. Here is no Moses communing with

God, who shows him his glory, but tells him to keep back the crowd, for, if they break through, they shall perish; no Jesus, the true door, denouncing all who enter some other way as thieves and robbers; no pope extending his pedal digits to be embraced by the sots of superstition; not even a priest to say "my people:" for communion with the spirit-world is open to all classes, — children of seven and old people of seventy. Peasants who never read a line are as highly favored as college-bred professors; and the sinner, in this respect, is as highly favored as the saint.

We have sects enough: why multiply them? Too long have we allowed men who never had any more authority than ourselves to drive down the stakes and enclose us within a creed-made fold. Luther found the pasture bare, or nothing left but bitter weeds; the streams soiled by the feet of millions and the impurities of ages: he looked over the pale, saw the fertile prairie in its virgin beauty, the best of pasturage, living streams flowing through it, and said to the hungry, thirsty, dog-bitten crowd, "Out where the living waters flow, and the pastures illimitable invite us to the feast." And out went a host, but only to drive down new stakes and enclose another flock. Wesley broke down the ecclesiastical barrier, and took the liberty to look for better fare; but no sooner had he found it, than the stake-drivers were set to work, the field enclosed, and the sheep solemnly warned against straying outside of the fold, where the wolves lurk to devour the straying lambs of the flock. Having taken the field for ourselves, we must allow all others the same privilege. Do not imagine, that, because we have outgrown Christianity, we have attained the highest and best of which the race is capable; that we have learned it all, and may henceforth embody our views in a creed, build our churches, and stand at the door and bark at all outsiders. We have done little more than master the alphabet of knowledge: its literature is all but unread.

Organizations we must have for work: let them be a thousand times multiplied. We must unite, or do but little of what is so much needed: but let it be a union of free men, not for the extension of a sect, but for the enlightenment and upbuilding of mankind; in that finding our satisfaction and sufficient reward, and rejoicing in all movements that aid this, by whoever made. Sectarians look at every thing as it affects their sect: if it will help that, then they will assist it; if it will injure their sect, however much it may benefit the race, "Curse it!" they cry: "for it blesses not us!" Thus the strongest sectarians have been the most deadly foes of progress.

We must stand where we can rejoice at all progress: whatever blesses mankind cannot but be worthy of our regard. We shall herald instead of denouncing reform. We shall aid temperance, labor-reform, social science, human suffrage, and all other progressive movements: they are agencies operated by the members of our grand church of humanity. We shall unite with those who do not recognize existence after death: they are our brethren also, — many of them most noble and true, who have stood by the truth amid obloquy, reproach, scorn, and bitter persecution. I can belong to no church that excludes them or any others who are honestly laboring to benefit the race.

Spiritualists need carefully to guard against making

spirits authority. The world abounds with lazy people, who do not wish the trouble of making up their minds, and are glad to have spirits do this for them. What the spirit says is swallowed as unadulterated gospel; and one idol, the Bible, cast down, only that another many-headed monster may take its place. Nothing can relieve us from the necessity of thinking. We must allow nothing to take us off the solid ground of reason, or growth is impossible.

Nothing can absolve us from the obligations of morality, the duties which we naturally owe to ourselves and others. We must prove that we have a better religion by living better lives. When ecclesiastical bonds are being snapped, people are sometimes ready to discard even the authority of Nature herself, and disregard the laws upon obedience to which our own and others' well-being depend. Spirits cannot prevent the consequences of wrong-doing from falling upon the head of the guilty; and a spiritualist sinner will be made to suffer as certainly as an Orthodox good-doer will be rewarded. With increasing intelligence, we shall learn that the wisest man is he who knows the most of what Nature teaches; and the best man, he who most faithfully reduces her lessons to practice.

Our vessel is afloat; the sails are set; heaven wafts a prosperous gale. Science is our compass, Reason our pilot, and angels point the way. Already the goodly land appears in view. See its sunny slopes! We can even hear its music in faint tones, as it comes wafted over the breakers. There stand the friends that in youth we loved, on whose cold graves we dropped a tear. They beckon to us! No dark cloud obscures our vision ; no mist like a curtain hides from us the home of the soul. We do not say, " I hope to join you, if God will but help me for the sake of Jesus ;" but we boldly say, " Ye, my brethren, live and love, and we shall live and love also ! "

GOD PROPOSED.

THE GOD PROPOSED FOR OUR NATIONAL CONSTITUTION.

It is said, that, "once upon a time," the frogs were desirous of having a king. On looking around for a suitable individual, they spied a fat ox feeding in the meadow. Admiring his majestic appearance, they sent a deputation to wait upon him, and ask him to accept the position. The ox, nothing loath, strode down to the marsh, and was properly installed king of frogdom. His happy subjects crowded around him to present their congratulations; but, unfortunately for them, as he moved his ponderous body to return the compliments that were croaked from every side, beneath his royal hoofs lay a dozen of his loyal subjects crushed to the earth. Too late they discovered that an ox, though a fine-looking animal, is no fit monarch for frogs.

Before we think of placing a God in the Constitution of these United States, it must be well to examine the character of the individual proposed for the position, or we may find ourselves in the condition of the frogs in the fable; death following every step of our God, and we powerless to stop the destruction.

Up to the present time, I have heard of but one God who has been proposed for the highest of all offices in the gift of the people; and that is the Christian's God, whom Jesus declared to be the God of Abraham, Isaac, and Jacob. The God, then, that we are asked to make the God of these United States, is Jehovah, the God of the Jews, whose sayings and deeds are recorded in their so-called sacred books and in the Christian Scriptures, from which we can, fortunately, obtain a knowledge of his actual character. It is furnished, if we are to believe what these books say, by himself and his friends, it is true; and this must be taken into account, as we may suppose them to represent him in a more favorable light than the facts will really warrant.

Moses gives us a portrait of him that is very beautiful: "He is the Rock; his work is perfect; for all his ways are judgment; a God of truth and without iniquity, just and right is he" (Deut. xxxii. 4). What an excellent example to place before the officers of our government! Of himself he says, "The Lord God is merciful and gracious, long-suffering, and abundant in goodness and truth" (Exod. xxxiv. 6). Who could object to such a God as this? He needs but to be known to be loved, but to be heard to be obeyed. It may be well, however, to see whether his deeds correspond with his words. Men accepted for what they claim to be, and State-prison convicts are patterns of all excellency. It may possibly be so with gods. Let us see.

Jehovah informs Adam (Gen. ii. 17), that, if he shall eat of the fruit of the tree of knowledge, in the day that he eats of it he shall surely die. But, instead of dying in that day, Adam lived more than nine hundred years afterward. Could Jehovah have made a mistake? That is, of course, impossible. Did he really intend to deceive the man? Was not some other kind of death meant? If truthful in every other respect, we will give him the benefit of the doubt; but, if otherwise, we shall suspect him, to say the least.

According to the sixteenth chapter of 1st Samuel, Jehovah told Samuel to go to Jesse the Bethlehemite, and anoint one of his sons, whom he had provided for king over Israel, in the place of Saul. But Samuel replies, "How can I go? If Saul hear it, he will kill me." Saul was king, and he would kill the man who thus sought to put another man in his place. Now, mark the advice of Jehovah: "And the Lord said, Take a heifer with thee, and say, I am come to sacrifice to the Lord." Was it for that Jehovah wished him to go? No such thing; but to anoint David king. What was he to take the heifer for? To deceive Saul, and thus escape the consequences of his deed by lying. You may call that a white lie. The crime of lying consists in the deception practised; and in this respect it was as black as any lie. The difference between that and an ordinary lie is, that it was a mean, cowardly lie. The man who tells an out-and-out lie stands on his feet when he tells it; but the man who tells a lie like that crawls on the ground like a snake. I have no respect for cowards, be they men or gods. How much better it would have been for Jehovah to say to Samuel, "Tell the truth, and I will attend to the consequences"! or, better still, "If you are afraid to do what I tell you, let it alone, and I will find a more courageous man"!

If we are to have a constitutional God of the United States, I think it will be generally acknowledged that he should be a *truthful God*. I know that politicians, as a class, care but little about truth, unless it can be made to subserve their purposes. I know that partisan newspapers, especially just before election, care as little about truth as a hungry hyena does about grace before meat. I know, also, that many priests and orthodox tract-society managers are not very scrupulous about lying, when they think it will help "the Lord's cause." This I know: but the body of the people love truth; feed on lies only because the truth is withheld from them; and, if they are to have a national God, want, as they must surely need, a God of truth; one who will neither lie himself, nor induce others to lie. I object to Jehovah, then, as our God, because *he is a liar.*

After the separation of Abram and Lot, Jehovah told Abram to walk through the length and breadth of the land of Canaan, and said, "All the land which thou seest, to thee I will give it, and to thy seed forever" (Gen. xiii. 15). He made this promise still more definite subsequently by saying, "Unto thy seed have I given this land, from the river of Egypt unto the great river, the River Euphrates" (Gen. xv. 18). The promise made and sworn to by Jehovah to Abraham was repeated to Isaac and Jacob. How was it fulfilled? Abraham himself never received a foot of it (Acts vii. 5). Nearly five hundred years passed away before his seed commenced the conquest of the promised country; and so slowly did it proceed, that it was not till nearly four hundred years after this that even Zion, the stronghold of Jerusalem, was taken from the Jebusites (2 Sam. v. 7); and less than four hundred years after this the kingdom of Judah was overthrown by Nebuchadnezzar (Jer. lii.). To-day the nine thousand

Jews that dwell in Palestine are foreigners; and they may see what the promises of Jehovah are worth, and how little dependence is to be placed upon his word. Even in the latter part of David's reign, and that of Solomon's, when the country of the Israelites was most extended, the northern part of the promised territory was in the hands of the Phœnicians and the Syrians, while the southern part was held by the Philistines and the Eygptians.

"From Dan to Beersheba," which designated the length of Canaan, even near the close of David's reign (2 Chr. xxi. 2), is only about a hundred and forty miles; while the distance from the river of Egypt to the Euphrates, the land promised to the seed of Abraham, is between five and six hundred miles. The little that the Israelites did possess was only for a few years at a time, fitful occupancy of a small territory, obtained by theft and murder, only held by continual fighting, and which they have lost possession of for more than two thousand years. This Jehovah, who thus swore to the fathers and lied to the children, is the very last of all gods to be chosen by a people who love truth, and desire it to become universal.

The same Jehovah lied to David and his descendants, lied plainly and unequivocally. In the 89th Psalm we read, "I have made a covenant with my chosen, I have sworn unto David my servant, Thy seed will I establish forever, and build up thy throne to all generations." And again, "His seed also will I make to endure forever, and his throne as the days of heaven." But the most definite promise is this: "If his children forsake my law, and walk not in my judgments; if they break my statutes, and keep not my commandments; then will I visit their transgressions with the rod, and their iniquity with stripes. Nevertheless, my loving-kindness will I not utterly take from him, nor suffer my faithfulness to fail. My covenant will I not break, nor alter the thing that is gone out of my lips. Once have I sworn by my holiness that I will not lie unto David. His seed shall endure forever, and his throne as the sun before me. It shall be established forever as the moon, and as a faithful witness in heaven."

If the sun had endured no longer than David's throne, we had never been; and, if the moon had been no better established, we had never seen it.

Long after this, when there seemed to be danger of the utter destruction of the kingdom of Judah, the promise is repeated to Jeremiah (Jer. xxxiii. 17): "Thus saith the Lord: David shall never want a man to sit upon the throne of the house of Israel; neither shall the priests the Levites want a man before me to offer burnt-offerings and to kindle meat-offerings, and to do sacrifice continually." Again he says, "If ye can break my covenant of the day, and my covenant of the night, and that there should not be day and night in their season; then may also my covenant be broken with David my servant, that he should not have a son to reign upon his throne; and with the Levites the priests, my ministers."

Let us see how these unconditional promises, from the God that would not lie to David, were fulfilled. David reigned about forty years, then Solomon forty; but his son Rehoboam lost the government of ten tribes, which were ruled over by Jeroboam, a man in no way related to David. And the kingdom of Judah, as the government of the remaining tribes, Judah and Benjamin, was then called, lasted under the dynasty of David about four hundred years, till Nebuchadnezzar destroyed Jerusalem, carried the people into captivity, and destroyed "the throne of David."

What kind of a forever is five hundred years? When Jehovah told Jeremiah that David should never want a man to sit upon his throne, he must have known, that within ten years, at the outside, there would be no throne of David to sit on. It is said that he who will swear will lie; and it appears to be as true of gods as men. Where is the throne of David to-day, that was to be as the sun before Jehovah? Where are the Levites offering burnt-offerings? and where are they doing sacrifice continually?

The condition of the Jew among us, which has been appealed to as a proof of the truth of the Bible, is one of the strongest evidences of the untruth of Jehovah. Destitute of a nation, destitute of the ceremonials of his ancient faith, he shows us the sad consequences of the trust of his race in the promise-making, but no less promise-breaking, Jehovah, who has ruined one nation, and whom traitors to freedom are inviting to ruin this country also, — the only refuge for the God-cursed of all lands.

Some children lie in their infancy, but, when their reasoning faculties become active, see the impropriety of it, and thenceforth speak the truth; but Jehovah does not seem to improve in this respect with age. I find Paul stating (2 Thess. ii. 11), that, because certain people would not receive the love of the truth, God should send them strong delusion, that they should believe a lie, that they all might be damned.

The God that Paul believed in was Jehovah; and, because people do not love the truth, he will lie to them, that they may believe the lie, and be damned! How much love of truth has that Being who adopts such lying measures? how much justice has he who lies to people, and then damns them because they believe him? and how much propriety is there in putting this lying Jehovah into our national Constitution?

Bad as was the treatment that the Jews received at the hands of Jehovah, it was the best ever vouchsafed by him to any people: for he is a *partial God;* and I bring this as another objection against him. He chooses Abram, out of all the Arab chiefs of his time, to be the father of his peculiar people; he loves Jacob rather than Esau, and that before either of them is born, "that the purpose of God, according to election, might stand," as Paul tells us. He chose the Israelites from all the nations of the earth, delivered them from Egypt by a series of most astounding miracles, blew a passage for them through the Red Sea, fed them with bread from heaven, and sent quails by the million, caused water to spring from the solid rock, and for forty years never allowed the clothes on their backs nor the shoes on their feet to grow old or worn. He says, "The Lord thy God hath chosen thee to be a special people unto himself, above all people that are on the face of the earth" (Deut. vii. 6). And again: "You only have I known of all the families of the earth" (Amos iii. 2). The peaceful and industrious Chinese, the philosophic Hindoos, the intelligent and religious Egyptians, the brave Assyrians, and the artistic Greeks, Jehovah never knew; for them he never cared. In the darkness, a thousand million of God's neglected sons groped through the centuries; but this handful of Israelites, his beloved children, lived in a blaze of divine glory, and were permitted, nay, commanded, to butcher their brothers who would not become their slaves, and bow down and worship their little-souled and partial God; and those who are moving for the Jehovah amendment in the Constitution not only worship this unjust Divinity, but seem to be desirous to compel their more enlightened and more manly neighbors to worship him also.

This country justly prides itself upon its general intelligence. The few do not shoot up like pines, and the many squat like toad-stools. The average culture of the people of the Northern States, at least, is probably as great as or greater than that of any other country on the globe. If we are to have a God for our nation, he should be an intelligent God, or how can intelligent people respect him? I object, then, to Jehovah, because he is an *ignorant God*, — so ignorant of geography, that he does not know either the shape of the earth or its size, and supposed that a forty-days' rain would drown it (Gen. vii. 4). He knows so little of astronomy, that he supposes the earth to be the universe, to which the heavens hold the same relation as a curtain does to a bed (Isa. xl. 22). He thinks the stars are "set" in this stretched curtain; and when he shall roll it up, as he threatens to do at some time, he supposes the stars will fall to the earth (Isa. xxxiv. 4; Rev. vi. 13). He has so little knowledge of the number of species of animals on the globe, that he supposed Noah could preserve, in a box about five hundred feet long, less than one hundred broad, and about fifty high, seven of every kind of bird, male and female, and two of every other kind of animal, and provisions for them for twelve months; one-fourth of which could never have got into it. He is so ignorant of zoölogy, that he tells the Israelites they must not eat the hare, because it chews the cud (Lev. xi. 6), — a thing that no hare does; thus mistaking a rodent for a ruminant. He knows so little of geology, that he supposes the earth was made less than six thousand years ago, and brought into a condition similar to the present in less than a week; and is so ignorant of the history of man, whom he pretends to have made, that he supposes all human beings descended from a single pair, who were made long after the valley of the Nile was occupied by civilized people; and then, to crown his imbecility, threatens man with damnation unless he believes that of which he fails to give him sufficient evidence. There is not a boy of fourteen years of age in any New-England grammar-school who does not know more than this Jewish Jehovah is represented in the Bible as knowing; and a man so ignorant would be a laughing-stock to his whole neighborhood. The Hottentots of Africa might debate whether a God as ignorant should be admitted into the constitution of their government; but the men who propose him for the United-States Constitution are the deadliest enemies of intelligence.

As a nation, the United States has been a grand success. The fathers of our country undertook to form a republic uncursed by kings and government priests; where all men could have liberty of conscience, for all religious faiths should be equal in the eye of the law. They sought to make a home for the oppressed, the king-cursed, the poverty-stricken, of all lands; and they did it. We undertook to rid the land of slavery, that it might be in spirit, as in name, the land of the free; and we have done it. Much remains to be done to make this country what the wisest and best desire: and, if we are to have a God for the country, it should be one who has been successful; one in whom we can have confidence that he will help us to succeed in carrying out still needed reforms. I object, then, to Jehovah, because *he has utterly failed in nearly every thing that he has undertaken.* Hell only exists in consequence of the failure of heaven. The very first human beings that Jehovah made failed so utterly, that he cursed them almost as soon as they were out of his hands. The world that he had made, and pronounced good, was such a dead failure, that it grieved him at his heart, and he destroyed it, and tried it over again with scarcely any better success. He chose the Israelites, that they might be a holy people unto him; yet they turned out to be the vilest of wretches, and made him so angry, that he cursed them in his wrath, and destroyed them in his fury. Mankind failed so utterly, that he left heaven to save them; and for this purpose became a Jewish baby, and subsequently a carpenter and a preacher; allowed men to kill him, and then sent his disciples unto all the world to tell people that they might be saved by believing the story. Yet so bunglingly did he manage the whole matter, that not one in fifty of the world's population since that time has ever believed the account; and the more intelligent people become, the less inclined they are to believe it, and the more certain they are to be damned, — the very fate from which Jehovah professes to have undertaken to deliver them, — and the myriads of hell's victims are to howl his failure to all eternity.

Shall we suffer a God who so mismanages his own affairs to manage ours? Obey such a God as this, and we should soon be in the condition of his chosen people when they wished to return to the Egypt they had fled from, or as they were when he sold them into the hands of Nebuchadnezzar.

One reason of Jehovah's want of success may be that *he is vacillating*, — lacking that strong will, governed by intelligence, which moves toward its object without flinching, because wisdom has determined the course marked out to be the best.

"It repented the Lord that he had made man on the earth, and it grieved him at his heart" (Gen. vi. 6). It is therefore presumable, that, if he had known how he would turn out, he never would have made him. After leading the Israelites into the wilderness, they so provoked him, that he declared he would smite them with the pestilence, and disinherit them; and would have done it, apparently, had not Moses expostulated with him, and led this vacillating Divinity to "repent of the evil that he thought to do unto his people" (Exod. xxxii. 14). Moses saw, that, if he did this, his reputation among other nations would be destroyed; and, on presenting this view of the matter to Jehovah, he appears to have seen the wisdom of the suggestion. A prime-minister often knows more than a king; and a prophet, we see, may be more intelligent than the God that sends him.

Jehovah sent word to Hezekiah, "Set thine house in order; for thou shalt die, and not live" (Isa. xxxviii.). But Hezekiah, as many others would have done, felt as if he would rather live than die: he said, "Remember now, O Lord! I beseech thee, how I have walked before thee in truth and with a perfect heart, and have done that which is good in thy sight. And Hezekiah wept sore." This appears to have led to a reconsideration of the matter on the part of Jehovah, and he sent word to him that he had lengthened his days fifteen years.

We read that the Ninevites at one time offended Jehovah greatly, and he sent Jonah to announce to them their unconditional destruction. Jonah was unwilling to go; and it required a three-days' residence in a whale to make him obedient to the heavenly voice. When "he reached Nineveh, he went through the streets crying, Yet forty days, and Nineveh shall be overthrown." But, at the preaching of this foreign prophet, the whole city repented, and fasted, and "cried mightily unto God;" and then God repented, and concluded to spare the repentant city, regardless of the feelings of Jonah, who thought he was badly used. If Jehovah knew the end from the beginning, he must have known that the Ninevites would repent, and the city be spared; and I think Jonah had just ground of complaint in being sent there with that lie in his mouth.

What confidence can we have in a God who is grieved at his heart at the foreseen consequences of his own actions, and undoes in a day what it took him more than a thousand years to accomplish, and then, after it is over, promises that he will not do it again? (Gen. viii. 21.)

I object to Jehovah's name in our national Constitution also, because he is a *male God*, and neither has, nor ever had, any female associated with him in the divine government. He is a stern father, chastising in anger every unrepentant son. But where is the tender-hearted mother, that with a kiss receives the erring child to her bosom, and melts him into repentance with her tears? God the Father, God the Son, God the Holy Ghost; three unmarried males, constituting a monkish trinity, from all eternity to all eternity. I object to him (them) as utterly unfit to reign over us, and especially when women shall have their political rights; and the day cannot be far distant. This is the God who thunders in the ears of the first woman, "Thy desire shall be to thy husband, and he shall rule over thee;" who made man first, and woman only because man needed somebody to help him; who set a trap for humanity, and baited it so that human nature could not resist the temptation, and then cursed all women because the first one went into it. A heavenly mother would never have cursed all her daughters with pain on account of the trivial fault of the first; nor would she ever have made the penalty for their misdoing unutterable woe forever. If we are to have a God in the Constitution of the United States, it must be a God in whom the sexes are equally represented, or our Government will be as one-sided as the Bible. It is altogether too much so now.

The fate of the Jews, who trusted in this Jehovah, should forever prevent us from following their example.

The Lord, we are told, delivered Israel out of the hand of the Egyptians, broke the yoke of their bondage, and became their guide to the land of promise. So near was it, that a man could have walked there in a couple of weeks; but, under the guidance of Jehovah, it took them forty years, and only two men arrived there who started from Egypt. So disgusted were the Israelites with the conduct of their God, that they desired to return to Egypt, preferring the slavery of Pharaoh to that of Jehovah. Nay, they even made a golden calf, and worshipped it in preference, and said, "These be thy gods, O Israel! that brought thee up out of the land of Egypt." And there is no doubt that the calf had as much to do with it as Jehovah. But Jehovah was so angry, that he caused the Levites, who were just as guilty as the rest, to murder three thousand of the people in consequence (Exod. xxxii. 28).

When their descendants arrived at the promised land, they were compelled to fight for many years in order to obtain possession of what Jehovah promised to give them. Whenever they failed in battle, it was because Jehovah was angry with them, of course; and, whenever they succeeded, it was because he helped them. But his help seems to have done them but little good. This is the way that he served them, as he himself has recorded for our instruction: "The anger of the Lord was hot against Israel, and he delivered them into the hands of spoilers, and he sold them into the hands of their enemies round about, so that they could not any longer stand before their enemies. Whithersoever they went out, the hand of the Lord was against them for evil; and they were sadly distressed" (Judges ii. 14, 15).

"The Lord strengthened Eglon, king of Moab, against Israel." "So the children of Israel served Eglon, king of Moab, eighteen years" (Judges iii. 12, 14).

Shall we, who have just liberated our slaves, put this Jehovah into our Constitution, who thus kidnapped a whole nation, and sold them for slaves?

"The Lord sold them into the hand of Jabin, king

of Canaan," "and twenty years he mightily oppressed the children of Israel." And so continues the disgraceful record. Out of three hundred and thirty years, in the time of the Judges, when Jehovah was their king, they were slaves, in the hands of their enemies, for one hundred and eleven years, or more than one-third of the time. We are told, it is true, that all this happened because the children of Israel did evil in the sight of Jehovah, and because they would not obey his commands; but when we read (Judges xiii. 1) that "the Lord delivered them into the hands of the Philistines forty years," the explanation is insufficient. In forty years, in a state of bondage, there could have been very few alive of those whose sins drove them into captivity; and what kind of a God can that be who kept innocent millions in slavery for the fault of a few? A sensible man would have modified his commands in the first place, or taken such measures as would have led the people to see that it was to their interest to obey them. As Jehovah did neither, he proved his unfitness to rule over the Israelites, and his infinite unfitness to rule over us.

On one occasion Jehovah sold them into the hands of the Philistines and the children of Ammon, who sorely oppressed them, so that they cried unto him. But he replied, "Ye have forsaken me, and served other gods: wherefore I will deliver you no more" (Judges x. 13). But even this was a lie; for the very next chapter tells us that the Lord delivered the children of Ammon into the hands of Jephthah, and they were subdued before the children of Israel. But the poor wretches were only delivered for a few years, to be sold again into the hands of their enemies by their Godly owner.

The Israelites did much better in the reigns of Saul, David, and Solomon, than at any previous time; for they had less to do with Jehovah, or rather with his priests, and more to do with men who understood their needs and attended to their supply. But their whole history, from the exodus to the destruction of Jerusalem, is one long, bloody trail down the ages.

Make Jehovah God of these United States, and let the people become obedient to his commands as they would be explained by his priests, and our history would be like theirs, and this paradise of liberty become a Pandemonium of tyranny, a plague-spot on the face of the earth.

A man may be known, it is said, by the company he keeps; and why not a god? Judging Jehovah by this, I cannot but regard him as utterly unfit for the office to which his American friends are so desirous of elevating him.

He is "the God of Abraham, Isaac, and Jacob." Abraham is styled in the Bible "the father of the faithful, and the friend of God;" an Arab chief, rude and hospitable, but crafty, superstitious, licentious, cowardly, and cruel. Twice he induced his wife to lie for him; and in both cases Jehovah cursed the men to whom she lied, but never rebuked either her or Abraham. He turned another wife with her child into the wilderness, where, according to the story, she would have perished, had not an angel saved her; and he receives more credit from Jehovah for his willingness to murder his son than for any other deed of his life.

Of Isaac we know but little; but, like his father Abraham, he was cowardly, lying, and selfish, putting his wife's chastity in hazard to save his life; though, as the event proved, there was no danger whatever. The blessing that he gave his son in his old age shows the character of the man. Part of it reads, " Let people serve thee, and nations bow down to thee: be lord over thy brethren, and let thy mother's sons bow down to thee." That is essentially Jewish and Jehovistic. Isaac had the same feeling for his pet son that Jehovah had for his pet nation.

Of Jacob we know considerable: he was an especial favorite of Jehovah: he loved him, if Paul is to be believed, even before he was born, and gave him, through life, many signal instances of his favor. Yet he was a liar, cheat, slaveholder, polygamist, and essentially mean man. He lied to his father, most shamefully lied, and in a way that showed him to have had large practice. He cheated his brother and his uncle; and when his sons murdered the men of a whole city, and took all the survivors captive, this is what the selfish old stock-raiser said: " Ye have troubled me to make me to stink among the inhabitants of the land; . . . . and I shall be destroyed, I and my house." No rebuke for the horrible crime committed, no word of pity for the widow and orphans; but, "*I* shall be destroyed, *I* and *my house*." "Ye have troubled *me*." If they had not troubled him, and he had been in no danger, it is evident that the deed would never have troubled him.

Yet this is the man whom Jehovah blesses, and with whom he converses; to whom he makes splendid promises, and with whom he wrestled a whole night, and lost, Jacob obtaining a blessing, which appears to have been the prize, though at the expense of a dislocated thigh.

Another of the favorites of Jehovah was Moses, a man, apparently, of a good deal of mental ability for the time in which he lived, and proud of his nation, yet crafty, harsh, exacting, and blood-thirsty. He murdered an Egyptian, fled to Midian, married the daughter of a Midianite priest, and lived there for forty years. One might suppose that he would have had some respect for the people of this land of his adoption. Yet, on the journey through the wilderness, he sent an army against Midian, that slew every man, but saved alive the widows, babies, and girls. As they returned from the massacre with the weeping captives, Moses meets them, and cries out, "Have ye saved all the women alive? Now, therefore, kill every male among the little ones, and kill every woman that hath known man by lying with him:" the girls they were to keep alive for themselves. What Camanche chief ever committed a greater atrocity than this? And yet he was one of Jehovah's favorites, talking with him for hours together as familiarly as one man talks with another.

After the death of Moses, Joshua became the leader of the people. His public life was that of a marauder and human butcher, who seems to have had no more pity than a hungry tiger. For years, at the head of a band of cut-throats, he went through Canaan among a peaceable people, destroying their cities, killing men, women, and children, and distributing their wealth and their country among his followers. "The Lord," we are informed, "was with him wherever he went;" and the result is told in the bloody record: "They utterly destroyed all that was in the city [Jericho], both man and woman, young and old, and ox and sheep and ass, with the edge of the sword." And again: "Joshua drew not his hand back until he had utterly destroyed all the inhabitants of Ai." So friendly was Jehovah with this man, and so much sympathy did he have with him, that on one occasion, when the people of the country united to defend themselves against this godly marauder, and were repulsed, and the daylight failed, as Joshua pursued the flying host, Jehovah stayed the sun in the heaven for about a whole day that the massacre might be complete, and rained down great stones from heaven upon the poor wretches who were fighting to save their families and their homes.

I question whether the whole world's literature presents a bloodier page than that of the tenth chapter of Joshua: —

"And that day Joshua took Makkedah, and smote it with the edge of the sword; and the king thereof he utterly destroyed, them, and all the souls that were therein.

"And he smote it [Libnah] with the edge of the sword, and all the souls that were therein: he let none remain in it.

"The Lord delivered Lachish into the hand of Israel, which took it on the second day, and smote it with the edge of the sword, and all the souls that were therein."

Then follows a list of other cities whose inhabitants were butchered, from the helplessly old to babes at the breast; and the document ends: "So Joshua smote all the country of the hills, and of the south, and of the vale, and of the springs, and all their kings: he left none remaining, but utterly destroyed all that breathed." There is good reason to believe that some who are clamorous for God in the Constitution desire just such a God as this. In a fair intellectual struggle, they acknowledge that they are no match for their opponents; but with soldiers, muskets, cannon, and this Israelitish Moloch, on their side, they would leave none remaining, "as the Lord God of Israel commanded."

There is another man of God who must not be forgotten in this connection, — the Jewish Hercules, Samson. An angel of Jehovah foretold his birth. When he was a child, Jehovah blessed him. On the occasion of his marriage, he wagered thirty changes of raiment with thirty young men that they could not find out the meaning of a riddle which he propounded to them. Having lost, the Spirit of Jehovah came upon him, and he went down to Ashkelon and slew thirty men, stripped them, and gave their garments to the young men (Judges xiv. 19).

Can those men who desire Jehovah to rule over this nation have read these passages? If they have, do they believe them? If they do, how dare they present this gamblers' companion, and instigator of murder, for our acceptance and worship?

On another occasion "the Spirit of the Lord came mightily upon him." We naturally look for some corresponding lordly deed; and we find it. He found a new jaw-bone of an ass, and put forth his hand and took it, and slew a thousand men therewith. We should like to know what the nine hundred were doing while he slew the first hundred. A man a minute gave him sixteen and a half hours of steady murder. There stands the butcher; here lie his victims; and he exclaims, "Heaps upon heaps, with the jaw-bone of an ass have I slain a thousand men." But now he is sore athirst: his long, unremitting labor has made him faint, and he is ready to die: unless he can obtain water, he must perish. What is he doing now? kneeling! praying! Can it be possible that such a murdering wretch as that can pray? Certainly: he has a God, the very image of himself: it is Jehovah. Listen to his prayer: "Thou hast given this great deliverance into the hand of thy servant; and now shall I die for thirst, and fall into the hand of the uncircumcised?" Jehovah heard the prayer of his faithful servant, and from the bloody, battered jaw-bone flowed water, that quenched his thirst, and his spirit revived.

Then comes Jehovah's great friend David, of whom he said, "I have found David, the son of Jesse, a man after mine own heart, which shall fulfil all my will" (Acts xiii. 22). He must have seen what a noble man he was destined to be. After the death of David, Jehovah says of him, "My servant David, who kept my commandments, and who followed me with all his heart, to do that only which was right in mine eyes" (1 Kings xiv. 8). He was fearless, firm, generous at times, pious, and poetic: but he was guilty of almost every crime; and it is quite safe to say that no criminal as great as he lives in any civilized country to-day. When he was not more than sixteen years of age, he murdered two hundred men to please his prospective father-in-law, and mutilated their persons in a way that would disgrace a man-eating savage (1 Sam. xviii. 27).

He was captain of a gang of banditti; and in return for the hospitality of the king of Gath, to whom he fled when Saul pursued him, killed the inhabitants of a whole city with whom that king was friendly, leaving not a soul alive, lest they should tell the tale of his villany (1 Sam. xxvii. 9–12). And yet, after this, he says, " The Lord rewarded me according to my righteousness; according to the cleanness of my hands hath he recompensed me " (2 Sam. xxii. 21).

This reminds me of an epitaph that I once saw in Wales over the grave of a prize-fighter and drunken scoundrel: —

"A man so true, there are but few,
And difficult to find;
A man so just, and true to trust,
There is not left behind."

But this was when David was a young man: perhaps he repented, and became a changed character, in his riper years.

In the latter part of his life, Rabbah, a city of the Ammonites, was taken; and David " brought forth the people that were therein, and put them under harrows of iron and under axes of iron, and made them pass through the brick-kiln; and thus did he unto the cities of the children of Ammon " (2 Sam. xii. 31). To find the equal of such a cruel wretch as this, we need to read the annals of the Fiji Islands.

But he certainly repented before he died. Not he: he had nothing to repent of. Jehovah acknowledges that he had done but one wrong deed in his whole life (1 Kings xv. 5); and that he had repented of long before. With his dying breath, the hoary sinner advised his son Solomon to kill the men whose lives he had sworn to spare.

Time fails me to tell of Rahab the harlot, who saved her life by betraying into the hands of murderers her own city; of Jephthah, who offered up his daughter a burnt-offering to Jehovah; Jael, who murdered the fugitive king, after receiving him hospitably into her tent; of Ehud, who slew the king of Moab, and who said, as he plunged the dagger into him, "I have a message from God unto thee;" of Jehu, who slew the seventy innocent sons of Ahab, his whole kindred and his priests, and of whom Jehovah said he did what was in his heart; and a host of lesser liars, thieves, and murderers, who are spoken of in terms of praise by Jehovah.

There is scarcely a man or woman mentioned in the Bible, with whom Jehovah was friendly, whose life was not stained by crime that would, in this day, send a person to the State-prison or to the gallows.

Even the prophets of Jehovah, who are generally supposed to have been patterns of all excellency, were far from being models of virtue. Samuel was a liar, as we have seen: he both murdered, and urged others to murder; and found fault with Saul because he saved the lives of kings whom he had captured. Elijah calls down fire from heaven, and kills men with no more concern than if they had been flies (2 Kings i.). Elisha curses children in the name of Jehovah; and bears tear forty-two of them (2 Kings ii. 24). Jeremiah never scruples to lie when the king advises him (Jer. xxxviii. 27); and some of his prayers are only second to the witch-curses of David. Hosea buys an adulteress to live with him (Hos. 1. 3), after having illicit intercourse by command of Jehovah with a prostitute. Is this the kind of God, a companion and abetter of liars, thieves, and murderers, whose name is to be placed in the Constitution of our country, and whose character is to be upheld as a model of all excellency?

I object to Jehovah in our Constitution because *he is fierce, jealous, cruel, vindictive, and even malignant.* We might as well be lost souls in the hands of a tormenting Devil as to be the subjects of such a God. Moses describes Jehovah correctly: "The Lord thy God is a consuming fire, even a jealous God" (Deut. iv. 24). The writer of Hebrews has a similar opinion: "God is a consuming fire." Watts, the Christian poet, draws his portrait for us: —

"Adore and tremble; for our God
Is a consuming fire:
His jealous eyes with wrath inflame,
And raise his vengeance higher.
Almighty vengeance, how it burns!
How bright his fury glows!
Vast magazines of plagues and storms
Lie treasured for his foes."

Nor is this portrait overdrawn. Jehovah himself, by Jeremiah, says, "I myself will fight against you with an outstretched arm, even in anger, and in fury, and in great wrath." No wonder the poor Jews suffered under such circumstances. To Moses he says (Deut. xxxii. 22), "A fire is kindled in mine anger, and shall burn unto the lowest hell;" and again, to Jeremiah, "Ye have kindled a fire in mine anger, which shall burn forever." If we heard a man talk so to his children, we should set him down as passionate, revengeful, unreasonable, and utterly unfit to be a parent. It is much less excusable in a God. Shall we make this eternally-angry and infinitely-furious Jehovah Lord of these United States?

The deeds of Jehovah are in correspondence with his words. He commences his career by a fit of cursing, of which woman obtains the largest portion. He follows this by drowning the entire human race because their conduct did not meet his approbation, and thus made himself king of murderers, who takes the life of the world as a human murderer takes the life of a man.

When he sent Moses to Pharaoh to tell him to let the people go, he said, "But I will harden his heart, that he shall not let the people go" (Exod. iv. 21): and then we are told that "the Lord hardened Pharaoh's heart, so that he would not let the children of Israel go out of his land" (Exod. xi. 10); and because Pharoah did not let them go, when he had so hardened his heart that he would not, he murdered the first-born of his entire nation.

There is a State-prison at Charlestown, where several hundred prisoners are held. Pres. Grant sends a letter to the superintendent, commanding him to let the prisoners go; but, before the letter reaches him, he surrounds the penitentiary with a guard of several thousand soldiers, who have strictest orders to allow no prisoner to go out. The superintendent receives the letter of the President, but, owing to the guard, is unable to set a single prisoner at liberty. "What! will you not let the prisoners go?" writes the President: "then I will show you my power, and make you glad to let them go." He hangs the oldest son of the superintendent in front of the prison, in sight of the heartbroken father and mother, as a punishment for his disobedience. Can anybody imagine the horror with which such a crime as this would strike the heart of the country? Multiply this by a million, and you have some idea of the crime of Jehovah.

Shall we make this greatest of wrong-doers a God, and our God? Forbid it, says humanity; and it must be forbidden.

When Jehovah came down on Mt. Sinai, he said to Moses, "Charge the people, lest they break through unto the Lord to gaze, and many of them perish," — as moths die when they fly into the flame: so Jehovah is a flaming fire, and the people must be kept out, or they will perish. The precaution was a necessary one. When the ark of Jehovah was sent from the land of the Philistines back to Judæa, the cattle that drew it went into a field near Bethshemesh. The Bethshemites were apparently inquisitive, and thought this a good opportunity to see what was in an old box, of which they had frequently heard; but, had it been Pandora's box, it could not have been more deadly. Jehovah was very angry at their intrusion, and slew of the men of Bethshemesh fifty thousand and seventy! This God can wink at lying, theft, murder, licentiousness, and praise the men who are guilty of these crimes; but, when inquisitive people look into one of his chests, he strikes tens of thousands with death. Shall we place the name of this almighty Bluebeard in our national Constitution?

In the fifteenth chapter of the First of Samuel, we are informed that Jehovah told Samuel that he remembered what Amalek did to Israel when he came up from Egypt: that was, remember, four hundred years before. For this he tells him to command Saul to smite Amalek, and utterly destroy man, woman, infant, and suckling; and, because Saul did not wholly execute the horrible command, Jehovah was angry with him, and repented that he had made him king over Israel.

During the reign of Queen Elizabeth, nearly three hundred years since, an immense Armada left Spain to conquer England. Suppose Jehovah should command Queen Victoria to kill every man, woman, infant, and suckling in Spain because he remembered this, and that she went with an army and did as she was commanded, but saved the king of Spain alive, and that Jehovah was angry because she had not killed him also: it would not be quite as bad as the conduct of Jehovah to the Amalekites; for they were a hundred years farther removed from the crime said to have been committed by their fathers.

Was viler deed than this ever done in the name of the child-devouring Moloch?

In the time of David, there was a three-years' famine in the land. David inquired of Jehovah what was the cause; and Jehovah answered, "It is for Saul and his bloody house, because he slew the Gibeonites" (2 Sam. xxi.). Here is a strange story. Saul slew the Gibeonites; and for this God torments a whole nation by famine in the days of David. What can be done? Saul is dead, and probably damned. David asks the Gibeonites how he can make an atonement for the crime done by Saul, and they reply by asking him to hang seven of Saul's sons. David hangs two sons of Saul, and five grandsons, — the sons being his brothers-in-law, and the grandsons his step-sons; and after that we are piously told that God was entreated for the land. After the seven innocent men were hung, Jehovah caused the famine to cease: his thirst for blood was satisfied.

Bad as are the representations of Jehovah in the Old Testament, those of the New are infinitely worse. Jesus, it is true, calls him "our Father;" and we are told by John that "God is love:" but such a father! and such love! Jesus, whom we are assured is the representative of Jehovah, tells us that those who believe not in him are to "be damned" (Mark xvi. 16); and those who have not administered to him in the person of his believers are to go "into everlasting fire prepared for the Devil and his angels" (Matt. xxv. 41). Again: he tells us that "all who do iniquity shall be cast into a furnace of fire, where there shall be wailing, and gnashing of teeth." There the doomed wretches, according to the apocalyptic seer, are to "drink of the wine of the wrath of God, which is poured out without mixture into the cup of his indignation; and they shall be tormented with fire and brimstone in the presence of the holy angels and in the presence of the Lamb, where the smoke of their torment ascendeth for ever and ever" (Rev. xiv. 10); where, as good Dr. Watts so beautifully expresses it, —

"Tempests of angry fire shall roll
To blast the rebel worm,
And beat upon his naked soul
In one eternal storm."

Jehovah made this hell of horror. Before him stand earth's millions, more numerous than her sand-grains. He calls up the few, the chosen few, who were mean, ignorant, or sycophantic enough to worship him, — not one in a thousand: to the rest he turns, and, with a voice that shakes the distant stars, he roars, "Depart, ye cursed!" Down drop the myriads, — men, women, fathers, mothers, beautiful maidens, noble men; the sweetest poets, the best of mechanics, the boldest navigators; painters whose creations have gladdened the eyes of many generations; musicians who have made the air more melodious for all time; true believers, miscalled infidels, who have broken the shackles of priestcraft and superstition from the limbs of millions, — down they go into that lake of fire, to hear Jehovah's laugh re-echo through the caverns of the damned, and his voice saying, "I told you in my Word that I would laugh at your calamity, and mock when your fear came." And to all eternity the jailer holds his captives, and applies his tortures; for "their worm dieth not, and the fire is not quenched."

This revelation of Jehovah we owe to Jesus, who, we are told, is Jehovah in another form; and he frequently anticipates the time when he shall execute his wrath upon the helpless victims that shall stand before his blazing throne.

The fact is, that this Jehovah is the idol of a Syrian mountain-tribe, that has been foisted upon the rest of mankind under the penalty of eternal torments, and modified from age to age, but his worst features retained even to our own day. I arraign him in the name of the millions who are held by him in spiritual bondage; in the name of the freemen of America, whose enslavement is sought by the incorporation of this tyrant's name into the charter of our liberties. Away with you, hideous monster, in whom meet the worst vices of the barbarous people who made you, and the ignorant and fearful who still believe in you! You may do for God of the wolves that prowl over our Western prairies and hunt down sick buffaloes, or the hyenas that make night hideous in your Holy Land. Your name may properly be inserted on the black flag of every pirate vessel, between the death's-head and the cross-bones. Infinite tyrant, king of miscreants, woman-curser, soul-tormentor, destroyer of the world, architect of hell, inventor of its tortures, and supplier of its eternal fires, go with your co-partner, the Devil! You belong to the ignorance, brutality, and lust of an age long past. Go to the hell to which you have so long consigned the best representatives of our race! and may your name and history alone remain for a warning and a lesson to all generations!

I am told that Jehovah was the highest ideal of the Divine that the Israelites could form at the time. I do not object to this: so Zeus was the highest ideal of the Greek, and all Hellas united to do homage to their god of gods. Shall we incorporate Jupiter with our Constitution, or acknowledge that he is god because an intelligent people once regarded him as such?

I have generally argued as if the Bible was a record of facts, and its God a reality. Most of you know better. The Bible is no more of an authority to you than the Book of Mormon. To you its God does not exist, and you may therefore think he is perfectly harmless. You may remember that the Greeks besieged Troy for weary years in vain, but at length accomplished by stratagem what they could not do by force of arms. They made a large wooden horse, and filled it with armed men, and retreated to a distance as if they had broken up the siege, and patiently waited for the result. The Trojans, finding their enemies gone, came out of the city, and soon spied the harmless wooden horse. "Let us draw it into the city," said they. It was done; but, that night, out issued the armed men, opened the gates to their companions, who had returned, and Troy fell.

This God may seem to be a very harmless fellow, since he is only a thought god or a paper god; but, admit him into our Constitution, and out will come the army of fifty thousand priests that are hidden in his bowels, the gates will be opened to our enemies, and religious freedom be no more.

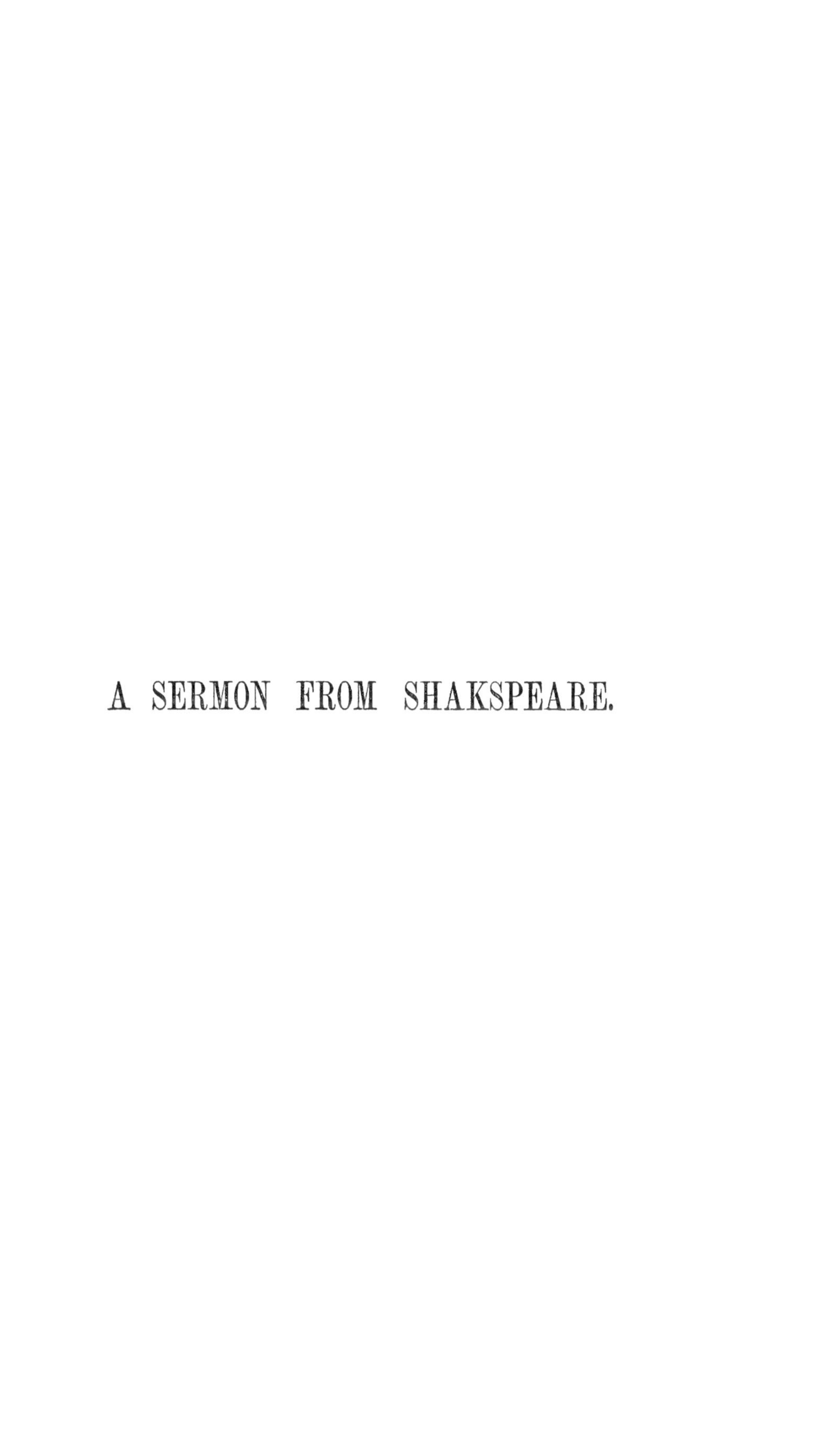

A SERMON FROM SHAKSPEARE.

A SERMON FROM SHAKSPEARE'S TEXT,

> "Tongues in trees, books in the running brooks,
> Sermons in stones, and good in every thing."

My text will be found in the play of "As You Like it," Act II., Scene 1: —

> "And this our life, exempt from public haunt,
> Finds tongues in trees, books in the running brooks,
> Sermons in stones, and good in every thing."

Shakspeare was a mental Argus, whose hundred eyes nothing could escape. Men see by their brains still more than they do by their eyes; and his were brains so developed that they enabled his eyes to see what mortal had never beheld before. He was a walking polyglot, with as many tongues as eyes; what his eyes beheld, his tongues had the ability to speak, — ability how rare! He peered through the palace walls and beheld the secret deeds of kings; and there was no dungeon so dark but his eye beheld the prisoner. He saw, too, the thought of each; he heard their uttered fancies; he beheld their aspirations, and embodied them in glowing language that speaks to every heart. In him the silent trees found utterance, the babbling brooks discoursed in rational speech, and the very stones cried out with eloquent tongue.

Nature, the ready-helper of genius, bowed to him, and opened wide the door of her domain for his observance and appropriation. She whispered her choicest secrets into his ear, and found him a worthy listener, — a true man, who proclaimed them aloud for the benefit of the world.

I can fancy William Shakspeare, after rambling by the banks of the flowing Avon, and watching the pellucid stream flow over its pebbly bottom, and the trees bending lovingly over it, returning to write, "And this our life, exempt from public haunt, finds tongues in trees, books in the running brooks, sermons in stones, and good in every thing." Let us, this afternoon, hear these tongued trees, read the books that are in the running brooks, listen to the sermons that the stones dispense, and find and appropriate the good that dwells in every thing.

It is autumn. We lie upon the velvet sward, and watch the squirrels skip. Grand old trees, lordly possessors of the soil, how I love you! You lift your myriad hands to heaven, and wave your tinted banners in your joy, as if a wintry wind could never blow. Generations of leaves have flourished, dropped, and decayed around you; but there you stand, renewing your beauty from year to year. You have put down your radiating roots deep into the soil, have sucked up by a million mouths the nourishment needed for your growth, and transformed the gross, dark mould into the regal garments you wear; and, though the storm has swept many a time around you, you have only knit your hearts the firmer, and soared daily nearer and nearer to heaven. Beautiful! trees, eloquent trees! we listen to your tongues, and we learn your lessons. So stands the true man: rooted in the earth, watered by its springs, fed by its soil, but using these only as a means to climb into the spiritual realm above him; shedding old opinions, false notions, barbarous creeds, as a tree sheds its leaves; but his firm heart grows but the firmer in the right, his aims the purer, new and true opinions take the place of the old, and he climbs year by year nearer and nearer to perfect manhood.

Down drop the acorns around us. What magical globes are these! The Chinese carve, with admirable skill, half-a-dozen ivory globes one within the other; but what are they to this forest-containing acorn? Folded within this shell is that life which makes the future tree, its leaves, its blossoms, its fruit, and the untold millions of its descendants; an artist lies sleeping here that may beautify a thousand worlds that are yet to be. So the truth, spoken or written, is a seed endowed with perpetual life, and the power to educe new truths and bless the world forever. Error is a stake driven into the ground. Every drop that falls tends to rot it, every wind to blow it down. All nature conspires against it; and its destruction is certain.

How these trees struggle upward for the light! How they "shoulder each other for the sun's smile!" Why are these crowded trees so tall, so straight, and their trunks so small? Every thing is sacrificed for light. The last words of the dying Gœthe are their motto, — "Light, more light!" Listen to that tongue, my brother, and learn. Let thy motto be, "Up to the sunlight!" What are riches, broad lands, magnificent house, honor, fame, when they go with an ignorant, undeveloped soul? Men squat and spread like toadstools under the dripping trees in the twilight, instead of soaring like pines to live in the sun's continual smile.

See on these trees the effect of surrounding conditions. Mark the one that has had light on every side: how symmetrical, how beautiful is that tree! It is, as the poet says, "a thing of beauty and a joy forever." But mark that tree shaded on every side but one, — uneven, warped, lopsided: toward the light it grew, toward the shade it refused to grow; and it would rather grow crooked than not at all. Far from it is the beauty and grace that go with the proper conditions for development. Here is an eloquent tongue. Tupper says, "Scratch the rind of the sapling, and the knotted oak will tell of it for centuries to come." There is a distorted ash, whose ugliness makes the raven croak, as it flies over it. The hoof of a flying deer trampled it into the earth when it was a tender sapling, and it will bear the brand of it while life lasts. That criminal you clutch by the throat, policeman, and strike with your billy, — he, too, was trampled upon in his infancy; nor is the hoof of society off him yet. Lift him up, give him a chance: room for him! air for him! sunshine for him! So much is assured: in the great hereafter, he shall have the chance for development that he never had here. This crabbed old woman, gnarled as a knotty oak, slanderer, liar, thief, — she, too, came to be so by causes. Once she was a smiling, prattling baby, the joy of her mother's heart, dearer to her than a cherub from paradise. She grew, she was tempted, fell, was trampled under the feet of the scrambling crowd of onrushing humanity. Charity for her! light for her! heaven for her, too, where all wrongs are at last to be righted, and the crooked made straight!

There is another tongue in these trees that discourses patience. The slower the growth, the firmer the tree, and the more enduring the wood. "See me grow," said the squash to the oak; "I shall cover a rod while your feeble head is rising a single inch." So it was: the squash covered the ground for many a yard, while the oak seemed an idler; but there stood the oak in its majesty when hundreds of generations of the squash had perished. The tree grows by steady, persistent effort: so can you. Do not hurry, do not idle; but steadily mount, and success, the highest success, is yours. Go into the woods now: how silent they are! Put your ear to the trunks of the trees; can you hear any thing? Not a whisper: they are still as death; yet engines are pumping, and sap is rushing through a million pipes to accomplish a most important work. The mandate has gone forth: every tree must be clad in velvet-green to greet the dawning spring; and there is but a month in which to do it. All the trees of the forest are busy preparing their new dresses in honor of the coming queen. Suppose a thousand young ladies were to be furnished with new dresses within the next month: what an excitement would there be! what a snipping of scissors, tearing of cloth, running of sewing machines, — yes, and of talking machines too, — before all were provided! And yet here are all the trees of the forest making their new dresses without contention, without noise, without the intervention of a French *artiste*, in the good, old-fashioned style which can never be improved.

The storm goes howling by. What a noise! It rouses the world! "Here am I: listen to me; see what I can do!" But when it is over, there lie a few rotten trunks prostrated by its power. Without bluster, or even sound, the million-columned woods arise, and God's first and best temples are reared. It is not the most noisy that accomplish the most. The armies march, the music sounds, the cannons thunder. "These are they that do the world's work," says the crowd. Some thinker in his silent study does more than they all. Bonaparte bestrides Europe like a colossus: his voice makes every throne tremble; all eyes are turned to him, and all ears are dinned with his name; but James Watt, obscurely laboring to perfect the steam-engine, has done infinitely more to change the face of the world, to revolutionize society, and, above all, to bless the human race.

Cut a tree down, and examine the rings of its growth, and you will find an eloquent tongue that gives the lie to many other tongues. The whole history of the tree, and of the times in which it flourished, is indelibly written in the grain of the trunk. Twenty years ago there was a cool, short, and dry summer: here is the narrow ring that answers to that summer. See that expanded circle: fifty years ago there was a warm, moist season; and you see the result. Not a day passed over this tree that has not left its record around its heart, never to be forgotten, never to be erased. I tell you, my brother, my sister, so is it with you. Thus we build up the inward man day by day. There is not an hour in your history that is not inwoven, ingrown into the very constitution of your soul, that does not exercise an influence on your destiny; and there is nothing that can make it be as though it had never been. I know how common it is for men to believe and teach that Jesus can wipe out, at one stroke, and in a moment, the consequences of their misdeeds,—that five minutes of prayer can remove the dark stains of fifty years of crime; but nothing can be more false. Nature tells us this in the grand eloquence of these trees. Do you think that any amount of waving on the part of the green leaves, this coming summer, can remove the effect of the dry seasons long gone by, and expand those contracted rings of growth to full dimensions? When conditions are unfavorable for their proper development, where are the Christs for the trees,—to remove the scars, straighten the bended trunk, and fill out the lean circumference? These very tree-tongues give the lie to this orthodox fable, that man can do wrong, thus hindering his spiritual growth and cramping his soul, and then escape the legitimate consequences of that wrong-doing.

Mark, too, the tendency in all trees to symmetry and beauty, each of its own kind. Take that young tree and hew off its limbs, — reduce it, if you please, to a naked, crooked stick. What does it do? It commences instantly to repair damages. The unsightly cuts are salved with new bark; to the right grows a branch, to the left a corresponding branch. A spirit of beauty presides over it, and employs her agents to adorn it; blossoms expand in their loveliness, fruit is developed, and the tree stands at last as perfect as its more favored neighbors. There is inherent in all nature this tendency to symmetry and beauty. The clay-stone no less than the crystal show it in the mineral kingdom; the vegetable kingdom displays it from the fucoid of the sea-bottom to the pine of the mountain-top; and is man destitute of it? He is and is to be its most glorious manifestation. Man, though king-curst and priest-curst and God-curst, —

> "Though sin and the devil hath bound him," —

has yet within him that divine spirit which, in spite of unfavorable conditions, shall push him onward to excellence, toward perfection.

Were I to tell all that the trees have to teach, how long would my sermon last? By what possibility could it ever have an end? It seems to me, as I go into the woods and listen to their tongues, that all other words are needless. They are the most eloquent of preachers; and, listening to them, we can well afford to let all others be silent. Multitudes who throng the piles of superstition on Sundays would be more blessed by attending the green temples of Nature, and entering into the spirit that breathes from every leaf.

I watch these trees, and see how they grow, day by day, year by year, becoming larger, fairer, as the seasons pass. But I am told that, when the tree arrives at its perfection, — which all may attain in a few centuries, like the stars when they culminate, — it begins to sink, and nothing can arrest its decay and death. It is resolved into its original components: it is gone as a tree, — entered into the dust from which it can never more emerge. And yet, out of the very dust of that tree up springs a new one, fairer and brighter for the richness of the soil gained from the ashes of its predecessor. Nor is that all. Extravagant as it may seem, I have learned that there is a future life even for trees. There is room enough in an infinite universe for all the trees that ever blossomed: somewhere they are blossoming still. How much more shall there be room for the men. They are all living still. A brighter sky than we ever saw bends over them; a more glorious sun sheds his rays on their heads; the winds of beneficent conditions play around them. Development in the grand future is their inalienable destiny.

But Shakspeare says there are "books in the running brooks;" and we must not listen too long to these trees, or we shall lose the lessons that are contained in those running brooks. Strange places to find books! No less strange, and quite as interesting, are the books themselves that we find in this alcove of Nature's library, free for all. There is a book on chronology, and a wonderful book it is: our longest chronological lists are invisible when compared with this. At Niagara, — one of our brooks, — you see an ocean of water pouring over the solid limestone into the foaming abyss beneath. At Queenstown, seven miles below, the cataract once was; and the deep channel between the two shows what the water has accomplished, fretting the solid rock through the ages. Though fifty thousand years were probably spent in the work, yet that is but a day in the geologic calendar. But what is this, compared with the record of other brooks? The Colorado has worn a *cañon* three hundred miles long, and in places more than a mile deep, and for a thousand feet through solid granite. Thousands of centuries must have been employed in the work. These grand brooks are older than Britain and the Druids, Greece and Etruria; older than the mummies; ay, older than Egypt itself, for it is made of the mud that one of these brooks laid down; older than the old serpent and the Christians that made him; older than Noah and his wonderful box; older, indeed, than the Jews and Jehovah, — "the Ancient of days," — their handiwork, or, rather, their headwork. These brooks have been rolling for ages where they now are, doing the work of the world, as they have prepared it for the habitation of mankind.

There is a volume on perseverance in the brooks that many might read with benefit. There was a time when the Gulf of Mexico extended to where Cairo in Illinois now is; and the Mississippi, by patient perseverance, has filled up the Gulf to New Orleans; and it is destined to annex Cuba to the United States, whether Spain favors the annexation or opposes it. They have carried to their graves in the ocean-depths mountains innumerable, and are now engaged in ferrying down all that remain. Not a day but they lay down part of Mont Blanc and Mount Washington, Cotopaxi and Chimborazo; and ere long, by their aid, the ocean shall roll over the heads of the loftiest peaks. They have made seven miles of fossilliferous rock, and formed the grand continents, on whose surface we dwell; and yet the process by which all this is accomplished is so gradual, that but few are aware of what is going on around them. There is a book on perseverance that it will do you good to read, young man, young woman. Never despair of accomplishing your soul's earnest wish. The very desire to be and to do indicates the power to be and to do what you desire: a day may do but little, but you have an eternity to operate in. A drop a day would drain the ocean in time; and you need never be discouraged.

I saw a silvery rill descending from the mountain; clear as crystal were its waters, as it leaped down with tinkling feet on its mission of usefulness and love. "I will stop its babbling," said the Frost, as he laid his cold hand upon it, icy as death; and it staggered and grew still. "I will bury it from sight," said the Snow; and down dropped its fleecy mantle and hid the rill from my gaze. "Alas!" said I, "for the beautiful stream, the envy of the Frost and Snow has destroyed it forever." But while I mourned, the south wind blew with genial breath, the sun looked through the craggy clouds, the bonds of the rill were broken, snow and ice did but increase its waters, and away danced its waters more merrily than before. On it sped; and wherever it went the trees arrayed themselves in their greenest dresses, they lifted up their heads and waved their banners in its praise; the birds sang to it in their leafy bowers, and the flowers kissed it with their sweet lips as it ran. But the hills saw it, and they were offended. "Why should we allow this vagrant to roam at large," said they, — "this leveller, this underminer and destroyer of all things old and sacred? Why should we allow it to chafe our sides, and set at defiance the limits set in the days gone by? Let us unite, and crush it forever." So saying, they encircled the brook in their close embrace, and presented a seemingly impassable barrier to its further passage; and again it was lost to my sight. But, though unseen, it was busy as ever, searching every crevice, flowing into every cranny, to find a passage through the frowning hills. "If I cannot get through, I must go over," said the brook. "Ah, ha!" laughed the hills; and they clapped their hands, and said, "Listen to the little fellow. We have stopped his mad career; no more shall he roam among the trees, and disport himself with the flowers; no more shall he remove the moss-grown rocks, invade our sacred retreats, and undermine the foundations of ages: his work is done, his life is ended." But, inch by inch, and foot by foot, the water rose above the woody sides of the hills; and, reaching a valley between two peaks, the hills saw, to their astonishment, the despised brook, now swollen to a river, go thundering down upon the plain with tenfold power. On it flowed, daily broader, deeper, receiving accessions from a thousand flowing streams, blessing thirsty lands, and administering to man's welfare, till it poured at last its majestic torrent into the all-embracing sea. There is a lesson for thee, my toiling brother. Starting from the mountains of truth-loving endeavor and manly resolve, what though the world's cold scorn falls on thee, and the bitter winds of persecution blow around thee, toil on, live to thy soul's ideal. There are noble hearts beating for thee, glorious rewards awaiting thee. There are no obstacles too high for thee to surmount; the greatest success of which thy soul ever dreamed is guaranteed thee.

But Shakspeare says there are "sermons in stones;" and, while there is time, we must look at some of these. You would never forgive me if I did not give you some of these sermons. These "hard-heads," as the bowlders have been called, are old heads and wise heads, and no less eloquent. They preach the longest, the truest, the wisest of sermons. These ministers of Nature are expounding continually, —

> With magical eloquence, day and night,
> Denouncing the wrong, upholding the right, —

by the road-side, in the swamp, in the foaming stream, and the ploughed field. They preached to the Indian, as he stealthily stole by to shoot the deer at the lick, as they had done to the dumb savages, his ancestors, who had not learned to form the rudest of implements for the chase. These preachers never stammer nor cough; they never rave nor rant; they never lie to please a congregation, or for the glory of God, as I'm afraid some of our gospel preachers do; they never get drunk nor blush for their record: they invariably tell the truth, and that is just what we need; and their bold, outspoken utterances have spoiled a thousand barrels of orthodox sermons in Massachusetts alone. Would that we were more awake to their glowing utterances!

When Shakspeare was living, geology was unknown. What wondrous sermons have been preached by the stones since his time, that have set the world a-thinking! Werner, Hutton, Bakewell, Buckland, Lyell, Mantell, Miller, and hosts of others listened to them, took notes of their discourses; and their rough notes, far from verbatim reports, have re-created the world, and bid fair to re-create the next. How silly the Genesical fable of creation appears in the light which their utterances reveal, — the six days of fatiguing labor of the Almighty Mechanic, dust-made grandfather Adam, and bone-made grandmother Eve, the chatting snake, and the cursing God! In these sermons that the stones preach, there is no God complacently congratulating himself on the success of his week's work, and, in a few days, cursing like a demon because his plans have been frustrated. What a story is that to be rehearsed in the nineteenth century, with the words of these stones ringing in our ears! There rolls the ruddy planet, as it came from the glowing furnace of the sun, a spirit within its concentrated fire-mist presiding over it, and able to produce, when conditions permit, plant and bird, beast and man. We see the solid rock, as the world cools, bare, black, and flinty ; and below, the boiling, turbid waters : from the deep, where the first rude forms of life appear, island after island emerges, lichens cling to the rocks upon them, moss-like plants carpet them, ferns fringe them, beetles hum over them, and fishes go flashing along their shores, or feed upon the sea-weeds that spread over the waters their long gelatinous arms. Tree-ferns unroll their fronds, club-mosses upraise their columns out of the dense swamps, lepidodendrons rear their scaly trunks, frogs hop along the margins of the lakes or vigorously swim in their waters, while above them dragon-flies flit on gauzy wings. Birds appear, rude, gross, stalking along the shores, fishing in the waters ; reptiles swimming, diving, crawling, basking on the rocks, roaming through the woods, soaring in the air ; mammals, huge and whale-like, follow them, living in the waters ; thick-skinned monsters wading in the rivers, crashing through the reeds ; horses roam over the virgin prairies ; deer feed on the newly-developed grasses ; monkeys, the fore-runners of men, feed on the luscious figs. Then comes savage man, low-browed, brutal, but human : within him the science, the art of the nineteenth century, and of a million centuries yet to be born ; and, at last, here are we, the freest congregation in the freest city, in spite of its fogyism, that our planet has yet seen, each one swearing that he will not rest till he has made this old world better than he found it.

This is one of the sermons the stones are preaching ; and where it is heard, most other sermons are preached in vain. Man has been advancing from the start, as the world had been for so many ages before him; then man never fell, and Jesus was never sent to raise what the devil was never permitted to knock down. Good and evil flow from humanity by virtue of its nature; the Devil is no longer needed, and his bottomless pit is filled to the brim. Jesus descends from the throne of his glory and takes his place on the platform occupied by his brothers; and we can say of a thousand living men and women, a better than Jesus is here.

Here, too, is a sermon on progress. From fluid fire to solid rock, from shapeless stone to symmetrical crystal, from crystal to polyp, from this sluggish stomach at the sea-bottom to the active fish, thence to the ground-treading reptile, first tenant of the soil; then life soars in the bird, advances toward man in the brute, and reaches him only to urge him on to higher and nobler positions. We are here with this infinite past beneath us, and an illimitable future above us, and ability within us to climb the heights apparently forever. All this to drop at death back to the dust from which life has ascended only by slow steps for millions of years? We are that we may be. All the past was that we might be in the present; and the present is that the future may be superior to it. Progress is not dead, nor God asleep. The ages have not sown that death or the Devil might reap: neither hell nor the grave is the granary of humanity. The everlasting arms are around us: over the stream of death they shall bear us, and land us in a sunnier clime.

But I must not preach too long from such sermons as these, important as they are. Few geologists have dared to tell the truth, — reveal to the world all that their science has taught them. Scientists, like theologians, are sad cowards. A great effort is made by many of them to make these old preachers talk orthodoxically; but the effort is a dead failure. Though many geologists seek with oblique vision to look upon old dogmas and new revelations at the same time, yet others are gaining courage to declare the whole counsel of Nature.

The stones are preaching their sermons in the streets of Boston to-day. Fort Hill is being cut down, and interested people gather to see the gradual disappearance of one of the interesting relics of historic times. Go and see the old "hard heads," as they are scooped from the soil by the steam excavator, or lie exposed once more to the light of day along the lessening crest. They are covered with marks and scratches. Not a stone to which they were introduced but left its mark: they tell us of the grinding ice-fields of the glacial period, when a Greenland winter locked the sea and buried the land; and you may learn from them that we have only fairly started to explore the past of our planet on which our present stands, and eternity will be needed to read what the eternity of the past has done.

But Shakspeare says there is "good in every thing." What an extravagant statement is this! Right, William, right: you, too, were wiser than you knew. Good in earthquakes, ground-shaking, rock-cleaving, city-swallowing, life-destroying earthquakes? Certainly. By earthquake throes the continents have been uplifted, the mountains reared, and the world adorned. We should never have been here in the glory of this day, if our planet had not been swept by fiery storms and shaken millions of times by the earthquake's jar. Their curses are inseparable from their blessings.

Is there good in volcanoes, those fearful hells that spout out glowing torrents that scathe and destroy, and with their clouds of ashes envelop cities in ruin? Yes: these are the safety-valves of the globe. Weight them down, as engineers sometimes do the safety-valve of the steam-engine, and but a short time would suffice to blow the crust of the globe to atoms.

Good in pain, that racks the nerves, that clouds the mind, — pain, the companion of sorrow, and herald of death? Assuredly there is. If we never felt pain, long before we reached maturity our bodies would be wrecks: a boy's hands would be burned to cinders before he was ten years old. The stomach would be injured beyond recovery by our excesses, before we were aware of our departure from correct living. Pain is a guardian forever attending us: for the child it is better than a hundred nurses. The mother's eye may wander from her charge; but pain never sleeps at its post. The child, attracted by the glare, puts its finger in the flame. Ha! it starts back with a sudden cry. It has learned a lesson that can never be forgotten. In a world without pain, not one human being in a hundred could ever arrive at maturity. Pain, often considered man's enemy, is but an angel in disguise.

But there is certainly nothing good in pestilences, that decimate cities and are the dread of nations? If no other good arose from them, they widen the streets of our cities, cause arrangements to be made for sewerage, and cleanse and beautify the close and otherwise filthy alleys. The general comfort arising from all these may be traced in considerable measure to the dread produced by those scourges of the human race.

The darkest features of some systems are often really the best portions of them, when properly understood. Ask a Protestant to name the darkest features of Catholicism, and he would probably say that portion of it which binds its members to life-long celibacy. Monk, nun, and priest must never marry; or, if they do, they receive the church's ban. "What a horrible system is this!" says the Protestant. Not so horrible as it looks. These monks, nuns, and priests are the most superstitious members of the Roman church. And how fortunate it is that their superstition dies with them, if true to their vows; and the most superstitious are the most likely to be. Thus, when superstition culminates in the Roman Catholic church, it is cut off forever. If the heretics could pass a law, and make it binding, that the most superstitious people should never marry, lest their superstition should be inherited by their children, what an outrage it would be deemed! Yet, thanks to the blindness of the most intolerant of all Christian sects, this is just what the church itself does; and there is good here, where we had least reason to expect it. When a man becomes as fanatical as a Shaker, he ought not to transmit his fanaticism to posterity. How carefully the Shaker, by virtue of his faith, guards against the possibility of it!

But is there any good in war? There must be, if Shakspeare is right; and I certainly think he is. Where did we stand but ten years ago? The North, a great hunting-ground for slaves, and every man by law a kidnapper; forty thousand preachers, and eighty thousand merchants, on their knees, licking the dust at the foot of the slave-power; the priests quoting scripture in favor of and apologizing for the vilest of all crimes; and the merchants defending the practices, that they might obtain the custom of the women-whippers and baby-stealers. Where are they now? The red whirlwind of war has swept the whole brutal system from the face of the land it insulted so long. Where now are those godly Boston ministers who with pious faces read their Bible-texts from the pulpit in favor of this stupendous crime? You can scarcely find a man from Maine to Mexico who dares lift up his voice in defence of chattel slavery; and the ministers are now hastening to prove that they were always in favor of freedom, and that Christianity has conquered and gained the victory alone! That war converted more than Christianity has done for a thousand years, and at the same time converted the Bible.

The villains that applied the torch of rebellion to the temple of our liberty expected to burn the fabric to the ground; but, instead of that, away went rags and scraps, hay and stubble, that blind priests and crafty politicians had been gathering and piling for years around it. And, when the smoke rolled away, there stood the temple in its grandeur, and the golden statue of Liberty above all, unharmed by the transient fire, and unblackened by the smoke; and now, within that temple, stands a redeemed people. This land has at length become in truth what it was only in name, —

> "The land of the free and the home of the brave."

This grand stumbling-block out of our way, we take, and shall henceforth keep, the foremost place in all the world. When I find war assisting so materially to bring about such a condition of things, I cannot but agree with Shakspeare, that there is "good in every thing."

"But the Devil, you know, is all bad," says my orthodox brother. Bring him here and we will dissect him, and I will show you that he has an angelic kernel in his heart. A king who has ruled so long over the largest population that was ever governed by any one potentate, must have some redeeming traits. It is only imaginary beings that are destitute of good. A soul of good seems to be essential to a thing's existence, destitute of which it must die, or rather, it never could have lived. If there is a devil, there must be good in him; but since, as the orthodox inform us, there is no good in the Devil, it is evident that he does not exist.

Good in death, — the terrible curse pronounced by Jehovah on all? Certainly, and the greatest of good. Death, the sick man's solace, the old man's hope, the good man's friend, the slave's release, the great uniter, the twin of sleep, and the door of heaven. We, as spiritualists, see the good there is in death as no other people ever did. We have come from the land of shadows, the gloomy wilderness, peopled by devils and lit by the fire of lurid hells. Up we have come to the "delectable mountains," fairer than those of which Bunyan dreamed; and we revel in the rays of a sun that never, never sets. The prospect is so clear that we can see beyond the swift-flowing stream the loved ones who have gone before; nay, we can hear their cheerful voices, and know that it is well with them, and must be well with us. In the light of this new morning we can take death by the hand and say: Thou art our benefactor, our unchanging friend. Sent by a higher life on the most beneficent of all missions, when our work is done on earth we will greet thee with joy, and look into thine eyes with a smile; for thou shalt usher us into the company of the immortal.

Is there good, then, in all that happens to man? I doubt not that we shall rise in the hereafter to where, looking over all the chequered scene of earth's universal history, we shall exclaim, from the fullest assurance of its truth, All is well! all is well!

www.ingramcontent.com/pod-product-compliance
Lightning Source LLC
LaVergne TN
LVHW010207110826
845151LV00002B/634